Radical Heroes

Studies in the History of Education
(Vol. 6)
Garland Reference Library of Social Science
(Vol. 1006)

Studies in the History of Education

Edward R. Beauchamp, Series Editor

Radical Heroes

Gramsci, Freire and the Politics of Adult Education

Diana Coben

Garland Publishing, Inc.
A member of the Taylor & Francis Group
New York & London
1998

Library of Congress Cataloging-in-Publication Data

Coben, Diana.
        Radical heroes : Gramsci, Freire and the politics of adult
education / Diana Coben.
            p.   cm. — (Garland reference library of social
science ; vol. 1006. Studies in the history of education ; vol. 6)
        Includes bibliographical references (p.   ) and index.
    ISBN 0-8153-1898-7 (alk. paper)
        1. Adult education—Political aspects. 2. Freire, Paulo, 1921–   .
3. Gramsci, Antonio, 1891–1937. 4. Critical pedagogy. 5. Socialism
and education. I. Title. II. Series: Garland reference library of social
science ; v. 1006. III. Series: Garland reference library of social science.
Studies in the history of education ; vol. 6.
    LC5225.S64C63 1998
    374'.01—dc21   98-11116

Printed on acid-free, 250-year-life paper
Manufactured in the United States of America

Contents

Foreword

It is certainly an honor to write the foreword for Diana Coben's careful, detailed analysis of the work of Antonio Gramsci and Paulo Freire in the political context of adult education. Coben presents a nuanced understanding of the contributions of Gramsci and Freire, their similarities and differences. Because of the critical insights Coben brings to *Radical Heroes,* the book holds important implications for both the field of adult education and all cultural workers who are concerned with social and economic justice. The book forces us to reassess the purposes of progressive adult education, as it analyzes the significance of Gramsci and Freire to the radical project. Published in the wake of Freire's death and the global outpouring of grief that followed, the book provides those of us who loved Paulo a timely assessment of his powerful role in adult education.

Though they lived in different social and historical contexts, the work of Gramsci and Freire is forever linked in the minds of political and educational progressives. The posthumous rise of Gramsci's fame roughly coincided with Freire's emergence on the world stage in the turbulent 1960s. Because of this coincidental timing, many scholars (myself included) came to read them at the same time, often one in light of the other. In these readings many of us found strength in our attempt to understand the ways that marginalized peoples achieve empowerment and self-direction. In our study of Gramsci and Freire we gained profound new insights into the study of power and the subtleties of its workings. For those of us in education, we learned how power and education were inseparable entities that would forever after have to be studied in relation to one another. The point here, of course, is that our lives were profoundly changed by our engagement with these two thinkers.

Coben clearly understands these dynamics, as she analyzes the "radical heroes" in relation to the ends of radical adult education. She deeply appreciates the help they provide in our critical effort to differentiate just from unjust social and educational practices, progressive from regressive deployments of power and empowering from disempowering human relationships. The ability to make such distinctions is central to any social or pedagogical practice that considers itself democratic. In this process Coben is careful not to appropriate Gramscian and Freirian ideas or the scholars themselves for some pure/authentic project. She understands the openness of their texts and the various ways they can be read. Buoyed by such insights, she appreciates the fact that her engagement with Gramsci and Freire is an interpretation and like any hermeneutic act is contingent and tentative. With these ideas in mind the author refuses to deify the heroes, and in the spirit of radical education subjects Gramsci and Freire to rigorous critique.

As the beloved educator, Freire often found himself beyond critique by his progressive admirers—a situation that frustrated him. Coben's critical analysis of Paulo therefore, is not motivated by a lack of respect for him, but just the opposite, by her reverence for what he taught. To honor Paulo we must critique him; we are obligated to point out his limitations as part of the larger effort to make sense of the nature of emancipation and justice in an ever-changing cosmos. In my personal interactions with Freire, he was genuinely thrilled by the frank critiques of those who shared his democratic and pedagogical passions. In her critical stance toward Gramsci and Freire, Coben problematizes the concept behind the title of her book, *Radical Heroes*. Here a central theme of the work emerges in her challenge to the fetishization of radical heroes in a manner that cuts off debate and disagreement. Coben refuses to approach the radical heroes with wide eyes and fawning deference.

Gramsci and Freire are central to the study of adult education in that both thinkers were interested in the ways that power wielders sought to engage citizens—educate them—in seeing the world in a manner that resonated with existing power relations. Dominant power consistently works to make meanings that reinforce the asymmetrical status quo. When it works best, dominant power gains the ability to help shape our interests and desires in a manner that precludes the need for visible coercion. In this sense, power becomes a conscience, an internalized authority that inaudibly whispers its admonition to play along, to avoid resistance. Gramsci's concept of hegemonic consent, Coben knows, can be viewed here as a pedagogical process, a central concern of adult educators. Power produces knowledge that helps shape identities—a central aspect of what those of us in progressive education understand pedagogy to involve.

If the act of bringing about social, economic and political change—as Coben, Gramsci and Freire maintain—is pedagogical, then the task of adult educators and educators in general is more central to the radical project than has been traditionally believed. Pedagogy in this articulation is always engaged on some level with power in the human struggle over the educational, emotional and value-related investments people make in the living of their lives. Adult education in this context devotes great attention to cultural pedagogy, a process that involves the education and acculturation that take place at a variety of cultural locations including but not limited to formal educational institutions. Such pedagogical concerns lead us directly to a closer, more detailed examination of power.

Coben's analysis of Gramsci and Freire provides us with important insights to these issues concerning the workings of power. Such insights are especially helpful when one understands the fact that the most powerful power is hidden from sight. Indeed, the success of power wielders is directly related to their ability to mask their acts of domination. Thus, the erasure of power is confusing to individuals who are at a loss to discern the reasons for the domineering and dehumanizing features of social life. The ways that men and women are regulated to act in opposition to their best interests remains mysterious to most citizens of Western societies. If we understand in a Foucauldian sense that power is everywhere, we are faced with the subsequent realization that everywhere is tantamount to nowhere. Coben is helpful in this dilemma, as she uses her analysis of Gramsci and Freire to expose the forces of domination as they invisibly operate in everyday interaction and communication.

For those of us concerned with the mutations of power and domination in the electronically mediated reality of the end of the twentieth century, Coben's analysis of Gramsci and Freire is helpful. Using her understanding of the relationship between Gramscian and Freirean insights, the author contributes to our effort to map the ways contemporary power operates to colonize desires and subjectivities and to undermine democratic impulses in everyday life. In an interesting and unusual way, the increasing nomadism of power in contemporary society with its globalized communications and economics makes Gramsci and Freire's work more relevant than ever. Adult educators who operate outside of these discourses have little understanding of how the lives of women and men are constrained or what pedagogical interventions are necessary to escape such constraints. The focus of radical adult education is to address these deficiencies, in the process enhancing the self-direction of the adult learner and catalyzing the exercise of human agency in general.

Coben's analysis is germane to these critical concerns, as she provides insights into domination that help us formulate pragmatic critiques of social practices and institutions. Such critiques are necessary for the development of practical forms of resistance, methods of challenging domination. By helping develop these methods, adult educators become facilitators of empowerment. In this context Coben chooses to include an analysis of Gelsa Knijnik's work with the landless people's movement in Brazil. Knijnik's pedagogical project is an excellent choice to illustrate the use of Gramsci and Freire in a contemporary social movement. I am very lucky at present to be working with Gelsa on a project and can personally report what a special, theoretically sophisticated and politically savvy scholar/activist she is. Analyzing Knijnik's work in light of the book's insightful analysis of Gramsci and Freire, Coben provides adult educators with a profound thought experiment in the understanding of and the struggle against oppression. *Radical Heroes* takes adult educators to critical spaces they rarely have the opportunity to explore in a subtle, accessible, and intellectually challenging manner. I hope it receives the attention it deserves.

Joe L. Kincheloe
Cultural Studies and Pedagogy
Penn State University

Acknowledgments

Many people have helped this book to see the light of day. My thanks to all those with whom I have discussed the ideas expressed here and whose interest has sustained me while I was writing. Warm thanks, especially, to Professor Gelsa Knijnik of the Universidade do Vale do Rio dos Sinos, Brazil, with whom I have enjoyed some memorable and thought-provoking conversations about Gramsci and Freire and the politics of adult education. Her reminder to me that a book is a provisional statement came at just the right time. My thanks also to Professor Seppo Kontiainen and Dr. Juan Carlos Llorente of the University of Helsinki, Finland, whose invitation to me to present a seminar on my research served to concentrate my mind wonderfully on the need to finish the book.

This book is based, albeit in a very substantially revised form, on my Ph.D. thesis. I was immensely fortunate to have as my supervisor Professor David McLellan of the University of Kent at Canterbury, to whom I owe a deep debt of gratitude. Since I submitted my thesis in 1992 my ideas have continued to develop and the literature on the education and training of adults has continued to grow. A number of books and articles have been published by and about Gramsci and Freire, including new books by Freire and the first volumes of a complete edition of Gramsci's prison notebooks in English translation. I am very grateful to friends who helped me to track down elusive items, especially to Professor Marilyn Frankenstein of the University of Massachusetts, with whom I have enjoyed some stimulating conversations and who drew my attention to material I might otherwise have neglected. I am also grateful to Dr. Kathy Safford of St. Peter's College, Jersey City, New Jersey, who kindly sent me books which were not available in the United Kingdom when I needed them. The International Gramsci Society has been a tremendous boon in helping me to keep track of the burgeoning publications on Gramsci and in providing a forum for the discussion of Gramsci's ideas. The "Signs of the Times" discussion group has also given me much food for thought during our meetings in the unlikely venue of a Swedish restaurant in North London. I am grateful, also, to my colleagues at Goldsmiths College, University of London, who have helped to create a culture in which ideas matter and in which attempts to bring together theory and practice are encouraged. Against this background, colleagues and students on my M.A. in adult education at Goldsmiths have helped me greatly by their searching questions, their enthusiasm and their willingness to challenge my every word.

I am sincerely grateful to Marie Ellen Larcada, Ed Beauchamp and all at Garland Publishing for their commitment to the book and their patience with its author. My thanks also to Dr. Carl Nelson of Northeastern University, Boston, who started the ball rolling in the direction of publication.

My special thanks to John Ashworth, without whose steadfast love and encouragement this book would never have been completed, and to Anders Bøhler, whose thoughtfulness I have much appreciated.

Any errors and imperfections that remain are entirely my own, as is my reading of the two "radical heroes" of adult education whose work forms the focus of this book.

List of Abbreviations of Works by Freire and Gramsci That Are Cited

CAF	*Cultural Action for Freedom*, by Paulo Freire. Harmondsworth: Penguin (1972).
EPF	*Education: The Practice of Freedom*, by Paulo Freire, translated by Myra Bergman Ramos. London: Writers and Readers (1976).
FSPN	*Further Selections from the Prison Notebooks/Antonio Gramsci*, edited and translated by D. Boothman. Minneapolis: University of Minnesota Press (1995).
GR	*A Gramsci Reader: Selected Writings 1916–1935 by Antonio Gramsci*, edited by D. Forgacs. London: Lawrence and Wishart (1988).
LGB	*Pedagogy in Process: The Letters to Guinea-Bissau*, by Paulo Freire, translated by C. St. John Hunter. London: Writers and Readers (1978).
LP	*Letters from Prison by Antonio Gramsci*, selected, translated and introduced by L. Lawner. London: Jonathan Cape (1975).
PE	*The Politics of Education*, by Paulo Freire, translated by Donaldo Macedo. London: Macmillan (1985).
PH	*Pedagogy of Hope: Reliving Pedagogy of the Oppressed*, by Paulo Freire, translated by Robert R. Barr. New York: Continuum (1995).
PNI	*Antonio Gramsci: Prison Notebooks* (Volume 1), edited with Introduction by Joseph A. Buttigieg, translated by J. A. Buttigieg and A. Callari. New York: Columbia University Press (1992).

PNII   *Antonio Gramsci: Prison Notebooks* (Volume 2), edited and translated by J. A. Buttigieg. New York: Columbia University Press (1996).

PO   *Pedagogy of the Oppressed*, by Paulo Freire, translated by Myra Bergman Ramos. Harmondsworth: Penguin (1972).

SCW   *Selections from Cultural Writings*, by Antonio Gramsci, edited by D. Forgacs and G. Nowell Smith, translated by W. Boelhower. London: Lawrence and Wishart (1985).

SPN   *Selections from the Prison Notebooks of Antonio Gramsci*, edited and translated by Quintin Hoare and Geoffrey Nowell Smith. London: Lawrence and Wishart (1971).

SPWI   *Selections from Political Writings (1910–20)*, by Antonio Gramsci, edited by Quintin Hoare, translated by John Matthews. London: Lawrence and Wishart (1977).

SPWII   *Selections from Political Writings (1921–26)*, by Antonio Gramsci, translated and edited by Quintin Hoare. London: Lawrence and Wishart (1978).

Radical Heroes

Chapter 1
Radical Heroes in an Age of Uncertainty

These are interesting times for radical adult educators—those who aspire to a progressive social and political purpose in their work, who want change in the original meaning of "radical," 'from the root'. The difficulty lies in trying to envisage the forms and directions that change from the root might take. At a time when Enlightenment ideas of progress are being reassessed and the very construction of the social and the self is being called into question (McRobbie 1994), what kinds of change do radical adult educators want, and change to what end?

The answers to these questions are no longer clear. Whereas the epithet "radical" was once synonymous with left-wing political ideals (Williams 1990), in the post-soviet, post-apartheid new world order the old oppositional certainties of "progressive left" and "reactionary right" appear to some to have melted away[1]. The new radicalisms associated with, for example, environmentalism, feminism or animal rights do not fit neatly into the left/right divide of conventional political analysis. Nor are all such social movements, however radical they may be, necessarily progressive in the sense of seeking to inaugurate a new and better future for humanity as a whole. The question is: progressive toward what end? Who is to judge, and on what grounds, which ends are better than others, and for whom?

Even if the desired end is taken to be social justice, an aim which many radicals espouse, this does not solve the problem, since, as David Harvey (1993:96) points out, "Social justice, for all the universalism to which proponents of a particular version might aspire, has long turned out to be a rather heterogeneous set of concepts."

He identifies various competing interpretations, including the egalitarian (entailing the equal treatment of unequals), the theory of positive law (the doctrine that law is just per se), the utilitarian (entailing the greatest good of the greatest number), and views based on notions of social contract, natural right, intuition, or relative deprivation (Harvey 1993:96)—any one of which might inspire a radical project.

Just as the new social movements are diverse and multifaceted, so the forms of political organization they have spawned are similarly various, with the political party arguably no longer dominant (Perryman in Perryman ed. 1994). Forms of political expression associated with the new social movements range from mass demonstrations such as the Million Man March in the United States, through myriad forms of group activity, to expressions of an individual's sexual or dietary preference. The relationships between the new social movements and adult education are similarly diverse (Finger 1989).

At the same time the centrality of the nation-state as the context for political action is being profoundly challenged by the process of globalization, defined by Giddens (1994:4) as "action at distance" exemplified by the emergence of new forms of global communication and mass transportation, the ascendancy of multinational corporations and the emergence of regional supranational political and/or economic formations, such as the European Union and the Pacific Rim.

Against this background, adult educators struggle with their experience of marginalization. For example, although six to seven million adults in the United Kingdom engage in formal or informal systematic programs of study each year and adult students are now in the majority in higher and further education, explicit provision for adults accounts for less than 1 percent of U.K. central government expenditure on education, and adult learning remains "almost invisible," according to the Director of the National Institute of Adult Continuing Education (Tuckett 1995:45). The picture elsewhere in the world varies (OECD 1992), but despite the increasing prominence of notions of lifelong learning, the learning organization and the learning society, nowhere is the education of adults a major priority. For would-be radicals, the key questions in any case are not only whether the education of adults receives sufficient public recognition or financial support, but also, crucially, about the social and political purposes of the education of adults.

There is growing interest in political theory in relation to adult education. The authors of a study of citation patterns in adult education point out that the main type of theoretical literature cited in the literature they surveyed was political (Field, Lovell and Weller 1991:15), although adult education has not yet generated significant "'invisible colleges' of scholars pursuing common debates and themes" (Field et al. 1991:20). As a result, the theoretical base of adult education is underdeveloped. Even within the field of education, adult education suffers from a low research profile and a degree of invisibility born of a widespread assumption that education is concerned primarily with what happens to children and young people in schools and colleges. Furthermore, the education of adults is dependent on knowledge derived from practice in a field in which theory is commonly treated as subordinate to practice (Jarvis 1990).

This would be less of a problem if the education of adults were a clearly delineated field of practice, but this is far from being the case worldwide (Charters 1989; Jarvis 1995; Titmus ed. 1989). Adult education is an exceptionally diverse field whose practitioners do not all share a common professional culture, or even a common term to designate what it is they do. Debates among adult education practitioners are accordingly informed—or ill-informed—by an inadequate theoretical base and distorted by terminological and conceptual confusions.[2] Where these debates are concerned with vital political questions of direction, purpose, the exercise of power and the allocation of resources, theoretical weakness can have serious practical consequences, making it hard for practitioners to understand the situations in which they find themselves and unsure of what action to take. Where politics is concerned, while knowledge may not always be power, ignorance is rarely bliss.

Against this background, this book is intended as a contribution to the development of political theory in the education of adults through an examination of the ideas of two radical heroes of adult education: Antonio Gramsci (1891–1937) and Paulo Freire (1921–1997). Gramsci and Freire are frequently cited in the adult education literature as thinkers whose ideas offer insights into the politics of the education of adults. They are among the top twenty-five most frequently cited authors in the literature of adult education. Indeed, Freire (equally with Malcolm Knowles) heads the list of the most frequently cited authors, and his *Pedagogy of the Oppressed* (PO),[3] described as "inspirational so far as practice is concerned," is the single most frequently cited publication (Field et al. 1991:13). Gramsci is referred to in the study as a "scriptural author," whose influence in a practice-orientated field is thought to reflect a generational, backward-looking academic culture (Field et al. 1991:15).

Gramsci and Freire are also frequently cited together, an association which implies that their ideas are compatible in some way. But are they? Gramsci was a revolutionary Marxist leader and political thinker, a steadfast opponent of Fascism and ultimately its victim, whereas Freire was an adult educator for whom education was political, a champion of the right to education of oppressed people everywhere, and particularly in the so-called Third World.[4] What significance might the ideas of these two radical heroes have for the development of a radical politics of adult education?

This question lies at the heart of this book. In order to answer it, I examine first Gramsci's educative concept of politics, focusing on his concepts of hegemony and the intellectuals. Then, in Chapter 3, I explore Freire's concept of education as political and the transformative role of adult education in liberating the oppressed. Chapter 4 looks at the points of contact and divergence of Gramsci's and Freire's ideas. Chapter 5 examines the references to Gramsci and Freire in the adult education literature and evaluates the linkage of their ideas in the context of a consideration of Gramsci's and Freire's status as radical heroes. In the final chapter I review the state of play thus far and look more closely at an account by one adult educator of her work with a social movement: Gelsa Knijnik's teaching and research in ethnomathematics with the landless people's movement in Brazil (Knijnik 1993, 1996).

Before proceeding, however, a word of warning is in order: in writing about a field as practice-orientated as adult education there is a constant danger of privileging the written, published form over the spoken and unspoken lived experience of adult educators and students. Often, exciting, innovative practice remains unknown to anyone outside the immediate circle of those engaged in it. Innovative interpretations of Gramsci's and Freire's ideas may be being worked out every day in different areas of adult education practice, but if they are not recorded they are not available for others to share insights and debate ends and means. The work that is researched, written up, presented at conferences or submitted for assessment toward a degree, and the even smaller amount of writing that is published, is a small and not necessarily representative sample of a much larger enterprise. Furthermore, those who theorize, research and write are not necessarily adult education practitioners, and those who practice may not have access to the books and journals in which such writing is published or be in the habit of reading widely in their field. In all this, the voice that is most rarely heard in debates about the politics and purposes of the education of adults is precisely that of the adult student.

The undertheorization of adult education limits the effectiveness of theoreticians and undermines research as well as impoverishing the practice of practitioners. It also makes it harder for adult educators to discuss with each other and with adult students and potential students what the purposes of adult education should be and how those purposes might be realized. As Carlos Alberto Torres emphasizes:

Time and again it should be stressed that without good theorization, reasonable good data for comparative studies, a consistent definition of the field and a political-sociological approach, the field of adult education will continue to be the domain for the operation of empirical practitioners and short-sighted thinkers and policy-makers. (Torres 1990a:283)

But the use of theory is not unproblematic either. Theory may be used to obfuscate debate, to mystify understanding, or to legitimize particular practices, rather than as a tool for the interrogation of practice or for the exploration of ideas. Rightly used, theory can help us to think through difficult issues, such as the relationship of adult education to social and political change.

All of this should be borne in mind in considering the discussion that follows. I have focused closely on Gramsci's and Freire's writings and on their treatment in the literature of adult education because that literature constitutes the forum in which ideas are debated beyond the local level. My focus is limited to the English-language literature because I cannot pretend to sufficient knowledge of relevant literature in other languages: others must take up that challenge. Discussions of Gramsci's and Freire's ideas, together with more casual citations, represent a significant part of the developing theoretical discourse of adult education, without which appropriate theory cannot be created or specific practices compared. The literature may or may not accurately reflect Gramsci's and Freire's standing among anglophone adult education practitioners on the ground, but it does reveal their standing in public among theoreticians and it sheds light on the ways in which their ideas have been interpreted over the last few decades.

First, however, it is necessary to establish what Gramsci and Freire have to say that may be relevant to adult education, and this is the business of the next two chapters, starting with Gramsci.

Notes

1.   See Giddens (1994) and Bobbio (1996) for two sides of this argument; Laponce (1981) provides a useful summary of previous analyses and sets out the basis for future research.

2.   For comprehensive discussions of terminology and associated concepts in the education of adults, see Tight (1996) and Chapter 2 of Jarvis (1995).

3.   Books frequently referred to in the text are designated by an abbreviation of the title. See "List of Abbreviations of Works" pp. 225. Please note: PO refers to the Penguin edition of *Pedagogy of the Oppressed*, first published in the United Kingdom in 1972 and since reprinted many times. The new revised Twentieth Anniversary edition, published in New York by Continuum, is referred to in the text and listed in the Bibliography as "Freire 1995."

4.   The term "Third World" is deeply problematic, hence my use of "scare quotes." See Hadjor 1993 for a full treatment of the difficulties—and some solutions.

Chapter 2
Antonio Gramsci: Politics As Educative

Antonio Gramsci was a revolutionary Marxist and victim of Fascism who has come to be regarded by many as the most original political thinker in Western Marxism and one of the outstanding intellectual figures of the twentieth century. He features posthumously as a radical hero in the literature of adult education, just one of the many fields in which his work has been influential.

In this chapter I shall explore the nature of Gramsci's legacy for adult educators, beginning with a brief biographical and bibliographical introduction[1] and a survey of the various "Gramscisms" that developed after Gramsci's death. This is followed by a discussion of Gramsci's educative conception of politics, focusing on two key concepts: hegemony and the intellectuals. Within this framework I shall discuss three strands in Gramsci's thought in response to the problem of the creation of revolutionary hegemony: the factory councils; the production of political and cultural journals, books and other writings; and education, particularly the education of adults.

Antonio Gramsci: Life and Writings
Antonio Gramsci was born in Ales, on the poverty-stricken island of Sardinia in 1891, the fourth of seven children. The family at first subsisted without hardship on Gramsci's father's salary as a minor government official in the Office of Land Registry in Sòrgono, only to be plunged into dire poverty during the years 1898 to 1904 when Gramsci's father was imprisoned on charges of misuse of public funds. Gramsci's health was poor throughout his life following an accident in infancy. What education he received was interrupted by illness and the need to earn money to augment the family income, since his

father worked only sporadically after his release. Nevertheless, the young Gramsci worked hard at his studies and in 1911 he won a meager scholarship to the University of Turin. There he studied Greek, Latin, geography, philosophy, modern history and Italian literature for a humanities degree, specializing in historical linguistics, the subject of his thesis, while suffering continuing ill-health exacerbated by extreme poverty.

The contrast between Sardinia and Turin in 1911 could hardly have been greater. Turin was a large industrial city, the home of the Fiat works, one of the most modern factories in Italy, with a workforce that was one of the most advanced, both technically and politically. Gramsci became deeply interested in the mass production process, as he reflected years later in his analysis of Americanism and Fordism (SPN:279–318). He also made frequent reference to the techniques of "scientific management" of the production process pioneered by the American engineer Frederick Taylor (1856–1915) and known as Taylorization (SPN:*passim*). In and around the university was a group of intellectuals who were active in the political struggles of the Turin proletariat. Gramsci made many friends and political contacts, joining the Socialist Party of Italy (*Partito Socialista Italiano,* PSI) late in 1913 (the precise date is not known).

Gramsci made a return trip to Sardinia in the summer of 1913. He supported the Sardinian nationalist movement in the general election of that year, the first in which literacy was not a condition of the franchise, and was moved by the sight of Sardinian peasants voting for the first time (Germino 1990:35). In the following year Gramsci took a course in Marxism and went on to study other works by Marx (Germino 1990:31).

In 1915 he left the university without completing his thesis (although he continued to work on it until 1918) in order to devote himself to his political and journalistic activities. Gramsci's writings of this period reflect the triumphs and setbacks of his political activity and his wide-ranging interests, spanning the theater, language, literature, education and folklore. He wrote for and later edited the Socialist papers *Il Grido del Popolo, Avanti* and *l'Ordine Nuovo* and was largely responsible for the emphasis on culture and education that was one of the salient characteristics of the *Ordine Nuovo* group,

as Joseph A. Buttigieg points out (PNI:19). This emphasis was reflected in *Ordine Nuovo's* slogan:

*Educate yourselves because we will need all your intelligence. Rouse your-
selves because we will need all your enthusiasm. Organize yourselves
because we will need all your strength.*

Ordine Nuovo became the crucial organizing and theoretical element
in the formation of the factory councils elected by the workforce
during the turbulent period of strikes and factory occupations in
Turin and Milan from 1919 to 1920. For Gramsci and others, this
period appeared as one of imminent revolution.

In the event, the revolution failed to materialize for reasons which
are still debated.[2] In Gramsci's eyes, a major cause was the PSI's
failure to resolve the relationship between the party and the councils. As a result, from 1920 on he directed as much attention to the
party as to the councils (Davidson 1977:135).

The Communist Party of Italy[3] (PCd'I) was formed by Gramsci
and others after a split with the PSI in 1921. The same year saw the
first period of Fascist terror in Italy, followed in 1922 by Mussolini's
seizure of power and the declaration of the world's first Fascist state,
supported by the monarchy, the army and Italian capitalism and the
middle classes. Gramsci left for Moscow as the PCd'I delegate to the
Comintern, where he stayed for eighteen months. During this time
he met and married Julca (Giulia) Schucht, a musician, with whom
he had two children. Meanwhile, a warrant was issued for his arrest
in Italy, preventing his return. In 1923 Gramsci moved to Vienna to
head a newly founded Comintern Bureau for anti-Fascist action. In
the following year, while still in exile, Gramsci became leader of the
PCd'I.

Gramsci was elected to parliament in Rome despite Fascist rig-
ging of the election and returned to Italy in 1924, only to be arrested on November 8, 1926, in breach of his parliamentary immu-
nity. He was eventually sentenced to twenty years imprisonment, a
term designed, as the prosecutor stated at his trial, to "prevent this
brain from functioning for twenty years" (Fiori 1970:230). Gramsci's
"Autobiographical Notes" in the prison notebooks (FSPN:lxxxiv–
lxxxvii) shed light on the reasons why he did not flee Italy to avoid

arrest and on his state of mind in captivity. On his decision to remain, he points out that unless the captain is prepared to go down with the ship,

what guarantee would there be that the captain had done everything possible: (1) to avoid the shipwreck; (2) to ensure that everything had been done in the event of a shipwreck to reduce damage to persons and things to a minimum? (FSPN:lxxxv)

Gramsci paid dearly for his decision. In prison he suffered physical and mental agony as his health collapsed. During the eleven years of his incarceration, he suffered from uremia, circulatory disturbances, hypertension, tubercular lesions in the right lung, gastroenterological disturbances, pyorrhea, fainting spells, chest pains, dizziness and hallucinations (Gramsci 1994a vol.1:16). Meanwhile, Giulia, who had returned to Moscow in August 1926 for the birth of their second child, had a series of nervous illnesses (probably compounded by a form of epilepsy) which confined her for much of the time to clinics in Moscow. Despite his appalling difficulties, Gramsci was able to read books and periodicals in prison, thanks to an open account with a Milan bookshop financed for him by his friend, the economist Piero Sraffa, who was an academic at Cambridge University. The selfless role played by Gramsci's sister-in-law, Tatiana (Tania) Schucht, who remained in Italy and supported Gramsci in a myriad of ways during his imprisonment, was crucial in keeping communication open between Gramsci, his wife and sons in Moscow, his family in Sardinia and his political allies in exile or in hiding. After the first two or three years of his imprisonment Gramsci was allowed to write, although only under conditions of strict censorship. Thereafter he continued to develop and record his ideas using coded phrases in order to deceive the Fascist censor.

Gramsci eventually filled thirty-three notebooks,[4] and wrote numerous letters to his family and friends.[5] The notebooks gave a focus to his inner life in prison and he filled them with political ideas, arguments and critiques of the prevailing modes of thought of his time, continuing to work on them up to the time of his death. They undoubtedly contain elements of his mature thought at its most incisive and creative as he reflected on and analyzed the lessons of defeat.

Gramsci died of a cerebral hemorrhage in the Quisisana Clinic in Rome on 27 April 1937; he was forty-six. He was unable to edit the notebooks and we can never know what his intentions were with respect to their final form, but that he considered the notes important is clear. In a letter to his sister-in-law, Tania, written early in his imprisonment, Gramsci told her that his intention was to write something *"für ewig"* (for ever) (LP:79). The prison notebooks stand as his political testament, but their fragmentary and partially coded form means that it is a testament peculiarly open to different interpretations. Gramsci's successors have been arguing over the nature of their inheritance ever since.

Against this background, I shall endeavor to make clear what I understand by Gramsci's key theoretical concepts, while recognizing that my interpretations are inevitably also partial. Accordingly, I shall examine hegemony and Gramsci's theory of the intellectuals, together with areas of Gramsci's writings that exemplify his educative approach to politics, including those which explicitly address educational issues, especially the political education of adults. Finally, I shall turn to a discussion of the various Gramscisms that emerged after Gramsci's death, since these may have a bearing on the uses to which Gramsci's ideas have been put in adult education.

Gramsci's Educative Politics
Hegemony

Gramsci developed the concept of hegemony in the prison notebooks—in a sense the notebooks are all about hegemony—but he did not define the term per se. Instead he used it in working through his ideas on relationships within and between political entities, including states, parties and groupings of various kinds. In Gramsci's prison notebooks, to use Laclau and Mouffe's phrase (1985:7), "hegemony" emerges not as the majestic unfolding of an identity, but as the response to crisis. His notes are elusive and fragmentary, subject to the constraints under which he wrote. As a result, as with so much of his work, the precise meaning is contested.[6] Nevertheless, commentators agree that Gramsci's concept of hegemony is a major contribution to Marxist theory and key to an understanding of his edu-

cative conception of politics. I shall begin by outlining the geneal-
ogy of Gramsci's concept of hegemony before going on to examine
it more closely.

Gramsci was not the first Marxist to use the term "hegemony,"
which was in common use by Russian Social Democrats from the
early 1880s. In this period "hegemony" denoted a strategy through
which an alliance of nonproletarian groups, including intellectuals
and peasants and led by the proletariat, would overthrow Tsarism.
Lenin developed the notion in his *What Is to Be Done?* in 1902, in
which he stressed the role of the revolutionary vanguard in developing leadership (Lenin 1947). From his early writing Gramsci also
stressed the importance of building class alliances (see, for example,
SPWI:66–7; SPWI:71–4) and he was certainly aware of, and approved of Lenin's usage, which, he said, "gave new importance to
the front of cultural struggle and constructed the doctrine of hegemony as the complement to the theory of the state as force" (Gramsci
quoted by Buci-Glucksmann 1980:390).

Gramsci's concept of hegemony also appears to echo Marx's and
Engels's (1974:64) statement in *The German Ideology:*

*The ideas of the ruling class are in every epoch the ruling ideas, i.e. the
class which is the ruling material force of society, is at the same time its
ruling intellectual force.*

However, *The German Ideology* remained unpublished until 1932,
six years after Gramsci's arrest, and there is no evidence that he knew
of it (Nemeth 1980:10).

Instead, Forgacs recounts Lo Piparo's argument that Gramsci's
lifelong interest in historical linguistics may have been an important
influence on his conception of hegemony (SCW:164). Lo Piparo's
persuasive thesis is that Gramsci extended into the political sphere
concepts developed to explain the process by which speakers of one
language influence speakers of other languages with whom they come
into contact. In other words, it may be, as Germino argues, that
Gramsci's theory of hegemony "had its roots prior to his intellectual
encounter with Marx" (Germino 1990:30).

In the notebooks, Gramsci developed a strategy for revolution
in countries where the state holds power, as it were, in reserve, through

the institutions of civil society, rather than through force alone. This revolutionary strategy he called "war of position" (the analogy is with trench warfare), by contrast with the "war of movement" or "war of maneuver," that is, direct assault on the state. The war of position entails the building of alternative, revolutionary forms of organization through which the "'spontaneous' consent given by the great masses of the population to the general direction imposed on social life by the dominant fundamental group" (SPN:12) may be transferred to the revolution. The hegemony of the dominant fundamental group pervades all aspects of civil society, including the law, education, morality and culture in the widest sense and so it is in these areas, as well as in the military field, that the revolution must be waged in order to form a new "historical bloc" (*blocco storico*). As Derek Boothman explains, the historical bloc is a dynamic concept through which Gramsci transcends Marx's two-dimensional metaphor of society as base and superstructure. It is "a bloc between structure and superstructure," a "social totality [. . .] rendered dynamic through the introduction of the aspect of hegemony and thus the inclusion of the direction in which a society is moving" (FSPN:xii).

In an important note, Gramsci recognized that the state successfully maintains hegemony insofar as it succeeds in articulating dominant class interests as if they were universal:

It is true that the state is seen as the organ of one particular class, destined to create favourable conditions for the latter's maximum expansion. But the development and expansion of the particular group are conceived of, and presented, as being the motor force of a universal expansion, of a development of all the "national" energies. In other words, the dominant group is coordinated concretely with the general interests of the subordinate groups, and the life of the state is conceived of as a continuous process of formation and superseding of unstable equilibria (on the juridical plane) between the interests of the fundamental group and those of the subordinate groups—equilibria in which the interests of the dominant group prevail, but only up to a certain point, i.e. stopping short of narrowly corporate economic interest. (SPN:182)

For Gramsci, hegemony is always contested; it is only ever a temporary resolution of a continual conflict. Gramsci rejected the simplistic idea of a purely instrumental class state, expressive only of the interests of the dominant class. As Andy Green (1990:94) points out, a hegemonic order comprises the formation of new alliances and the attempted incorporation of subordinate groups, even the granting of concessions, though never such as would damage the vital interests of the dominant group; it is "not the homogeneous substance of an imposed class ideology."

In maintaining hegemony, the state exercises an active, ethical and educational function, an idea Gramsci borrowed from Croce and which was also used by the Socialist-turned-Fascist, Benito Mussolini (SPN:258n). For Gramsci, "every State is ethical in as much as one of its most important functions is to raise the great mass of the population to a particular cultural and moral level" (SPN:258). This level corresponds to the needs of the productive forces for development, and hence to the interests of the ruling classes.

The state is defined broadly as "the entire complex of practical and theoretical activities with which the ruling class not only justifies and maintains its dominance, but manages to win the active consent of those over whom it rules" (SPN:244). It is an active, organizing force with an educative and moral role in ensuring the hegemony of the dominant classes. The state is essentially proactive in all spheres, it is "an instrument of 'rationalisation', of acceleration and of Taylorization. It operates according to a plan, urges, incites, solicits, and 'punishes'" (SPN:247).

As Anderson (1976–7) makes clear, the boundaries between the state and civil society are always ambiguous in Gramsci's thought. For Gramsci, the state works through civil society, so that its power continually permeates those institutions beyond the boundaries of the state, as Green (1990:93) points out. Institutions such as the school perform on behalf of the state what Gramsci described as "a positive educational function," whereas the courts perform "a repressive and negative educative function." However, "in reality, a multitude of other so-called private initiatives and activities tend to the same end," forming "the apparatus of the political and cultural hegemony of the ruling classes" (SPN:258).

Gramsci described the parliamentary regime as a classical example of the normal exercise of hegemony (SPN:80 n49). The parliamentary regime is "characterised by the combination of force and consent, which balance each other reciprocally, without force predominating excessively over consent." Should force become necessary, the parliamentary regime will always attempt to elicit the consent of the majority for its use through the influence of newspapers and other organs of public opinion, attempting thereby to remain hegemonic.

For Gramsci, the antithesis of hegemony—state coercion, "political government" or "direct domination"—comes into play when spontaneous consent has failed, "legally" enforcing discipline on those groups who do not "consent" either actively or passively (SPN:12). For a revolution to be successful necessitates victory in both the spheres of hegemony and direct domination, and Gramsci was thus able to see the revolutionary process as an intellectual and educational phenomenon, as well as a matter of practical politics. Indeed, for Gramsci,

Every relationship of "hegemony" is necessarily an educational relationship and occurs not only within a nation, between the various forces that comprise it, but in the entire international and world field, between complexes of national and continental civilisations. (FSPN:157)

It is a process in which intellectuals play a key role as the organizers of hegemony.

The Intellectuals

Gramsci used the term "intellectual" in different ways throughout his writing. For example, he referred early on in his political career to the problem posed by intellectuals in the revolutionary movement, using the term in the conventional way to describe those who are primarily thinkers rather than practical activists. Writing in this vein in 1917 he stated that "the intellectuals represent a dead weight in our movement because they do not have a specific role in it which fits their capabilities" (SCW:21).

Gramsci developed his solution to the problem of the "dead weight" of the intellectuals in the context of his analysis of the relationship between the industrial north of Italy and the agrarian south, first outlined in his essay "Some Aspects of the Southern Question" (SPWII:441–62; Gramsci 1995). The essay was written for the planned relaunch of *Ordine Nuovo* at a time of political turmoil in Italy and remained unfinished because of Gramsci's arrest. Gramsci regarded the essay as short and superficial (LP:79) and later, writing in prison with time to reflect, he expanded the concept.

In "Some Aspects of the Southern Question" Gramsci differentiated between "southern intellectuals" and the "new type of intellectual" bred by industry: "the technical organizer, the specialist in applied science" (SPWII:454). Southern intellectuals comprised most of the state bureaucrats, while the new breed of industrial technocrats was based in the north. Gramsci characterized southern society as made up of three social layers: "the great amorphous, disintegrated mass of the peasantry, the intellectuals of the petty and medium rural bourgeoisie" and finally "the big landowners and great intellectuals" (SPWII:454). In Gramsci's formulation, the middle layer of intellectuals responded to impulses from the peasant base, whereas the landowners and great intellectuals, such as Croce and Giustino Fortunato, dominated and centralized the whole complex of phenomena through their mastery of the political and ideological fields. As such, they were "the two major figures of Italian reaction" (SPWII:454), capable of defusing a potentially revolutionary situation. Gramsci described Croce as fulfilling "an extremely important 'national' function" by detaching the radical intellectuals from the peasant masses and forcing them to take part in national and European culture (SPWII:460). Croce was, for Gramsci, in a reference to Machiavelli's classic renaissance text (1965), the "Prince" of the bourgeoisie, just as the Communist Party was the "modern Prince" of the revolutionary working class. But Croce was a Prince whose weakness Gramsci perceived. As Buci-Glucksmann (1980:396) points out, Gramsci saw that Croce's idealistic historicism was incapable of promoting a genuinely expansive intellectual and moral reform that would reach the masses "precisely because it made culture into an 'autonomous subject', unable to inspire a 'constructive psychology';" by contrast, the modern Prince "would make culture one of the places where the unity of theory and practice is realised."

However, Gramsci was not only interested in analyzing the role of those whose intellectual powers were employed in the service of the dominant forces in capitalist society, he was also essentially concerned with the difficult task of the formation of intellectuals committed to the revolutionary movement. In an important passage, Gramsci reflected that

Intellectuals develop slowly, far more slowly than any other social group, by their very nature and historical function. They represent the entire cultural tradition of a people, seeking to resume and synthesize all of its history. (SPWII:462)

It is therefore very difficult for intellectuals *en masse* to "break with the entire past and situate themselves totally upon the terrain of a new ideology" (SPWII:462).

Nevertheless, what Gramsci called "a break of an organic kind, historically characterized" was essential in order that the necessary political alliance between the northern proletariat and the southern peasant masses might be forged by intellectuals committed to the revolutionary cause (SPWII:462). The alliance would be backed up by a program of the division of land among the peasants, provision of credit, the setting up of cooperatives, guarantee of security of person and property against looters and the establishment of public works of reclamation and irrigation (SPWII:442). This was in the interests of both workers and peasants, because only through such an alliance would it be possible to mobilize the majority of the working population against capitalism and the bourgeois state and oust the bourgeoisie from state power (SPWII:443).

In the prison notebooks Gramsci developed this theme into his theory of the intellectuals. Gramsci started by rejecting the idea that intellectuals exist as a distinct social category, independent of class and social context. Instead, he stressed that, "All men are intellectuals, [. . .] but not all men have in society the social function of intellectuals" (SPN:9). Those who are intellectuals by social function were divided by Gramsci into two groups: organic and traditional. The distinction is, as Quintin Hoare (1980:321) reminds us, a conceptual rather than simply an empirical one, the categories not being mutually exclusive. Organic intellectuals are so called because they perform an educational and organizational role on behalf of their class, giving it "homogeneity and an awareness of its own function not only in the economic but also in the social and political fields" (SPN:5). Gramsci was a student of philology and would have been aware of the etymological link between the words "organic" and "organizing" which exists in both English and Italian. The working class must produce its own organic intellectuals in order to perform the task of articulating and disseminating the hegemony of their class over society as a whole. For Gramsci, "critical self-consciousness means, historically and politically, the creation of an *elite* of intellectuals" (SPN:334).

In Gramsci's formulation, the working-class organic intellectual is an active participator in practical—industrial and political—life "as constructor, organiser, 'permanent persuader' and not just a simple orator" (SPN:10). Technical education, "closely bound to industrial labour even at the most primitive and unqualified level must form the basis of the new type of intellectual" (SPN:9). These new intellectuals must be "'specialised' in conceptual and philosophical elaboration of ideas" (SPN:334), because

consciousness of being part of a particular hegemonic force (that is to say, political consciousness) is the first stage towards a further progressive self-consciousness in which theory and practice will finally be one. (SPN:333)

In this way, organic intellectuals of the working class would be "the whalebone in the corset" (SPN:340), able to make politically possible the intellectual progress of the mass through working out and making coherent, "the principles and problems raised by the masses in their practical activity, thus constituting a cultural and social bloc" (SPN:330).

In a highly condensed passage in the prison notebooks (SPN:9), Gramsci delineated the task of creating this new stratum of intellectuals. It was emphatically not a question of filling empty vessels; instead, the task consisted "in the critical elaboration of the intellectual activity that exists in everyone at a certain degree of development." That entailed integrating the physical and mental domains, modifying the relationship of intellectual activity with muscular-nervous effort towards a new equilibrium in which "the muscular-nervous effort itself [. . .] becomes the foundation of a new and integral conception of the world."

Gramsci recognized the difficulty of the task, writing in the prison notebooks of the "unprecedented difficulties" to be overcome in order to produce "a new stratum of intellectuals including those capable of the highest degree of specialisation, from a social group which has not traditionally developed the appropriate attitudes" (SPN:43). Despite the difficulties, the creation of such intellectuals was essential because "there is no organization without intellectuals, that is without organisers and leaders" (SPN:334). Gramsci recognized that the Church knew this better than many on the left. As he wrote:

The Pope knows the mechanism of cultural reform of the popular-peasant masses better than many secular left elements: he knows that one cannot convert a great mass in molecular fashion but that, to hasten the process, it is necessary either to conquer the natural leaders of the great masses, in other words the intellectuals, or to form a group of intellectuals of a new type, hence the creation of native bishops. (FSPN:123)

Unlike in the Church, however, in the revolutionary movement the relationship between the masses and working-class organic intellectuals, between leaders and led, must be reciprocal and complementary rather than static and unidirectional. This is necessary because, as Gramsci pointed out:

The popular element "feels" but does not always know or understand; the intellectual element "knows" but does not always understand and in particular does not always feel. (SPN:418)

By contrast, traditional intellectuals are intellectuals of the ruling class, "the dominant group's deputies," whose intellectual status and power are so great that they constitute a quasi-autonomous elite, able to assume the mantle of permanence and claim insight into eternal truths (SPN:7). The working class must "struggle to assimilate and to conquer 'ideologically' the traditional intellectuals" by absorbing ideas and individuals where these intellectual defectors are of value in its struggle for hegemony. This will be achieved more quickly and effectively the more the working class "succeeds in simultaneously elaborating its own organic intellectuals" (SPN:10).

Intellectuals are thus, for Gramsci, not fixed in the social class from which they originated, nor are they an elite detached from the exigencies of political reality. His belief that the intellectual function is common to all humanity and therefore must be developed, like other faculties, through experience and education, dispels the mystique surrounding intellectuality. The intellectual, for Gramsci, is not only one who knows: feeling, knowing and understanding are all essential attributes of Gramsci's revolutionary intellectuals. The key point is that intellectuals perform a leadership function in the organization of a hegemonic historical bloc. Leadership, for Gramsci, is not a matter of position in a hierarchy, rather it is a matter of analysis and direction in relation to the political situation pertaining at the time. But how is the capacity for such leadership, the new intellectualism, to be developed—and, more broadly, how is hegemony to be organized? Gramsci does not supply a recipe, although, in a sense, the answers are to be found throughout his work. Some of these are examined in the next sections.

The Organization of Hegemony
In a note for a study on how "the ideological structure of a dominant class is organized, in other words the material organization intended to maintain, defend and develop the theoretical or ideological 'front'," Gramsci stated that the largest and most dynamic part of the structure is printed matter in general. He elaborated this to include

publishing houses (which either explicitly or implicitly have a programme and are linked to a given tendency), political newspapers, journals of all sorts—scientific, literary, philological and so on, periodicals down as far as the parish newsletter. (FSPN:155)

But printed matter was only one part of the structure; in addition, it included everything that has a direct or indirect influence on public opinion, such as "libraries, schools, groups and clubs of different kinds, right up to architecture, street lay-out and street names" and that supremely hegemonic institution, the Church (FSPN:155–6).

Gramsci asked the questions that haunt the prison notebooks: what can the innovatory class oppose "to this formidable complex of trenches and fortifications of the dominant class?" (FSPN:156) and how can it spread its influence to "the classes that are its potential allies" (SCW:390)? Gramsci's answer was that the innovatory class must organize its own hegemony, its own blend of force and consent, including its own organization of the ideological front and the development of its own intellectuals. It is this insight, above all, that makes him essential reading for radical adult educators.

In order to see what this might mean in practice, I turn now to three areas of activity (Gramsci would call them "terrains") which may be particularly relevant to adult educators: his political and cultural journalism, his work on the factory councils and his writings on education, in particular, adult education.

Political and Cultural Journalism

For Gramsci, political and cultural journalism[7] is a vital factor in the organization of hegemony. It is a field that he knew well from his time as a journalist in Turin and his interest never left him. For example, he wrote to the PCd'I executive committee from Vienna in 1923 to propose that "a kind of yearbook of the working class be compiled" containing in brief "everything that might interest a party member or sympathiser," including a review of the international political and trade union movement; an examination of the Italian economic, political, military, labor and financial situation; Marxism and its history, particularly in Italy; the political organization and economic situation of Russia, the history of the Bolshevik Party, and the theory and tactics of the Comintern (SCW:404 n35). Later, writing in prison, Gramsci returned to the idea of a yearbook (SCW:421). He advocated the publication of an almanac that, in addition to the usual annual information, would "emphasize those subjects considered to be of the greatest educative and formative importance" (SCW:404).

In a series of prison notes, Gramsci developed this idea in a scheme for what he called "integral" journalism:

one that seeks not only to satisfy all the needs (of a given category) of its public, but also to create and develop these needs, to arouse its public and progressively enlarge it. (SCW:408)

This kind of journalism was "the manifestation of a group which aims to spread an integral conception of the world through various journalistic activities" (SCW:403). Such a group would be "a more or less homogeneous cultural grouping" with "a given general orientation" which could be used "to construct a self-sufficient, complete cultural edifice, by beginning directly from [. . .] language, from the means of expression and reciprocal contact" (SCW:408–9).

Gramsci must have had in mind the editorial board of journals such as *Ordine Nuovo,* which "function at the same time both as editorial committees and as cultural groups" (SPN:28). The method is one of "collective discussion and criticism (made up of suggestions, advice, comments on method, and criticism which is constructive and aimed at mutual education)" (SPN:28). The group "criticises as a body, and thus helps to define the tasks of individual editors, whose activity is organised according to a plan and a division of labour which are rationally arranged in advance" (SPN:28). Gramsci stressed the need for "an unyielding struggle against habits of dilettantism, of improvisation, of 'rhetorical' solutions or those proposed for effect" (SPN:29). To counteract these tendencies, work should be written in the form of terse succinct notes. These methods would create "ever more organic conditions of work: files, bibliographic digests, a library of basic specialised works, etc." (SPN:28–9). Intellectual work of this type is necessary, "in order to impart to autodidacts the discipline in study which an orthodox scholastic career provides, in order to Taylorize intellectual work" (SPN:29).

Although the activity is collective, it is nevertheless organized in a stratified way with "work-groups under the guidance of the most highly-skilled and highly developed, who can accelerate the training of the most backward and untrained" (SPN:29). Each member's area of expertise complements that of other members and helps to complete the expertise of the collectivity. In this way, "the average level of the individual editors is in fact successfully raised so that it reaches the altitude or capacity of the most highly-skilled" (SPN:28). This process benefits the review and creates the conditions for the emergence of "a homogeneous group of intellectuals, trained to produce a regular and methodical 'writing' activity" (SPN:28). Such an editorial group contributes to raising the level of the revolutionary movement through its processes and ways of working as well as through its product, the newspaper or review. As Gramsci commented, *Ordine Nuovo* "worked to develop certain forms of new intellectualism," a fact which was "not the least reason for its success" (SPN:10).

Gramsci's scheme for an integral journalism included three types of periodicals (PNI:120–1). The first type was "theoretical: especially 'historiography'. Very unified," exemplified by Croce's prestigious bimonthly philosophical journal, *La critica* (Hughes 1979 *passim*). Periodicals of the second type were "devoted to current events" and their articles "have a popularizing, expository character." At worst, these are "addressed to everyone and no-one and after a while become entirely useless" (SCW:401). They must be rescued from sterility and become "the motive and formative force of cultural institutions of a mass associative type, i.e., not of closed cadres" (SCW:402).

The third type of periodical Gramsci found particularly interesting. It was "critical-historical-bibliographical" (PNI:121), exemplified by the more successful issues of Luigi Russo's influential but erratic review, *Leonardo* (Cannistraro ed. 1982 *passim*). Periodicals of the third type would provide

critical information, for the benefit of a public of average culture or just entering cultural life, with a coverage of all the publications on the group of topics likely to be of greatest interest to it. (SCW:402)

This type was necessary because "individually nobody can follow all the literature published on a group of topics or even on a single topic" (SCW:402). It would be geared to the needs of the general, nonspecialist reader who needs specific facts, coherently presented. In this way,

A complex historical movement may be broken down in time and space and also into different levels (special problems) which can themselves be broken down in time and space. (PNI:122)

This type of periodical would also contain "an encyclopedic political-scientific-philosophical dictionary" of monographs. These "should be truly practical, that is, they should adhere to genuinely felt needs and their expository form should be suited to the average reader" (PNI:126). Such periodicals would also contain "political-intellectual autobiographies," outlining "how one overcomes his environment, through what external impulses and what crises of thought and of feelings" (PNI:127). An important feature would be "historical-bibliographical analysis of regional situations," since, as Gramsci pointed out, many people would like to study local situations but lacked knowledge of how to conduct research (PNI:127). As a result,

one has to provide the general outline of a concrete problem [. . .], indicating the books that have dealt with it, the articles in specialised journals, etc., in the form of bibliographical-critical reviews, providing access especially to uncommon or foreign language publications. (PNI:127)

Gramsci advocated the creation of "a unitary cultural organization" that would organize the three types of periodical, in conjunction with a publishing house for book series associated with the periodicals that "would satisfy the needs of that mass public which is intellectually more active and which it matters most to make think and to transform" (PNI:121). Integral journalism of this kind would create an informed and critical public, an important element in the organization of hegemony, but only part of the picture. Hegemony must also be organized on the industrial front; here, Gramsci's work on the factory councils comes into play.

The Factory Councils
The factory council movement[8] established by Gramsci and his comrades in Turin in 1919 was intended as a key political, educational and technical instrument for the maintenance of production and the creation of the revolution. The councils consisted of elected workplace representatives; the electoral system could vary according to the size of the workshop concerned, but the aim was to elect one delegate for every fifteen workers to a committee of factory delegates representing every aspect of work (manual, clerical and technical) (SPWI:67). They were independent of the trade unions and included nonunionized workers as well as union members; this was regarded as heresy by much of the Italian left at the time.

For Gramsci, the factory councils were intended to be just the beginning of a much wider organization of the working class. Factory council delegates, together with delegates from other categories of workers living in an area, such as waiters, cab drivers, tramway and railway workers, roadsweepers, private employees, clerks and others, would form the "ward council of workshop delegates, the ganglion co-ordinating and centralising all the proletarian energies in the ward" (SPWI:67). The ward committees would be an expression of the whole of the working class living in the ward and would grow into urban commissariats, controlled and disciplined by the Socialist Party and the craft federations (SPWI:67). The commissariats, integrated with the corresponding peasants' organizations, would form the basis of the proletarian state. As Gramsci wrote in September 1919:

the central organs that will be created for every group of factories, every city and every region, right up to a supreme national Workers' Council, will pursue and broaden and intensify the job of controlling and preparing and organising the whole class for the tasks of conquest and government. (SPWI:97)

For Gramsci, therefore, every council was "a step on the road to communism" (SPWI:92).

The factory is a fertile ground for the development of a new proletarian hegemony because, as Gramsci pointed out, "the more the proletarian is specialised in a job, the more he feels the need for order, method, precision;" society comes to appear as "one immense factory, organized with the same precision, method, order that he sees as vital in the factory where he works" (Gramsci quoted in Cammett 1967:79). The factory councils would establish "a shop floor *way of life* [. . .], initial germ of a true and effective labour legislation, i.e., laws which the producers will enact and lay down for themselves" (SPWI:96).

Gramsci believed that the factory councils would make workers aware of their capacity "to produce and exercise sovereignty [. . .], without need for the capitalist and an indefinite delegation of political power" (SPWI:91). As he saw it:

Once they are bonded together in productive communities, the workers will be led automatically to express their will to power in terms of prin-

ciples which are strictly organic to the relations of production and exchange. (SPWI:92)

Gramsci went on in optimistic vein to predict the effect this would have on working-people's psychology:

All mythical, utopian, religious and petty-bourgeois ideologies will drop away from the average proletarian psychology. A communist psychology will become rapidly and lastingly consolidated, as a constant leaven of revolutionary enthusiasm, tenacious perseverance in the iron discipline of work and resistance against any open or underhand assault of the past. (SPWI:92)

Gramsci also emphasized the technical, information-gathering function of the factory councils, which would collect "data and factual material for both the trade federations and the central directive bodies of the new factory organisations" (SPWI:96). The councils could also perform the essential function of technical education, preparing workers to become autonomous producers (Cammett 1967:81). Thus, in an article of 13 September 1919, Gramsci urged the workshop delegates of the Fiat Centro and Brevetti plants to establish "appropriate instruction departments, real vocational schools" inside the factory (SPWI:96). Such schools were accordingly organized by the commissars to increase the workers' skills in their own trades or industrial functions.

In the event, however, the revolution failed to materialize and the reaction led to the Fascist takeover in 1922. Piccone's stark assessment is that Gramsci "recklessly projected his elegant philosophical scheme onto the Turin labor struggles without any realistic evaluation of the nature of predominant power relations" (Piccone 1983:127). Gramsci's own verdict was equally harsh, but he saw the failure as one of political leadership, rather than as endemic to the factory councils per se. As he wrote in 1924:

In 1919–1920 we made extremely serious mistakes which ultimately we are paying for today. For fear of being called upstarts and careerists, we did not form a faction and organize this throughout Italy. We were not ready to give the Turin factory councils an autonomous directive centre, which could have exercised an enormous influence throughout the country, for fear of a split in the unions and of being expelled prematurely from the Socialist Party. (SPWII:189)

Accordingly, after 1920, Gramsci turned his attention to the role of the revolutionary political party, but this was a widening of focus rather than a change of direction. He saw that revolutionary leadership must entail the development of organic links between leaders and led, party and masses. He saw the councils as an important means of achieving this, but they would only be able to do so if the party were "controlled from the bottom" by an informed, articulate membership, and acted as "the coordinator of revolutionary assaults on a national level" (Davidson 1977:139).

Gramsci never renounced the factory council ideal. It is clear from his prison writing that he believed the type of educative experience represented by the councils could produce organic intellectuals of the working class, without whom the revolution would be no more than a *coup d'état* without a mass base, coercive rather than hegemonic. But he saw that educative political experience must be bolstered by appropriate education, and it is to Gramsci's work in education that we turn next.

Education

Gramsci's conception of education was informed by his Socratic idea of culture: as he wrote in 1917,

I believe it means thinking well, whatever one thinks, and therefore acting well, whatever one does. And since I know that culture too is a basic concept of socialism, because it integrates and makes concrete the vague concept of freedom of thought, I would like it to be enlivened by the other concept, that of organization. Let us organize culture in the same way that we seek to organize any practical activity. (SCW:25)

As we have seen in the earlier discussion of journalism and the factory councils, it is when culture is "enlivened with organization," when it is educative, that it becomes, at least embryonically, hegemonic.

For Gramsci, education and culture were integral to issues of hegemony and the formation of intellectuals. His conception of education is thus much broader than the conventional one and includes specifically educational issues, as well as much more. It also includes the education of adults; indeed, much of Gramsci's political activity could be seen in terms of the education of adults. It is in this context that his writings on education should be read and his record as "a tireless popular educator," as Green (1990:97) describes him, considered.

The very breadth of Gramsci's conception of education, however, makes it difficult to present a coherent account of his ideas without forcing them into a straitjacket. This is particularly problematic given the fragmentary nature of his writing in the prison notebooks, especially since, as Green points out, Gramsci "often slides from the descriptive to the prescriptive without any clear signals as to what he is doing" (Green 1990:97). My approach here is to look first at Gramsci's own experience as an adult educator and then to look at his writings on education, focusing particularly on his writings on the education of adults.

Throughout his life, in his reflective and analytical writing in the prison notebooks, in his personal relationships and in his journalism, Gramsci strove to explore, to explain, to educate. His letters to his wife about the development of their sons are a moving testimony to his abiding interest in education (see, for example, LP:161–2, 195–7). Even when produced for immediate polemical purposes, Gramsci's writing is characterized by a seriousness, depth and range unusual in political polemic. As he wrote in 1916: "Culture is a privilege. Education is a privilege. And we do not want it to be so" (SPWI:25–6).

Gramsci relished the cut and thrust of political debate. As he wrote to his sister-in-law early in his imprisonment,

Only rarely do I lose myself in a particular train of thought and analyze something for its inherent interest. Usually I have to engage in a dialogue, be dialectical, to arrive at some intellectual stimulation. I once told you how I hate tossing stones into the dark. I need an interlocutor, a concrete adversary. (LP:193)

Given this cast of mind and his acute awareness of the need to educate people (including those with little formal education) for political change, it is not surprising that Gramsci's prolific political activity often took the form of adult education. In the period 1916–1922 alone, he lectured to workers' cultural circles and helped to run a discussion group, a workers' school and an Institute of Proletarian Culture (SCW:16).

In those years, Gramsci was sometimes accused of being too interested in education, and of seeming to assign to education the crucial role in creating the revolution. Some of his early writing appears to bear the accusation out; for example, in an article in *Avanti* in 1916, he stated that "the first step in emancipating oneself from political and social slavery is that of freeing the mind" (Gramsci quoted in Davidson 1977:77). But in his later work Gramsci made it clear that he had no illusions about the power of education *alone* to bring about the revolution. In 1924 he stated that pedagogic methods could not resolve "the great historical problem of the spiritual emancipation of the working class" (SPWII:227). He rejected the idealist notion that the consciousness of the entire working class could be changed completely before the conquest of the state, stating that class consciousness is only changed when the way of living of the class itself has been changed, "in other words when the proletariat has become a ruling class and has at its disposal the apparatus of production and exchange and the power of the State" (SPWII:288).

However, even in his early days, Gramsci's interest in education was tempered by practical political considerations. For example, calling for the creation of a proletarian cultural association in Turin in 1917, Gramsci argued that the cultural association would make up for a serious deficiency in the movement in which

we wait for the present moment to discuss problems and to determine the direction of our action. Out of urgency, we provide hurried solutions to problems, in the sense that not all those who take part in the movement have mastered the exact terms of the problems. (SCW:21)

As a result, when people did follow the strategy established, it was because they trusted their leaders, rather than out of a deep conviction, so that "at every important hour of history there occurs a breaking of the ranks, a giving in, internal disputes, personal issues. [. . .]

There is no widespread resolute conviction" (SCW:21). Since "Socialism is an integral vision of life [with] a philosophy, a mystique, a morality" (SCW:21), the cultural association would be a forum in which to discuss the moral, religious and philosophical problems posed by political and economic action, which trade unions and political parties are unable to discuss and to which they cannot disseminate proper solutions.

Gramsci noted that in England and Germany there were "powerful organizations of proletarian and socialist culture," and he singled out the Fabian Society for praise:

Its task is to offer a forum for a thorough and popular discussion of the economic and moral problems which life brings or will bring to the attention of the proletariat. It has succeeded, moreover, in involving a large part of the English intellectual and university world in this work of civilization and liberation. (SCW:23)

Gramsci envisaged that such cultural associations in Italy would become "the third organ of the movement for the vindication of the Italian working class" (SCW:23).

Gramsci's own first practical experience of adult education came with the Club for Moral Life, established in 1917 by the Turin Branch of the PSI. The club comprised Gramsci and several young men who had been forced by poverty to leave school early. Gramsci described the club's method in a letter written in 1918: one member would introduce an analysis of an essay or book and give it to the others for their comments with the aim of achieving the "intellectual and moral communion of everyone" (FSPN:xxxii). A surviving member has described how they met and talked informally as they walked in the street, passing round a copy of Marcus Aurelius's *Meditations* (Germino 1990:34). The club broke up when two members were drafted into the army in 1918 but, as Dante Germino (1990:34) points out, the fact that ordinary workers, with only elementary education, could rapidly absorb great ideas of the past, must have led Gramsci to see such clubs as a possible model for generating revolutionary change.

The following year, through *Ordine Nuovo*, Gramsci established a School of Culture and Socialist Propaganda, attended by both

university students and workers, which examined the idea of "a new
State completely replacing the liberal State by a 'system of councils'"
(Cammett 1967:81). This initiative generated a great deal of interest and enthusiasm, and Gramsci considered that its success was due
to its organic links with the party and the Turin factory councils:

*Study and culture for us are none other than the theoretical conscious-
ness of our immediate and supreme goals, and the way in which we will
succeed in translating them into action. (FSPN:xxxiii)*

The school was ultimately overwhelmed by the numbers of people
coming forward, and Gramsci commented that "a school adequate
to the importance of that movement would have required not the
activity of a few people but the ordered, systematic effort of an entire party" (FSPN:xxxiii).

In the changed circumstances of 1924, with Fascist repression
increasing and many party members in prison or in exile, Gramsci's
focus switched to the education of party members: "Our task is limited to the Party [. . .] to improve our cadres; to make them capable
of confronting the forthcoming struggles" (SPWII:227). He launched
an appeal to guarantee *Ordine Nuovo*'s independent existence and to
underwrite the initial expenses of a correspondence school for party
activists as the first phase of a movement to create small party schools.
The aim was "to create organizers and propagandists who [. . .] have
brains as well as lungs and a throat" (SPWII:227). Gramsci saw work
of this kind as particularly appropriate for the party members in
exile, where the older and more skilled members should "bring the
younger comrades to share in their experience, and thus contribute
to raising the political level of the mass of the members" (SPWII:227).

The course was to consist of three sections: on historical mate-
rialism; on general political questions; and on the Communist party
(FSPN:xxxiii). Also planned was an Italian edition of *The Communist Manifesto* and "a collection of the most significant passages from
Marx and Engels" (SPWII:228). In the introduction to the first set
of study notes, Gramsci stated that the party must "make it a duty
for the militant to know Marxist-Leninist doctrine, at least in the
most general terms" (SPWII:289). But doctrine alone was not
enough: militants must also know "how to derive from reality the

elements with which to establish a line, so that the working class will not be cast down but will feel that it is being led and can still fight" (SPWII:290).

The correspondence school was duly established, although only two sets of study notes were produced and distributed, both written entirely by Gramsci, before the PCd'I was declared illegal on 5 November 1926.

Even after his arrest, Gramsci probably did not abandon the plan for a correspondence school: Boothman argues convincingly that some of Gramsci's prison notes were intended as notes toward a continuation of the program (FSPN:xxxiv). Neither did Gramsci abandon his practice as an adult educator: while imprisoned on the island of Ustica for six weeks from December 1926 to January 1927, he and fellow PCd'I member Amadeo Bordiga, the leader of the left grouping within the PCd'I, organized education courses for their fellow political detainees. Gramsci directed the literary–historical section and Bordiga the scientific section of this party school (FSPN:524 n36). The courses included all levels of elementary education as well as more advanced study; Gramsci wrote to his friend Piero Sraffa that their students, "even if sometimes semi-literate, are intellectually well-developed" (FSPN:xxxiii). The prison school on Ustica started a movement which spread to other places where political prisoners were confined by the Fascist government (LP:68 n2).

Gramsci's critique of the Popular Universities (*Università Popolari*) gives further insight into his approach to adult education. The Popular Universities were independent philanthropic institutions for the education of adults (SPN:329 n10). Gramsci's interest in them was long standing. As he wrote in 1917, instead of philanthropy "let us offer solidarity, organization. Let us give the means to good will, without which it will remain sterile and barren" (SCW:25). He also regarded the lecture-based mode of delivery of the Popular Universities as inappropriate. What was needed instead was "the detailed work of discussing and investigating problems, work in which everybody participates, to which everybody contributes, in which everybody is both master and disciple" (SCW:25).

Despite their flaws, however, Gramsci pointed out that the Popular Universities "demonstrated on the part of the 'simple' a genuine enthusiasm and a strong determination to attain a higher cultural level and a higher conception of the world" (SPN:329–330). The problem was that the Popular Universities betrayed the trust of the "simple." Gramsci likened the educational transaction involved to the first contacts between English merchants and Africans: "trashy baubles were handed out in exchange for nuggets of gold" (SPN:330). For Gramsci, the Popular Universities were fatally flawed by the lack of "any organic quality either of philosophical thought or of organisational stability and central cultural direction" (SPN:330). The principle behind Gramsci's own initiatives in adult education is clearly stated in his critique of the Popular Universities. These could only have worked properly if

the intellectuals had been organically the intellectuals of those masses, and if they had worked out and made coherent the principles and problems raised by the masses in their practical activity. (SPN:330)

By contrast, Gramsci's initiatives in adult education were all, as we have seen, in the service of revolutionary hegemony, the political development of which, he states,

necessarily supposes an intellectual unity and an ethic in conformity with a conception of reality that has gone beyond common sense and become, if only within narrow limits, a critical conception. (SPN:333)

Gramsci strove to create this "intellectual unity" beyond "common sense" and he draws a distinction between "good sense" and "common sense"[9] in various prison notes.

Gramsci described common sense as the "diffuse, uncoordinated features of a general form of thought common to a particular period and a particular popular environment" (SPN:330n). It is a collective noun since "there is not just one common sense" (SPN:325). Despite its incoherence, common sense nevertheless contains "a healthy nucleus of good sense [. . .] which deserves to be made more unitary and coherent" (SPN:328). It is good sense which must be developed.

Good sense is to be developed in three main ways: through the study of Marxism; through an analysis of common sense in order to retrieve and develop the elements of good sense inherent in it; and through an analysis of the ideas of traditional intellectuals. Gramsci made the case for studying Marxism on the grounds that it is "a philosophy of praxis" (the term Gramsci uses to deceive the prison censor) rather than a set of doctrines to be accepted uncritically. As such, Marxism "cannot but present itself at the outset in a polemical and critical guise, as superseding the existing mode of thinking and the existing concrete thought (the existing cultural world)" (SPN:330). Indeed, all ideas must be examined critically: Gramsci criticized Bukharin for assuming that the ideas of traditional intellectuals were irrelevant to revolutionary workers (SPN:419). Instead, they should be rigorously examined and subjected to criticism in order to recover whatever might be useful. In the struggle for hegemony, the incoming class must conquer the "commanding heights of the adversary's culture," as Boothman puts it (FSPN:xxx).

The incoming class must also look critically at its own culture, particularly at its own common sense. Gramsci pointed out that in Italy religion provided the principal elements of common sense, and consequently the relationship between common sense and religion was much more intimate than that between common sense and the philosophical systems of the intellectuals (SPN:420). Even within one religion, such as Christianity, however, there is a mass of distinct and contradictory tendencies. Common sense is likewise not monolithic; it is contradictory and difficult to chart. It is at one and the same time, as Timothy Ireland puts it, the "seed-bed of the dominant ideology as well as being the battleground of the new ideology in elaboration" (Ireland 1987:72). Critical thought means criticizing one's own conception of the world in order to make it, "a coherent unity and to raise it to the level reached by the most advanced thought in the world" (SPN:324). It entails the discovery that one belongs to a fundamental social class, with all the implications of that discovery for one's historical role in society. The starting point for this is

the consciousness of what one really is, and is "knowing thyself" as a product of the historical process which has deposited in you an infinity of traces without leaving an inventory. (SPN:324).

This does not entail "introducing from scratch a scientific form of thought into everyone's individual life, but of renovating and making 'critical' an already existing activity" (SPN:331).

In the absence of a history of common sense, the study of the history of philosophy must be the main source of reference, in order to develop in the individual the ability to evaluate ideas "as superseded links of an intellectual chain, and to determine what the new contemporary problems are and how the old problems should now be analyzed" (SPN:331). For Gramsci,

Critical understanding of self takes place through a struggle of political "hegemonies" [. . .] first in the ethical field and then in that of politics proper, in order to arrive at the working out at a higher level of one's own conception of reality. (SPN:333)

Thus it is politics that links common sense and the upper level of philosophy, just as it is politics that "assures the relationship between the Catholicism of the intellectuals and that of the simple" (SPN:331). But the two cases are antithetical; whereas the Catholicism of the intellectuals leaves the "simple" in their primitive philosophy of common sense, "the philosophy of praxis" tends instead "to lead them to a higher conception of life" (SPN:332). It affirms the need for contact between intellectuals and the simple "precisely in order to construct an intellectual-moral bloc which can make politically possible the intellectual progress of the mass and not only of small intellectual groups" (SPN:332). The instrument for the construction of such an intellectual-moral bloc is the revolutionary party of the working class, and it is to the educative role of the party that we turn next, before going on to look at Gramsci's aims for education after the revolution.

For Gramsci, the revolutionary party of the working class acts as a "collective intellectual," elaborating and diffusing conceptions of the world, working out the ethics and the politics corresponding to these conceptions and acting as "their historical 'laboratory' [. . .] the crucibles where the unification of theory and practice, understood as a real historical process, takes place" (SPN:335). Indeed, Gramsci's insistence on the necessity for the unification of theory and practice presupposes an educational role for the party. The party must be dialectically related to the masses, so that its actions are informed by the experience of the masses. The revolutionary movement must find in its contact with the "simple" "the source of the problems it sets out to study and to resolve" (SPN:330). Similarly, the actions of the masses must be informed by the analysis and direction worked out by the party. As Gramsci stated,

one can construct, on a specific practice, a theory which, by coinciding and identifying itself with the decisive elements of the practice itself, can accelerate the historical process that is going on, rendering practice more homogeneous, more coherent, more efficient in all its elements, and thus, in other words, developing its potential to the maximum. (SPN:365)

Gramsci emphasized that the party is "essentially political and even its cultural activity is of a politico-cultural kind" (SCW:402). He accordingly distinguished between "cultural policy" and "cultural technique," illustrating the point with the example of a party that contains illiterate members and has a policy of fighting against illiteracy. He pointed out that "a group for the struggle against illiteracy is not exactly the same thing as a 'school for the illiterate'." A school for the illiterate "teaches people how to read and write;" this is a matter of cultural technique. A group for the struggle against illiteracy "prepares all the most effective channels for eradicating illiteracy from the great mass of a country's population;" this is a matter of cultural policy (SCW:402).

Gramsci's vision was in stark contrast to that of the Fascist Minister of Education, Giovanni Gentile, whose reforms rigidly separated instruction from education (FSPN:72) and technical training from philosophical education. Instead, Gramsci stressed that

democracy, by definition, cannot mean merely that an unskilled worker can become skilled. It must mean that every "citizen" can "govern" and that society places him, even if only abstractly, in a general condition to achieve this. (SPN:40)

Accordingly, the new society would ensure "for each non-ruler a free training in the skills and general technical preparation necessary to that end" (SPN:40–1).

Within this framework, Gramsci envisaged a postrevolutionary education system, arranged in stages geared to different ages, from early childhood to adulthood. The process would begin with a network of "kindergartens and other institutions" in which "children would be habituated to a certain collective discipline and acquire pre-scholastic notions and attitudes" (SPN:31). After this, the stages of education would comprise,

First, a common basic education, imparting a general, humanistic, formative culture; this would strike the right balance between development of the capacity for working manually (technically, industrially) and development of the capacities required for intellectual work. From this type of common schooling, via repeated experiments in vocational orientation, pupils would pass on to one of the specialised schools or to productive work. (SPN:27)

The common school would be an "active school," meaning one in which the pupil is a truly active participant in the school—something which, Gramsci states, could only happen if "the school is related to life" (SPN:37) (i.e., hegemonic). This is a reference to the concept of the active school developed by Montessori and others, which Gramsci regarded as "still in its romantic phase, in which the elements of struggle against the mechanical and Jesuitical school have become unhealthily exaggerated" (SPN:32–3). It would therefore be necessary to "place limits on libertarian ideologies in this field and to stress with some energy the duty of the adult generations, i.e. of the State, to 'mould' the new generations" (SPN:32). In order to develop the new form of the active school, it would be necessary to go beyond the romantic to the "'classical', rational phase, and to find in the ends to be attained the natural source for developing the appropriate methods and forms" (SPN:33).

In the later stages of the common school, Gramsci envisaged that the pupil would proceed to the "creative" phase of schooling, where, "the aim is to expand the personality—by now autonomous and responsible, but with a solid and homogeneous moral and social conscience" (SPN:33). The creative phase is characterized by work in seminars, libraries and laboratories, where "learning takes place especially through a spontaneous and autonomous effort of the pupil, with the teacher only exercising a function of friendly guide—as happens, or should happen in the university" (SPN:33).

Beyond the common school, Gramsci aimed to break down the rigid separation between the universities and the professional academies (or vocational schools). The professional academies

ought to become the cultural organization [. . .] of those who, after the common school, will go on to a professional job, as well as becoming a meeting ground between them and university people. (FSPN:145)

Such professionally trained people should have access to specialized institutes which would undertake research in a wide range of fields. There would be "centralisation of expertise and specialisation on a territorial basis" with a network of national, regional and provincial sections and local groups in the towns and countryside (FSPN:146). There should be close collaboration between the new cultural organizations and the universities (FSPN:147). Activities such as industrial conferences and experimental laboratories in factories would be scrutinized and a mechanism set up "to select and advance the intellectual capacities of the masses of the people that are today being sacrificed and are losing their way in a maze of errors and blind alleys" (FSPN:146). Local groups (by which Gramsci presumably meant local Communist Party branches) would all have a "moral and political science section" which would

organize other special sections to discuss the technical aspects of industrial and agricultural questions, problems of the organization and rationalisation of work, the factory, farm and office and so on. Periodic congresses at different levels will bring the most capable people to general notice. (FSPN:146)

In another note, Gramsci stated that a list should be drawn up of all the "institutions which are to be considered useful for public education and culture" and which, without state intervention, could not be accessible to the public. These should include the "theatre, libraries and museums of different types, the art galleries, zoological and botanical gardens, etc." (FSPN:153). Gramsci praised the Italian Society for the Advancement of Science as the prototype of the new cultural organization, bringing together "all the 'friends of science', [. . .] specialists and 'amateurs'" just as, in a different field, the Touring Club brings together the "friends of geography and travel" (FSPN:152). In such organizations

the work of the academies and universities must meet and join together with the need the national-popular masses have for scientific culture, thus uniting theory and practice, intellectual and industrial labour: an organ which could find its root in the common school." (FSPN:152)

Gramscism after Gramsci

In the years since Gramsci's death, his ideas have eventually reached a wide audience through the publication of the notebooks and his prison letters and the re-publication of much of his earlier writing. A host of publications has appeared in many languages commenting on his work from a variety of political standpoints and carrying forward his ideas in a wide range of fields. The comprehensive two-volume international bibliography of works on Gramsci produced by Cammett (1991) and Cammett and Righi (1995) lists more than 10,400 items in thirty-three languages, the majority of which have appeared since 1966 (International Gramsci Society[10] 1995:31).

Gramsci's posthumous career has been marked by controversy: he has been variously interpreted as a Leninist, a Hegelian, a social democrat, a humanist Marxist, or an idealist. His position in relation to the Italian idealist philosopher Benedetto Croce and the Marxist Antonio Labriola is also hotly debated. The question of continuities or disjunctions between the Gramsci of the prison notebooks and his earlier writing is unresolved also, and likely to remain so, given that the notebooks are an "open text," one on which the writer himself has not had the final word.

The prison notebooks did not have an easy path into publication. After Gramsci's death they were smuggled out of the clinic, probably by Tania, and then out of Italy to Moscow. A preliminary edition of the notebooks was published in Italy between 1948 and 1951 by the Turin publisher Einaudi together with collections of his earlier (pre-1926) political writings and some of his prison letters. Valentino Gerratana's critical edition of the prison notebooks, based on a chronological reconstruction of the manuscripts and including rejected drafts as well as revised pieces, was not published in Italy until 1975, thirty-eight years after his death.

In the period following the end of World War II, Gramsci was virtually canonized by the Italian Communist Party (PCI), the successor to the PCd'I (Shore 1990:35). However, commentators, including Paul Piccone (1983:109–10 n9), have pointed out that his ideas were distorted for many years through the suppression of those parts of the notebooks and prison letters that appeared to run counter to the Party line. Debates about his political heritage have been dominated by arguments about his political relationship to his PCd'I and Comintern comrades and more broadly to Leninism, Stalinism and Trotskyism.[11] These debates came to a head with the development of Eurocommunism in the 1970s, when the PCI found in such Gramscian notions as the formation of historical-cultural blocs and the war of position, guidelines for a strategy of "historic compromise," i.e., an electoral pact with the ruling Christian Democrats (Shore 1990; Piccone 1983).

It was not until a selection of Gramsci's writing was translated into English and published in Britain and in the United States twenty years after his death that he began to be known to a small circle of Marxists in Britain and North America (Gramsci 1957a; Gramsci 1957b). The timing was fortuitous: as David Forgacs puts it in his review of Gramsci and Marxism in Britain, "Gramsci was thus conveyed into the culture of the left on the tide of the post-1956 thaw, destalinization and the formation of the first New Left" (Forgacs 1989:73).

Forgacs (1989:74) identifies two directions from which "intellectual brokerage" was instrumental in bringing Gramsci's work to the attention of a wider British audience in the early 1960s, both of which are still resonant today. These were the work on culture and class by Raymond Williams (1958, 1961) and E.P. Thompson (1963) and theoretically innovative writings on the British state and the labor movement by Perry Anderson (1964) and Tom Nairn (1964a, 1964b, 1964c), published in *New Left Review*.

Forgacs considers that the first set of "brokers," Raymond Williams and E.P. Thompson, were only indirectly influenced by Gramsci. He contends that they were nonetheless influential because their work on culture illuminated a certain way of looking at Gramsci which fitted in very well with the Marxist humanism and the "culture and community" outlook which began gaining ground throughout Western Europe as a reaction to the invasion of Hungary by Soviet troops in 1956. Whether Gramsci's influence was indirect or not, it was certainly there. For example, Raymond Williams drew on Gramsci's concept of hegemony in his analysis of the processes of social and cultural incorporation of the working class that he saw around him in Britain. In an article first published in 1975, Williams cites Gramsci in support of his affirmation that

the essential dominance of a particular class in society is maintained not only, although if necessary, by power, and not only, although always, by property. It is maintained also and inevitably by a lived culture. (R. Williams, quoted in Morgan 1996:71)

E.P. Thompson (1978), similarly, cites Gramsci's concept of hegemony in a closely argued article against Nairn and Anderson's reductive interpretation of the term, as he sees it. According to Thompson (1978:283), Nairn and Anderson had merely reworked the old distinction between "revolutionary" and "reformist" into a distinction between "hegemonic" and "corporate." He warns that "Gramsci wrote, not about hegemonic classes but the hegemony of a class" (E.P. Thompson 1978:283). Consequently, "the most that we are entitled to say is that a subordinate class may display an embryonic hegemony, or a hegemony within limited areas of social life" (E.P. Thompson 1978:284). It may be noted here that both Raymond Williams and E.P. Thompson were active adult educators and accordingly influential in introducing Gramsci to the field. It is ironic, therefore, that a similarly reductive interpretation of Gramsci's concept, often using the term "counterhegemony," has gained currency in adult education, as we shall see in Chapters 4 and 5.

Meanwhile, in the French Left, Forgacs contends that a similar equation between Gramsci and humanism was made, so that for a time in both France and Britain Gramsci came to be seen primarily as a humanist Marxist. As Forgacs makes clear (1989:75n), it was this humanist interpretation of Gramsci which was subsequently attacked by Louis Althusser and Nicos Poulantzas (both of whom were profoundly influenced by Gramsci) in the mid-1960s.

Forgacs contends that his second set of "brokers" (1989:76), Nairn and Anderson, posed an important alternative both to the culturalism of the Williams/Thompson project and to the economistic Marxism-Leninism of the Communist Party of Great Britain (CPGB). Nevertheless, Forgacs points out that their Gramscism remained at an abstract level, isolated within a discourse of "professional intellectuals" with no concrete political project through which it might be tested and developed.

He contends that the result of this competition between interpretations of Gramsci was a highly selective, mainly culturalist and rather abstract reading of Gramsci (Forgacs 1989:77) which set the scene for his reception from the late 1960s on, when a wider selection of his work began to be published in English. In particular, the publication in 1971 of *Selections from the Prison Notebooks* (SPN) aroused considerable interest and the 1970s and 1980s saw the publication of further key texts in English translation.[12]

Gramsci is now recognized as a major Marxist, and one who was unusual among Communist leaders of his period in that he was both a major Marxist theorist and a leader of what was for a time in the 1920s a mass revolutionary party, as Eric Hobsbawm (1987) has pointed out. His writings are now widely available in English in selections, and the first volumes (PNI and PNII) of a complete English translation of the prison notebooks, based on the Gerratana edition and edited by Joseph A. Buttigieg, have been published.

In Britain, three main contemporary Gramscian strands have been identified by Forgacs (1989:79) as, first, the New Left, associated with the journal *New Left Review*, second, Gramscian currents in the Communist Party, and third, academic studies of culture and the media associated with Stuart Hall and others at the Centre for Contemporary Cultural Studies at Birmingham University and the Popular Culture group at the Open University. The culture and media strand continues strongly on both sides of the Atlantic, with, for example, Marcia Landy's book, *Film, Politics and Gramsci* (1994), David Harris's study of the effects of Gramscianism on cultural studies (1992) and Epifanio San Juan Jr.'s *Hegemony and Strategies of Transgression: Essays in Cultural Studies and Comparative Literature* (1995).

The New Left strand developed from the Nairn and Anderson analyses of the 1960s and *New Left Review* continues to feature articles on Gramsci, including Forgacs's article. In the Communist Party of Great Britain (CPGB, now re-formed as Democratic Left), Gramsci's name was associated with the Eurocommunist faction and, more recently, with the magazine *Marxism Today*, which, until it folded in 1992, argued for a redefinition of the political in broadly Gramscian terms. The CPGB's *Manifesto for New Times* (1990) and Stuart Hall and Martin Jacques's book *New Times* (1989) attempted to set a new agenda for the Left, inspired by a reading of Gramsci and engaging critically with postmodernist writers such as Baudrillard, Jameson and Lyotard.[13] Although *New Times* politics is more a politics of analysis than of strategy, the implied strategy entails the creation of an alliance of disparate elements such as the green movement, antinuclear protesters, gay and lesbian activists and feminists.

This "politics of difference" entails a diminution in the central role of class in socialist politics, a view which has been energetically propounded by Ernesto Laclau, Chantal Mouffe and others, who have found inspiration in Gramsci for their development of post-Marxism.[14] With the rise of interest in postmodernism in the 1990s, Gramsci has emerged as a precursor of postmodernist and feminist critical theory (Holub 1992) and as the theorist of a new, postliberal form of democracy (Golding 1992).

This new wave of interest in Gramsci is as heterogenous as previous Gramscisms have been. For example, in relation to feminism, Renate Holub's verdict on "Gramsci's relation to feminist theory, to feminism, to women" is mixed. His relations to women (particularly his wife, Giulia, and sister-in-law Tania), carry "the distinct mark of a pernicious historical rationality that exerted, and often still exerts, a destructive influence on the lives of women" (Holub 1992:191). This damning indictment is relieved somewhat by her remark that

I find it difficult to insist on feminist practices when it comes to a thinker and man such as Gramsci whose experiences were not confronted, the way ours now are, with a series of continuous radical, complex and extensive feminist discourses. (Holub 1992:195)

I would concur with the latter statement, while taking issue with Holub about the severity of her indictment of Gramsci's treatment of his wife and sister-in-law. It seems to me that Gramsci's letters to both women, and to his mother reveal above all his love, concern and respect for them (Gramsci 1994a *passim*). He is certainly not faultless: he is sometimes angry with Tania when she takes an initiative on his behalf without first obtaining his permission; often deeply hurt, mystified and frustrated by Giulia's vagueness and prolonged silences; always concerned to minimize his mother's anxiety. He is undoubtedly at times harsh and unjust in his letters to Tania and Giulia, but I find it hard to recognize Gramsci from Holub's description of him in his letters to them as "often [. . .] harsh, authoritarian and condescending" (Holub 1992:194).

Holub's statement that Tania's "care and services follow a rationality and expediency of their own, uninterrogated by Gramsci, who, after all, rarely lacks an interrogative will when it comes to other matters" is more telling (Holub 1992:194). But if Gramsci sometimes seems to take Tania's help for granted, that is not to say that he does so because she is a woman, any more than if he takes his friend Sraffa's help for granted it is because he is a man. Perhaps it is because he has become accustomed to depending on Tania, especially (since she was in Italy and able to visit him), as the linchpin of his tormented existence in prison.

On feminism, as Holub (1992:195) points out, only a few paragraphs of the prison notebooks deal with feminist issues. These raise as many questions as they answer. His discussion of female sexuality in relation to the process of production in his notes on "Americanism and Fordism" (SPN:294–306) is a case in point. In a note entitled "Some Aspects of the Sexual Question" Gramsci avers that

The formation of a new feminine personality is the most important question of an ethical and civil order connected with the sexual question. Until women can attain not only a genuine independence in relation to men but also a new way of conceiving themselves and their role in sexual relations, the sexual question will remain full of unhealthy characteristics and caution must be exercised in proposals for new legislation. (SPN:296)

Thus far, Gramsci sounds like a fairly libertarian feminist, but he goes on to insist that, despite the difficulties this would entail, it is still necessary to attempt to regulate sexual relations and to attempt to create a new sexual ethic. He concludes the note by affirming that

The truth is that the new type of man demanded by the rationalisation of production and work cannot be developed until the sexual instinct has been suitably regulated and until it too has been rationalised. (SPN:297)

Gramsci's use of the male referent here may indicate that he is think- ing of a male subject, or it may be that he means "the new type of human being," either way, his emphasis on rationality here appears to betray his distinctly modernist thinking on questions of indus- trial production and, by implication, the new form of civilization to be inaugurated by the revolution. For example, he seems to regard the Ford motor company's interest in its employees' sex lives and family relationships as legitimate (SPN:296). Part of the problem is, as with various other of Gramsci's prison notes, it is not always easy to know when he is writing about what is (in this case, in companies such as Ford in the United States) and when he is writing about what will be, or what he considers ought to be, in the hoped-for new society. This note could—and I think definitely should—be read as an argument for the regulation of sexual relationships in the new society, an argument which is clearly not libertarian and not neces- sarily feminist either (although that would depend on who made the rules and on what basis). Gramsci's earlier comments in the same note (SPN:295) about the high incidence of incest in rural areas clearly indicate the need, in his view, to regulate sexual practices. However, whereas regulation might be regarded as acceptable in the case of incest, many present-day readers would balk at the idea that general surveillance of sexual relations could be legitimate, whether undertaken by a capitalist employer or by the workers' state or the Communist Party. Furthermore, the implication is that sexual rela- tions are determined ultimately by the means of production: it is unlike Gramsci to be deterministic and reductive, as he seems to be in this formulation.

Nevertheless, in posing the sexual question in relation to the production process, Gramsci is raising an important question, addressed much later and in much greater detail by Foucault, about the disciplining of the body in accordance with the prescriptions of society. Holub is surely right to state that Gramsci and Foucault share "the notion that power and domination function in so far as those dominated consent to that domination" as also "their understanding of the production of that consent;" where they differ is in "the directedness of the production of that consent" (Holub 1992:199). She points out that for Gramsci, unlike Foucault, it is important to know why power exists (Holub 1992:200). Therefore, armed with Gramsci as well as Foucault and recent feminist theorists, "feminist theory can make out who is powerful and who is not" (Holub 1992:201). Thus Gramsci emerges in Holub's reading, in spite of his poor record on feminism and in his relations with women, as a crypto-feminist.

In my reading Gramsci has less ground to make up. I find his concept of hegemony adaptable to analyses of power in terms of gender—although to explain why and how would take another book. Also, while his revolutionary organic intellectual was probably envisaged by Gramsci as male, "he" is not irredeemably so—the organizing principle that "he" embodies may be embodied by a woman, given the "optimism of the will" with which Gramsci sought to overcome his "pessimism of the intellect" (Gramsci 1994a vol.1:18).

Other commentators, such as Laclau and Mouffe (1985), venture beyond Gramsci in their construction of a new radical democratic politics. They reject Gramsci's "insistence that hegemonic subjects are necessarily constituted on the plane of the fundamental classes" as well as "his postulate that, with the exception of interregna constituted by organic crises, every social formation structures itself around a single hegemonic centre" (Laclau and Mouffe 1985:137–8). Thus, for them,

Hegemony is, quite simply, a political type of relation, a form, if one so wishes, of politics; but not a determinable location within a topography of the social. In a given social formation there can be a variety of hegemonic nodal points. (Laclau and Mouffe 1985:139)

This is a long way from the notion of hegemony as articulated by a class championed by E.P. Thompson. It opens the way to a consideration of the significance (in this instance, to adult educators) of the so-called new social movements. However, this too is problematic. As Laclau and Mouffe (1985:159) make clear, they regard the term "new social movements" as unsatisfactory because it groups together a series of highly diverse struggles, differentiating them from "workers' struggles, considered as 'class' struggles." As Laclau and Mouffe state:

What interests us about the new social movements, then, is not the idea of arbitrarily grouping them into a category opposed to that of class, but the novel role they play in articulating that rapid diffusion of social conflictuality to more and more numerous relations which is characteristic today of advanced industrial societies. (Laclau and Mouffe 1985:159–60)

What that "novel role" may be, and how adult educators may engage with it, is considered in the case of one adult educator's accounts of her work with one organization within one social movement (part of the landless people's movement in Brazil) in Chapter 6. For now, I want to note how, in this statement, Laclau and Mouffe both reiterate Gramsci's concept of hegemony and go beyond it. As Laclau insists, in relation to his and Mouffe's designation of their thought as "post-Marxist":

the reason for the term "post-Marxism" is that the ambiguity of Marxism—which runs through its whole history—is not a deviation from an untainted source, but dominates the entire work of Marx himself. (Laclau 1990:236)

The same could be said of Gramsci's thought. This is not to belittle its cogency, but rather to recognize that there are ambiguities within Gramsci's thought which have, in a sense, sanctioned the emergence of a multiplicity of Gramscisms since Gramsci's death, just as Marxisms have proliferated since the death of Marx (McLellan 1979).

Conclusion

Gramsci's theory and practice of an educative politics is infinitely suggestive for present-day adult educators. Gramsci teaches us to analyze relations of power in their unique conjuncture of time and place and in terms of their educative force. He teaches us to see the education of adults as a multifaceted activity, part of the complex set of institutions and forces of civil society which constitute the bulwarks of the state and potentially form part of the revolutionary terrain. The education of adults, broadly conceived in Gramscian terms, is a means through which revolutionary organic intellectuals may be developed and equipped to undertake the crucial, painstaking work of organizing revolutionary hegemony. But there is no guarantee that this will succeed—indeed, the evidence so far is rather the other way. Gramsci tried and failed to create an educative, humane, Marxist revolution; he cannot give us a model for revolutionary success. Rather he shows us, through his example, how to learn from defeat, carry on working and survive, at least for a while, under the most difficult circumstances. The uncertainty of our times makes reading Gramsci, who struggled to make sense of what were to become catastrophic uncertainties in his own life and times, peculiarly apposite. Gramsci's writings continue to resonate with our times as his continued currency in debates on postmodernism and feminism shows.

But reading Gramsci as a crypto-feminist or crypto-post-modernist is quite as problematic as reading Gramsci the Leninist, Gramsci the idealist Crocean, Gramsci the Eurocommunist, Gramsci the culturalist—or Gramsci the theorist of the education of adults. In some readings of Gramsci, such as the Nairn-Anderson theses, there is no obvious connection with adult education outside the confines of courses in political science. Although Gramsci's ideas are, in a sense, all about the education of adults, he was not a theorist of adult education per se. Interpretation is necessary in order to derive a theory of adult education from Gramsci's work, and given the open nature of Gramsci's text, interpreters are bound to disagree. Against this background, some writers on adult education have developed Gramscian analyses of the education of adults and many more have made generally positive references to his work; these are examined in Chapter 5. First we turn to a consideration of the ideas of that other radical hero, Paulo Freire.

Notes

1.   Biographical information for this section is drawn primarily from Fiori's *Antonio Gramsci: Life of a Revolutionary* (1970), Davidson's *Antonio Gramsci: Towards an Intellectual Biography* (1977) and Rosengarten's Introduction to his edition of Gramsci's prison letters (Gramsci 1994a). Bibliographical details are drawn from Cozens (1977); Eley (1984); Forgacs (1989); Cammett (1991) and Cammett and Righi (1995).

2.   For a range of views on why the revolution failed to materialize, see for example, Piccone (1983); Cammett (1967); Davidson (1977); Fiori (1970); Spriano (1975); Clark (1977).

3.   The Communist Party of Italy (*Partito Comunista d'Italia*, PCd'I), was the Italian section of the Third Communist International, also known as the Comintern. The PCd'I changed its name to *Partito Comunista Italiano* (Italian Communist Party, PCI) in 1943 when the Third Communist International was dissolved.

4.   A complete English translation of the prison notebooks on the basis of Valentino Gerratana's 1975 edition (*Quaderni del carcere*) is being prepared by Joseph A. Buttigieg of Notre Dame University for publication by Columbia University Press; Volume 1 (PNI) was published in 1992 and contains notebooks 1 and 2 and Volume 2 (PNII), containing notebooks 3, 4, and 5, was published in 1996. Gramsci's prison notebooks are also available in English in selections, of which the best known is SPN (1971). Gramsci's "Notes on Language" are in Gramsci (1984). A new translation, by Pasquale Verdicchio, of Gramsci's essay *The Southern Question* has recently been published (Gramsci 1995). Other selections are published in Gramsci (1957a, 1957b); Cavalcanti and Piccone eds. (1975); SCW (1985); David Forgacs's *A Gramsci Reader* (GR); Gramsci (1994b) FSPN.

5.   The most complete and definitive English edition of Gramsci's letters from prison, edited by Frank Rosengarten and translated by Raymond Rosenthal, is published by University Press, New York (Gramsci 1994a). Selections are available in English in Lynne Lawner's LP, in an edition edited and translated by Hamish Henderson (Gramsci 1988).

6.   The *Shorter Oxford English Dictionary* defines hegemony as "Leadership, predominance of one state of a confederacy . . ." For different treatments of the concept of hegemony in Gramsci's work, see for example, Bocock (1986), Laclau and Mouffe (1985), Anderson (1976–77), G.A. Williams (1960).

7.   See SPWI and SPWII for examples of Gramsci's preprison journalism. Some of Gramsci's most important writings about political and cultural journalism in English translation are collected in SCW (386–425) and GR (379–90); others are scattered throughout SPN and PNI.

8.   The history of the factory councils is described by Clark (1977), Cammett (1967), Spriano (1975). Gramsci's writing on the factory councils is in SPWI and SPN.

9.   Gramsci uses the distinction drawn by Alessandro Manzoni (1785–1873) between "good sense" and "common sense" in his popular historical novel, *The Betrothed* (*I promessi sposi*, first published 1827). The reference reads as follows: "good sense was not lacking; but it was hiding for fear of common sense" (Manzoni 1956:446). Gramsci made the concept his own, as he did also with hegemony, but it is interesting to note that, while the origin and development of the latter concept has inspired considerable comment, the provenance of the distinction between good sense and common sense has not been explored in the English language literature.

10.   The International Gramsci Society (IGS) exists to disseminate knowledge and understanding of Gramsci's work; the Society publishes a newsletter. The

IGS secretary is Joseph A. Buttigieg, Department of English, University of Notre Dame, Notre Dame, Indiana 46556, U.S.A.

11.   See, for example: Shore (1990); Piccone (1983); Togliatti (1979).

12.   An authoritative history of the publication of Gramsci's writings in Italian and in English is given in Buttigieg's Preface to his edition of *Antonio Gramsci: Prison Notebooks* vol.1 (PNI:ix–xix).

13.   For a discussion of postmodernism in relation to "New Times" see Hebdige (1989). For a development of the "New Times" strand in the 1990s, see Perryman, ed. (1994) and Squires ed. (1993); see also Chapter 5, endnote 2, on Signs of the Times.

14.   See Laclau and Mouffe (1985) and the ensuing debate in *New Left Review*: Geras (1987); Laclau and Mouffe (1987); Mouzelis (1988).

Chapter 3
Paulo Freire: Education As Political

Paulo Freire was a Brazilian adult educationist whose fame rests on his vision of education for liberation. This is a process through which, it is claimed, oppressed people undergo changes in their consciousness so that they understand that they are oppressed and can act to change their situation. This process Freire calls *conscientização* in Portuguese, a term normally translated as "conscientization." Freire's approach rests upon the belief that education is never politically neutral and that it can help to bring about and sustain the revolutionary transformation of oppressive societies.

Freire is a controversial figure. He has generated international interest as an inspirational educator, and he has a cult status for many radical adult educators, yet debate continues on the coherence of his ideas, the efficacy of his educational methods and the nature of the politics embodied in his "pedagogy of the oppressed." In the absence of an accredited biography,[1] even Freire's life has been mythologized—indeed, the word "myth" has been used of Freire by several commentators. Pierre Furter (1985:301) describes him as "a myth in his own lifetime" and Kathleen Weiler (1996) has written a perceptive article entitled "The Myths of Paulo Freire."

The most authoritative reading of Freire to date, Paul V. Taylor's critically sympathetic bio-text, indicates areas of myth, hiatus and conflicting information in a variety of published sources, some apparently sanctioned by Freire himself (Taylor 1993). Heinz-Peter Gerhardt's brief biographical study for the UNESCO journal *Prospects* fills in some of the gaps, while inevitably leaving some areas unresolved (Gerhardt 1993). Weiler (1996:353 n4) points out that until recently most English-speaking students of Freire have relied on Dennis Collins's (1977) brief life, or Cynthia Brown's (1975) even briefer account of the Brazilian literacy campaign. The problem is compounded by the hagiographic nature of some of the writing about Freire (*viz.* Gadotti 1994), which is long on approbation and short on references, with the result that the source of biographical information on Freire is often unstated or unclear. John L. Elias's uneven sympathetic account of Freire's pedagogy of liberation falls into this trap (compounded by poor proofreading), with conflicting, unreferenced information on the duration of Freire's imprisonment in Brazil appearing on the same page (Elias 1994:7). Freire himself has done little to clarify matters, although his *Pedagogy of Hope* (PH) is noticeably more autobiographical than his earlier published work. Weiler points out that "the details of [Freire's] early history and accomplishments are confused and contradictory partly because of his own rewriting and reinventing of himself" (Weiler 1996:356). Tracing Freire's bibliography[2] is similarly complex, with pieces appearing under different names and in different translations.

Such difficulties are compounded by the fact that Freire's writing is rhetorical: at best, poetic, and at worst, prolix and inaccessible. His published work has been accurately described as having "the quality of concentric ripples in a pool in which a stone has been thrown," with successive publications elaborating a central core of principles or beliefs, sometimes with reference to other authorities or areas of knowledge (Leach 1982:185).

In this chapter, while acknowledging these difficulties, I shall attempt to identify the main themes of Freire's work, beginning with a brief biographical and bibliographical introduction and going on to discuss Freire's vision of education as a political process.

Paulo Freire: Life and Writings

Paulo Reglus Neves Freire, the youngest of four children, was born into a comfortable, middle-class family in 1921 in Recife, a large port city, capital of the state of Pernambuco in northeast Brazil. He was brought up as, and remained, a practicing Catholic (Taylor 1993:21). His family endured poverty in the depression of 1928–32 and Freire has said that his performance at school suffered as a result of hunger at this time[3] (Shor 1987:29). To save money, the Freire family moved to Jaboatão, eighteen kilometers from Recife, where a further severe emotional and financial blow came with the death of his father in 1934 when Freire was thirteen (Freire 1993:96). After repeating two years of schooling, Freire graduated from the private high school where he had been allowed a free place by the director (Taylor 1993:15). While still at school Freire taught supplementary Portuguese to some of his fellow pupils (Freire 1993:54; Taylor 1993:15). In 1941 he began the Pre-law Secondary Cycle, the standard preparation for a career in the human sciences in Brazil at that time. In 1943 Freire enrolled at Recife University where he studied law, philosophy and linguistics (Freire PH:210–1). Gerhardt (1993:440) says that his studies were interrupted several times by the need to earn his living and contribute to the family finances.

At the age of twenty-two Freire met Elza Maria Oliveira, who came to him for tuition in Portuguese syntax in order to pass a test for promotion in her work as a teacher in early childhood education (Freire 1993:96). They married a year later and Freire has acknowledged that her influence in his life was enormous (Freire 1993:97). He has said that his linguistic studies and meeting Elza led him to pedagogy (Freire PE:175). In his later writing (for example, LGB, PH) he refers to her collaboration in his work, although the nature and extent of her contribution is never specified.

Freire's law degree qualified him to teach in secondary schools, and Gerhardt (1993:440) records that Freire taught Portuguese language in 1944–5, while also working as a lawyer for the state-run trade unions and giving lectures on legal matters for union members in the suburbs of Recife. Freire states that he soon abandoned his legal career, turning instead to teaching (PH:15). According to Robert Mackie (1980a:3), for a time Freire and his wife worked in Catholic Action (*Ação Católica*) among well-off people in Recife, before becoming disillusioned with the moral compromises that they felt the work entailed. In his book *Catholic Radicals in Brazil*, Emanuel de Kadt describes Catholic Action as being in the doldrums at this time (1970:59). Taylor states that Freire turned to work instead with the poor and illiterate through the *Comunidades Eclesiales de Base* (Basic Church Communities, CEBs[4]), a Catholic organization seeking to relate biblical study to local social and personal issues (Taylor 1993:22). Taylor states that this move came about through Freire's close relationship with Bishop Helder Câmara.[5]

Taylor also states that it was through Freire's involvement with the CEBs that he was invited to join Social Service for Industry (*Serviço Social da Indústria*, SESI) in Recife in 1947, as head of the Department of Education and Culture (Taylor 1993:22). SESI was a private sector institution set up by the National Confederation of Brazilian Industries, and Gerhardt traces Freire's appointment to his trade union contacts. Whatever was the key factor in his appointment, Freire stayed at SESI for eight years, becoming director in 1954, before resigning "after criticism of his democratic, open and free style of administration" (Gerhardt 1993:440).

Freire's work at SESI involved coordinating the work of teachers and working with families in what was essentially a postliteracy education program based on "culture circles" (Taylor 1993:22). Gerhardt reports that "study groups, round-table discussions, debates and the distribution of themed flash cards" were typical of Freire's work in the parish projects (Gerhardt 1993:441). It was in this period that the Paulo Freire Method evolved. Gerhardt gives the principles informing Freire's work at this time as "dialogue, 'parliamentarization' and self-government" (Gerhardt 1993:441). Freire has affirmed that "it was precisely my relationships with workers and peasants then that took me into more radical understandings of education" (Shor 1987:29), a point he reiterates in *Pedagogy of Hope* (PH:16). He described this period as "an indispensable moment in the gestation of *Pedagogy of the Oppressed*" (PH:16).

According to Gerhardt (1993:441), Freire was appointed to a part-time teaching post in pedagogics at the University of Recife, presumably after his resignation from SESI, in or around 1955. There he came into contact with the Recife branch of the Catholic Students' organization, the JUC (*Juventude Universitària Católica*, a special section of Catholic Action). De Kadt remarks that in 1957–8 the Recife JUC*istas* were particularly active in both discussing social issues and going out into the slums to put their ideas into action (de Kadt 1970:62). At the university Freire also encountered the ideas of nationalist intellectuals associated with the Higher Institute for Brazilian Studies (*Instituto Superior de Estudos Brasilieros*, ISEB) in Rio de Janeiro. For Freire and others of his generation of Catholic radicals, ISEB represented "the awakening of the national consciousness, advancing in search of the transformation of Brazil" (EPF:40). The ISEB intellectuals were influenced by European sociologists and philosophers such as Karl Mannheim, Karl Jaspers, Gunnar Myrdal and Gabriel Marcel (Gerhardt 1993:441–2). Gerhardt (1993:442) reports that Freire, unlike many of his colleagues, considered it important to discuss national problems at the university as part of the country's transition to democracy. Also gaining influence at the time in the social sciences was theoretical work on the relationship of dependence between Latin America, on the one hand, and North America and Europe, on the other, that was being formulated by André Gunder Frank (1969) and others. As Torres (1993:123) points out, "to this extent, Freire represents and reflects in his writings a particular ideological momentum in Latin American societies."

But if these intellectual and political interests may be considered positive legacies from his early university career, other influences were arguably less positive. Gerhardt's (1993:442) judgment is that Freire's avowed eclecticism, together with the theory requirements of the university, may explain his "tendency to obfuscate his practical work through 'leaden philosophical prose'." Even this view is disputed, however, Torres (1993:120) praises his "exceptional talent as a writer," blaming any difficulties for anglophone readers on some of his translators and the fact that "Freire's dialectical thinking evolves into a pattern of reasoning and logical analysis different from positivist explanations, thus outside mainstream writing in English-speaking countries."

Freire states that he defended his doctoral dissertation on "Educação e Actualidade Brasileira" (Education and the Brazilian Present) at Recife University in 1959 (Freire 1995:17). He does not actually say that the dissertation was approved and Taylor (1993:152 n6) notes that his doctorate may have been awarded *honoris causa* on account of his successful literacy program. Mackie (1980a:4) and Elias (1994:3), after Collins (1977), state that Freire was appointed Professor of the History and Philosophy of Education at the university shortly afterward, which implies that it was approved. However, Gerhardt (1993:443) states that the thesis did not receive the approval of the university committee, a decision he finds "somewhat logical" given Freire's criticism therein of the undeveloped state of Brazilian university structures. Despite this setback, according to Gerhardt (1993:443), Freire continued working at the university through the good offices of his friend João Alfredo Gonçalves da

Costa Lima, who was first vice-chancellor and then, from 1962, chancellor of the university. Gerhardt states that Freire first became special counselor for student relations—a post which sounds as if it might have been created for him.

At the university, together with graduate students, Freire conducted research into teaching illiterate adults in urban and rural areas of northeastern Brazil. Both Gerhardt and Taylor agree that from early 1961 Freire went on to become director of the newly created Cultural Extension Service of the university. Citing Cynthia Brown (1975) as his source, Taylor reports that from October 1962 to January 1964 the Cultural Extension Service received considerable financial assistance from the United States Agency for International Development (USAID), clearly with Freire's knowledge and approval (Taylor 1993:24).[6]

The national Movement for Popular Culture (*Movimento de Cultura Popular*, MCP) developed in this period and *Centros Populares de Cultura* (CPCs) sprang up all over Brazil (de Kadt 1970:105). Freire was enthusiastically involved in the MCP in Recife from its inception in 1960 to 1963 and Gerhardt (1993:444) reports that his literacy method was first developed in an MCP culture circle which he coordinated in a suburb of Recife. In 1961 Freire was invited by the mayor of Recife, Miguel Arraes, to undertake an ambitious MCP initiative to construct a literacy program on behalf of the city council (Taylor 1993:23). The program was intended to bring about the socioeconomic transformation of the northeast (de Castro 1969:170). Freire developed his method, exploring such themes as nationalism, remission of profits, development and illiteracy through group discussion (a process Thomas G. Sanders likens to group psychotherapy), using visual aids to schematize the issues (Sanders 1973). De Kadt notes that subsequently (around December 1962) Freire transferred his literacy program from the MCP to the Cultural Extension Service at the university, partly in response to his unease at the increasing influence of communists in the MCP (de Kadt 1970:104).

In 1963 Freire was invited to represent the Ministry of Education on the important Northeast Development Board (*Superintendência do Desenvolvimento do Nordeste*, SUDENE) where he worked with SUDENE officials and officials from USAID, considering proposals for educational projects in the northeast. Freire was appointed coordinator of an adult literacy project in the north-eastern state of Rio Grande do Norte, funded by the USAID Alliance for Progress program. In the pilot project, in the town of Angicos, 300 formerly illiterate people were taught to read and write in three months, according to one commentator (Mashayekh 1974). Elias (1994:4) puts the time at an even more impressive forty-five days; the title of Cynthia Brown's account of Freire's literacy work in northeast Brazil, *Literacy in 30 Hours* (1975), speaks for itself.

The success of the Angicos project was such that Freire was invited by his friend, Paulo de Tarso, newly appointed minister of education in the populist government of President João Goulart (1961–4), to become the director of the Brazilian National Literacy Program (Elias 1994:5). In that capacity Freire drew up plans for 20,000 circles of culture to involve two million people by 1964, extending the pattern of literacy work throughout the country (Mackie 1980a:4). In a period of three or four months, Freire and his team worked with thousands of illiterate workers. By his own account, they organized "three hundred cultural circles, around Brasília in the satellite towns, with excellent results" (Freire in de Figueiredo-Cowen and Gastaldo 1995:65). However, Weiler reports that it is not clear how successful the national campaign was, overall (Weiler 1996:359).

The literacy program was modeled on the Cuban literacy campaign, which had been successfully completed the previous year (Kozol 1978; Leiner 1987; Morales 1981; Skidmore 1967:244–56; Taylor 1993:24). The Brazilian National Literacy Program was a key element in President Goulart's bid to democratize the country, since under Brazil's constitution literacy was a condition of the franchise (Gerhardt 1993:445). A mass extension of literacy was thus bound to create a corresponding extension of democracy among the mass of the people.

Freire seems to have been in accord with the aim of democratization (de Kadt 1970:104), although perhaps rather naive about the process in practice. For example, Moacir Gadotti (1994:31) reports that Freire's demand that the state governor should not visit Angicos during the literacy project in order to avoid electioneering was "not entirely respected." Taylor reports Gerhardt's judgment on Freire's literacy campaigns, which carries weight since he observed the process at first hand: "the educators had espoused the political objectives of the programme organizers, that is, the reformist provincial government. The reality is that the goals of the campaigns were blatantly political" (Gerhardt, quoted in Taylor 1993:26).

Freire's work in the northeast spanned the end of a period of rapid growth in the Brazilian economy which lasted from 1945 to 1960 (Wynia 1990:214–48). During that period, a policy of industrialization based on import substitution primarily benefited the southeast of the country, exacerbating a division between what Gary W. Wynia (1990:217) calls the "two Brazils." The policy relied heavily on foreign capital and imported business practices and growth could not be sustained. By 1964, approximately one-third of Brazil's manufacturing industry was owned by foreigners and the economy was in crisis, with illiterate peasants and the urban poor (Freire's constituency of learners) making up 50 percent of the population. The economic crisis was matched by a political crisis as President Goulart tried to find a way out of the impasse through populist policies, including the encouragement of Freire's literacy campaign.

This was also the period in which Liberation Theology[7] emerged in Latin America, a process apparently sanctioned by Pope John XXIII (1958–63) and the Second Vatican Council (1961–5). The movement reached its apogee in 1968, when the Latin American Bishops' Conference in Medellin, Colombia, proclaimed its "option for the poor." Freire, although a layman, was part of this movement through his involvement with the CEBs and his association with Bishop Helder Câmara, who was a leading Liberation theologian.

In this climate of religious ferment and rising political tension, Freire's work was one of a number of initiatives in the 1950s and early 1960s aimed at the poor. Some were official government initiatives, others were initiatives of the various political parties, including the illegal Brazilian Communist Party (*Partido Communista Brasiliero*, PCB) and the Maoist *Partido Communista do Brasil* (de Kadt 1970 *passim*). Some, such as Catholic Action, the CEBs and JUC, were official Catholic organizations, although the JUC later (in 1966) declared itself an independent lay movement (de Kadt 1970:80). In 1961 the *Movimento de Educação de Base* (MEB) was established, a Catholic network of radio schools aimed at the poor and illiterate in deprived regions of Brazil, including the northeast. MEB was sponsored, like Freire's literacy work, by the federal government (Elias 1994:5).

The MEB's nondirective pedagogy had some affinity with Freire's pedagogy: both rejected what Freire calls the banking mode of education in favor of conscientization and both favored process over content, insofar as both believed that content should come from the learners. However, Freire's educational process, as we shall see below, is highly structured, whereas MEB's approach was partly derived from ideas on group dynamics originating in the United States which positively value structurelessness. But the MEB was also influenced by the Jesuit tradition of three stages of prayerful meditation, utilized in its see-judge-act method: "what is the case, why is it so, and what can be done about it?" This method was common to the CEBs and MEB and Taylor describes it as paralleling Freire's three-stage pedagogical method. He states that Freire was thus using a tried and tested method "as Cartesian as it was Catholic" (Taylor 1993:74). But it is a moot point who influenced whom: Fernandes (1985:83) describes the see-judge-act method as used by the CEBs in the 1980s as containing elements of Freire's method. De Kadt (1970:156) mentions that from late 1962, when MEB took up a more radical stance, there was some "mutual influencing" between Freire and MEB, particularly in the northeast. Carlos Alberto Torres (1993:122) puts it more strongly, stating that in 1963 MEB adopted Freire's method as its own.

The years 1961–2 also saw the launch of a new political movement (not a political party), *Ação Popular* (AP), by former JUC militants and others, dedicated to conscientization of the poor. As well as its student supporters, AP drew support from within SUDENE, the MCP and Freire's literacy campaign. It was, in de Kadt's terms, a populist movement "of intellectuals for the people" (de Kadt 1970:82). Although AP had no formal ties with the church, it was widely regarded as a "para-Christian organization" (de Kadt 1970:83). It also had an uneasy relationship with the Communists. De Kadt reports that AP "shared the post-Stalinist disenchantment of the world's neo-Marxists and socialist humanists with the results of the Russian Revolution" and attacked the PCB "mainly for its lack of a true revolutionary perspective" (de Kadt 1970:99). The PCB's policy of *frente única* (united front) meant that many popular initiatives involved Communists, as well as non-Communist radical Catholics and others, to varying degrees. As de Kadt points out (1970:119), the Communists "played a whole range of roles depending on their ally" and were regarded by non-Communists as manipulative. Although Freire's philosophy was elaborated independently, it was in many respects closely related to AP (de Kadt 1970:103), and it seems likely he shared the suspicion of many Catholic AP activists for the activities of the PCB since, as we have seen, he removed his literacy work from the Communist-influenced MCP in Recife. It is also possible that he feared that any association with Communists would jeopardize the continuation of his USAID money.

When in April 1964 the military staged a successful *coup d'état*, almost certainly with U.S. backing, the democratization program abruptly ended, and with it Freire's literacy program—his USAID funding had already been withdrawn in January 1964. At the time of the coup, Freire's work was "still characterized by potential rather than actual achievements" and he was certainly not inciting the masses to revolt (de Kadt 1970:104). Taylor's verdict is telling: he was not a social agitator but an educator, "an intellectual occupying that position of neutrality which later he came to condemn" (Taylor 1993:23). Nevertheless, Freire was listed as anti-American and pro-Communist and he was one of the 10,000 or so government officials who lost their jobs as a result of the coup (Taylor 1993:27).

Gadotti (1994:34) states that Freire took refuge for a time in the house of a friend who was a parliamentary deputy and that when he returned to Recife in June 1964 he was arrested and imprisoned for seventy days. As Taylor points out (1993:27–8), accounts of the duration of his imprisonment vary and the story of his passage into exile is also confused. Freire himself discusses his feelings at this time in *Pedagogy of Hope* (PH:31*ff.*). It appears that on his release from prison he sought refuge in the Bolivian Embassy and arranged to travel to Bolivia, where he had been granted political asylum, only to arrive, in October 1964, shortly before that country also underwent a *coup d'état*. Freire left Bolivia for Chile, where he was allowed to stay by the newly elected Christian Democrat government of Eduardo Frei, which was pursuing a policy of literacy and agrarian reform.

In Chile, Freire was reunited with his family (Elza and their five children) (PH:34) in January 1965. Soon after his arrival, he began work as a consultant for the economist Jacques Chonchol, president of the Institute for the Development of Animal Husbandry (*Instituto de Desarrollo Agropecuario*, INDAP) (PH:34), working in "the area of what was then called in Chile human promotion" (PH:39). In this capacity he collaborated with people working in adult literacy in the Ministry of Education and with the Ministry of Agriculture's Agricultural Reform Corporation (CORA). Later he worked as a consultant for INDAP and CORA from a UNESCO post in the Institute for Ways and Means and Research in Agrarian Reform (*Instituto de Capacitación e Investigación en Reforma Agraria*, ICIRA), a joint organization of the United Nations and the Chilean government (PH:39). Here he organized research and training with groups of small farmers and peasants (Gadotti 1994:359; Taylor 1993:27–9).

Reflecting on his time in Chile, Freire writes (PH:42) that he experienced there the "respect for cultural differences, respect for the context to which one has come, a criticism of 'cultural invasion', of sectarianism, and a defense of radicalness" of which he wrote in *Pedagogy of the Oppressed.* Chile certainly does seems to have been a radicalizing experience for Freire. He recalls:

We learned of analyses, reactions, and criticisms by Colombians, Venezuelans, Cubans, Mexicans, Bolivians, Argentineans, Paraguayans, Brazilians, Chileans and Europeans—analyses ranging from an almost unrestricted acceptance of Christian Democracy to its total rejection. There were sectarian, intolerant criticisms, but also open, radical criticisms in the sense that I advocate. (PH:44)

While in Chile, Freire wrote various essays and articles, including *"Educação como prática da liberdade"* (Education As the Practice of Freedom), which he has described as a reworking of his doctoral dissertation (PH:17) and *"Extensão ou comunicação?"* (Extension or Communication?). These were written in 1965 and 1968 and first published in 1967 and 1969, respectively; they were later translated into English and published together under the title *Education for Critical Consciousness* and then as *Education: The Practice of Freedom*

(EPF). In 1968 he completed the book for which he is most famous, *Pedagogy of the Oppressed* (PO), described as "a handbook for revolutionary education" by Elias (1994:6). Freire describes the process of writing *Pedagogy of the Oppressed* in *Pedagogy of Hope* (PH:Chapter 2). This was his first work to be published in English translation, in the United States in 1970 and then in Britain in 1972, and with its publication Freire's ideas began to spread to a worldwide audience. It has since been translated into many other languages including French, German, Japanese, Korean and Spanish, and is regarded as the classic Freire text. A New Revised 20th Anniversary Edition was published in 1995 (Freire 1995) in which Freire attempted to correct the "sexist mark" he left on the original (PH:65).

In 1969 Freire left Chile to take up a post as visiting professor at Harvard University's Center for Studies in Education and Development and became a fellow of the Center for the Study of Development and Social Change in Cambridge, Massachusetts. While in the United States, Freire wrote the essays "The Adult Literacy Process As Cultural Action for Freedom" and "Cultural Action and Conscientization," published as a monograph by the *Harvard Educational Review* in 1970 and later as a book under the title *Cultural Action for Freedom* (CAF).

His period in the United States also brought him into contact with radical educators, including Ivan Illich and Jonathan Kozol. Freire and Illich collaborated on a series of seminars at the Center for Intercultural Documentation in Cuernavaca, Mexico, during the summers of 1969 and 1970 (Mackie 1980a:6). As Taylor (1993:30) points out, this was a period of challenge to orthodoxies, particularly in education, and the publication of *Pedagogy of the Oppressed* and the *Harvard Educational Review* monograph "quickly established Freire's international reputation as a radical, even revolutionary, pedagogue," notwithstanding the absence of any published, quantifiable results from his literacy programs.

In 1970 a government led by the Marxist Salvador Allende was elected in Chile. Freire revisited Chile twice during Allende's period of office (PH:35). He has described one brief visit in June 1973 as "one of the most unforgettable I have ever made" and said that it taught him a lot about the class struggle (Freire 1993:186). When Allende's government was overthrown later that year, Freire was one of those declared *persona non grata* by the new regime of General Pinochet (Mackie 1980a:6). Meanwhile, his approach grew in popularity in Latin America, as Torres (1993:123) reports, "being experienced almost everywhere, on a small scale or incorporated into national experiences of adult education," such as in Uruguay, Argentina, Mexico, Peru and Ecuador. However, the instability of the region, as evidenced by the coups in Chile and Argentina in 1973, cut short many such experiments.

From the United States, Freire moved to Switzerland in 1970 to take up the post of special consultant to the Office of Education at the World Council of Churches (WCC) in Geneva. He stated in his letter accepting the post: "You must know that I have taken a decision. My case is the case of the wretched of the earth. You should know that I opted for revolution"[8] (Simpfendorfer, quoted in Gerhardt 1993:449). In Geneva, in 1971, Freire, together with other Brazilian exiles, established the Institute of Cultural Action (IDAC), an organization dedicated to the establishment of a political pedagogy based on conscientization.

Freire's position at the World Council of Churches enabled him to disseminate his ideas throughout the world through consultancies, seminars and conference appearances. Weiler contends that this is when "the myth of 'Freire the revolutionary' was in a sense created, not only through his books, but also through his charismatic personal appearances" (Weiler 1996:359). His advice was sought by the governments of many newly independent former colonies struggling to educate largely illiterate populations, including Guinea-Bissau, São Tomé and Príncipe, the "New Jewel" government in Grenada and the Sandinista government of Nicaragua (evaluations of these campaigns are discussed in Chapter 5). His book about one such involvement, *Pedagogy in Process: The Letters to Guinea-Bissau* (LGB), published in 1978, consists of a series of his letters to Mario Cabral, Commissioner of State for Education and Culture and brother of Amílcar Cabral, and other members of the Commission, between January 1975 and May 1976. The São Tomé and Príncipe campaign is described by Freire himself in Freire and Macedo (1987:Chapter 4) and in Freire (1981). The Grenada and Nicaragua campaigns are described by Torres (1991) and Cardenal and Miller (1981).

Freire's growing international influence at this time may be seen in the report of the UNESCO international symposium on literacy held in Persepolis, Iran, in 1975. The report distinguished between "economic" and "cultural" functions of literacy, the latter "encouraging the development from primary consciousness to critical consciousness (the process of 'conscientization')" (quoted in Street 1984:187).

Freire has said that his world travels through the WCC enabled him to "overcome the risk which exiles sometimes run of being too remote in their work as intellectuals from the most real, most concrete experiences" or of becoming "lost in a game of words" (Freire and Faundez 1989:13). In 1980, while still in exile in Geneva, Freire became a founder-member of the Workers' Party of Brazil (*Partido dos Trabalhadores*, PT) (Freire 1993:57), for the first time committing himself to a political party.

An amnesty in 1979 enabled Freire to return on a visit to his homeland and from 1980 until his death in 1997 he once again lived and worked in Brazil. He worked initially at the *Centro de Estudos em Educação* (Center for Educational Studies) and then took up the post of Professor of Philosophy of Education at the *Pontifícia Universidade Católica de São Paulo* and the public *Universidade de Campinas* in São Paulo. In 1985 Freire's *The Politics of Education* (PE) was published, a collection of mainly previously published articles, including the 1970 "Cultural Action and Conscientization" from *Cultural Action for Freedom*. The one new piece in the book is a taped dialogue with the book's translator, Donaldo Macedo (PE:175–99). Also in 1985, Elza and Paulo Freire were awarded the Prize for Christian Educators in the United States. Freire was awarded the UNESCO Peace Prize in 1986, the year in which Elza died.

Many of his recent books to be published in English are coproductions with sympathetic partners: with Ira Shor, *A Pedagogy for Liberation: Dialogues on Transforming Education* (Shor 1987); with Donaldo Macedo, *Literacy: Reading the Word and the World* (Freire and Macedo 1987), both published in Britain in 1987; in 1989 with António Faundez, *Learning to Question: A Pedagogy of Liberation* (Freire and Faundez 1989) published by the WCC; in 1990, with Myles Horton, *We Make the Road by Walking* (Horton and Freire 1990) and in 1994 with Miguel Escobar, Alfredo Fernandez and

Gilberto Guevara-Niebla, *Paulo Freire on Higher Education.* The first is a "talking book," transcribed from taped conversations between Shor and Freire and concentrates on the problems of teaching large classes of recalcitrant full-time students. The second book is a collection of various pieces, including essays by Freire, reproduced from earlier publications and talks in which he elaborates his theory of literacy, together with dialogues between Freire and Macedo in which they discuss Freire's work and Freire responds to his critics. There are also historical accounts of literacy campaigns in São Tomé and Príncipe and a review of the campaign in Guinea-Bissau, the subject of his earlier book, *Pedagogy in Process: The Letters to Guinea-Bissau* (LGB). *Learning to Question* (Freire and Faundez 1989) is another spoken book, this time recording a conversation with Freire's successor at the Education sub-unit of the WCC, the Chilean philosopher and follower of Gramsci, António Faundez.

Freire married again in 1988. His second wife, Ana Maria Araújo ("Nita"), is a former student of his and the daughter of his old headmaster (Freire 1993:55). She collaborated in his work, sharing the stage with him at his public appearances and writing the Afterword and extensive Notes to Freire's *Pedagogy of Hope* (PH).

In 1989 Freire was appointed to the post of Secretary for Education of São Paulo by the mayor of the PT municipal administration, Luiza Erundina, a period discussed in a series of transcribed interviews in his book *Pedagogy of the City* (Freire 1993) and in an interview with Torres (Torres and Freire 1994:101–2). In that capacity he established four priorities for the PT educational reform program: (1) democratization and access; (2) democratization of administration; (3) new quality of teaching; (4) youth and adult education (Freire 1993:150). Under the fourth heading he established MOVA, a literacy movement which aimed to educate 60,000 people in 2,000 culture circles (Taylor 1993:32). In his accounts of this period, Freire emphasizes his commitment to school autonomy, permanent professional development of teachers, reorientation of the curriculum, dialogue with parents, students and education professionals and the involvement of university academics in the reform program. He also emphasizes his determination to improve the deplorable physical condition of many of São Paulo's public schools and deal with the "illogical and threatening bureaucracy"

(Freire 1993:35). However, the PT subsequently lost the municipal elections in the city in 1992 and it is not clear how far-reaching the changes initiated during Freire's period of office were (Torres and Freire 1994:102).

After resigning from his Secretary for Education post in May 1991, Freire returned to his university post and his writing (Taylor 1993:33). During his long career, he was awarded numerous honorary doctorates and prizes, including the Organization of American States Simon Rodriguez Prize in education in 1992.

Taylor comments that none of the work Freire published in English after his return to Brazil shows a radical change in his thought or practice (Taylor 1993:32) and his last major book, *Pedagogy of Hope: Reliving Pedagogy of the Oppressed* (PH), is no exception. In it he reflects on his experience and reaffirms and seeks to clarify the themes of his most famous book.

Freire's vision is of education as a preeminently political process: what kind of education and what kind of politics he promotes are explored in the rest of this chapter. I shall start with a brief review of some of Freire's key concepts: conscientization and the "culture of silence"; praxis and dialogue; "banking education" and "problem-posing education." Against this background, I shall then outline Freire's pedagogical method before turning to explore the nature of the politics and theology embodied in Freire's vision of education as political.

Freire's Vision of Education As Political

I use the term "vision" rather than "theory" here because Freire is reported to have claimed not to theorize, but instead to "reflect on his experiments" (Furter 1974:119). He has also said that his work should be seen as part of a process and not as a finished product; Faundez speaks of his constant need to explain himself (Freire and Faundez 1989:101). For these reasons and because, in his published writing, Freire tends to reiterate rather than develop his ideas, it is hard to speak of his work unequivocally in terms of a body of theory.

However, Freire insists that "there is no practice that does not have a built-in theory" (Freire 1993:132) and his practice is informed by many theories: he is an eclectic thinker *par excellence*. His eclecticism is not random, however, but historically specific, reflecting his formation as a radical Catholic intellectual in the period from the mid-1940s to 1964 and his subsequent experiences. Freire's historical situatedness is evident in de Kadt's (1970:102) statement about the "unity of theory and practice," praxis, regarded by many adult educators as a distinctly Freirean concept:

Marxists acknowledge the "unity of theory and practice"; the Catholic radicals shared the principle with them, not only as a result of their common roots in Hegelian dialectic, but also as a result of the concern for "commitment" in existentialist thought.

Freire acknowledges influences from a prodigiously wide range of sources, including Aristotle, Hegel and Rousseau, a connection convincingly demonstrated by Taylor (1993:45–50).

Like other Catholic radicals of his generation in Brazil,[9] Freire incorporates aspects of Marxism, including ideas from Marx himself, and, to an extent which will be explored in Chapter 4, Gramsci, as well as a host of neo-Marxist thinkers and activists. These include Louis Althusser, Agnes Heller, Georg Lukács, Mao Zedong, Che Guevara, Erich Fromm, Leszek Kolakowski, Herbert Marcuse, Karel Kosík, Gajo Petrovic and Lucien Goldmann and the anticolonialists Frantz Fanon, Albert Memmi and Amílcar Cabral. Freire also cites existentialists such as Jean-Paul Sartre, Emmanuel Mounier and Gabriel Marcel, the phenomenologists Edmund Husserl and Maurice Merleau-Ponty and the political philosopher and analyst of totalitarianism, Hannah Arendt.

His influences do not all come through his reading either, Freire has thanked "all who inspired me with their word" during his exile in Chile:

Marcela Gajardo, Jacques Chonchol, Jorge Mellado, Juan Carlos Poblete, Raúl Velozo, and Pelli, Chileans. Paulo de Tarso and Plínio Sampaio, Amino Affonso, Maria Edy, Flávio Toledo, Wilson Cantoni, Ernani Fiori, João Zacariotti, José Luiz Fiori, and Antonio Romanelli, Brazilians. (PH:62)

He also writes warmly of the "knowledge of living experience" of the rural workers he encountered in Chile (PH:44) and of his debt of gratitude to Elza (PH:64).

Freire has described his literacy work as "embedded in the theoretical foundations of psycholinguistics and sociolinguistics" (Freire in de Figueiredo-Cowen and Gastaldo 1995:66). Speaking in 1993, he said that he had discovered Vygotsky ten years earlier and now felt that "it is impossible to think about literacy without reading Piaget and Vygotsky" (Freire in de Figueiredo-Cowen and Gastaldo 1995:63).

In some cases the influence of a thinker is obvious once the source is identified. For example, de Kadt (1970) traces the influence of Hegel's dialectic, mediated through the Jesuit philosopher and theologian, Henrique C. de Lima Vaz, SJ, on Catholic radicals in Brazil. Vaz, writing about his concept of "historical consciousness" in a publication of 1962, could easily be mistaken for Freire. He contends that historical consciousness emerges when man begins to look critically at his world, becoming aware of the fact that "history unfolds in an empirical time-span, which is given substance by the action of man in the form of historical initiative; action, that is, which transforms the world" (Vaz, quoted in de Kadt 1970:87–8). Similarly, the personalist Christian existentialism of Emmanuel Mounier, with his emphasis on man and the unfurling of his potential (de Kadt 1970:91), clearly had a profound influence on Freire.

Taylor argues convincingly that key features of Freire's philosophy, such as his utopianism and use of the concept of praxis, may be traced from the writings of humanist Marxists such as Kolakowski, Petrovic and especially Kosík. Freire's debt to Kosík is evident in Taylor's (1993:44–5) analysis of the parallel structures of *Pedagogy of the Oppressed* and Kosík's *Dialectic of the Concrete* (1976) and in his careful reading of Freire's direct and indirect references to Kosík. Taylor identifies the following themes as common to both books:

*social reproduction and the reality of oppression; social banking structures and educational banking systems; reading the world and dialogic conscientization; the praxis of freedom and the practice of education.
(Taylor 1993:45)*

Taylor (1993:34–51) also highlights the major influence of French academics on Freire's early reading, in particular the influence of *l'éducation nouvelle,* with its central tenet that "education is nothing less than life itself" and its roots in French and German education in the 1920s (Taylor 1993:37). He identifies Lucien Febvre as the source for Freire's conception of consciousness as stratified and capable of acceleration or retardation and traces Freire's technique of decoding back to Febvre's introduction to discourse analysis; he identifies Freinet as the inspiration for Freire's literacy-centered pedagogy (Taylor 1993:35).

Taylor's meticulous study shows that it is one thing to identify Freire's probable sources of ideas and inspiration, but quite another to trace the nature and extent of their influence and the ways in which they interconnect in his thought. Freire is selective in his appropriations. He is quoted by Gerhardt (1993:442), for example, as saying, in an interview in 1978, that he was not willing to adhere to Marxism or existentialism because of some questionable points he found in the writings of Marx and Jaspers. With respect to Marx, Freire's memories of the PCB in Brazil before 1964 may also be a factor in his holding back from a full commitment to Marxism. In my judgment Freire is *Marxisante,* in the Brazilian idiom, meaning "not fully Marxist, but inspired by and sympathetic to Marxist revolutionary ideas" (de Kadt 1970:110), a position not uncommon among those influenced by Liberation Theology. Perhaps he is also *existentialisante.* If so, he would still be well within the Liberation Theology camp, since, as McLellan (1987:150) states, the movement was strongly influenced by the tradition of existentialism espoused by progressive theologians prior to the mid-1960s, while rejecting its characteristic individualism in favor of a more structuralist approach. Certainly, Freire is a syncretic thinker, in keeping with those strands of Catholicism which weave together disparate elements, short of actual heresy.

Freire's philosophical contradictions are thus, to a great extent, the contradictions of Liberation Theology, or at least, of the milieu of which Liberation Theology was a part. Likewise, his language, which has been condemned as impenetrable, reaches, at best, toward a poeticism which is also a hallmark of Liberation Theology. As McLellan points out, this characteristic *has enabled a realization of alienation and oppression (and therefore resistance to it) to take place within religious consciousness among people who would be quite untouched by the rational tones of a pure Marxist discourse. (McLellan 1987:155)*

Perhaps Freire's particular gift has been to enable such a realization to take place within the professional consciousness of adult educators.

Given all these theoretical and stylistic influences, it is not unreasonable to seek a theoretical framework in Freire's work, even if only an implicit one. Perhaps the framework metaphor is not well-chosen, however, for one who weaves together such a multiplicity of ideas and sources—Freire himself speaks of "fabric" and "tapestries" in his reflections on his life and work in *Pedagogy of Hope* and these more flexible metaphors seem appropriate. What, then, is the fabric that Freire has woven and how has it developed since his early work in Brazil?

Conscientization

The key motif in Freire's theoretical fabric is his concept of conscientization (*conscientização*). Freire did not invent the term, which emerged from ISEB deliberations in the late 1950s and was popularized abroad by Bishop Helder Câmara (O'Gorman 1978:53). De Kadt (1970:98) states that *conscientização* was in common use amongst Catholic radicals in Brazil before the coup and it was an express goal of initiatives such as the MCP and MEB.

Despite its currency in Brazil before the coup, conscientization is an elusive concept in Freire's writing. An early published statement of the concept is arguably Freire's most succinct: *"Conscientização represents the development of the awakening of critical awareness"* (EPF:19). He stresses that this development "must grow out of a critical educational effort based on favourable historical conditions," it is not the inevitable result of "even major economic changes" (EPF:19).

If the concept is elusive, the process, as described in Freire's writings, is nothing if not elaborate. Conscientization involves passage through several stages corresponding to different levels of consciousness which Freire describes in *Education: The Practice of Freedom* (EPF) and *Cultural Action for Freedom* (CAF). The lowest level Freire describes as "semi-intransitive consciousness." This he considers typical of poor people, peasants and bonded laborers living in the *latifundios* (large land holdings) and *favelas* (urban slums) of Brazil. In this situation people are "submerged in the historical process," concerned only with survival, consequently "they confuse their perceptions of the objects and challenges of the environment, and fall prey to magical explanations because they cannot apprehend true causality" (EPF:17). If the explanation for their ills is seen by poor and oppressed people as lying in a superior power, or in their own "natural" incapacity, "their action will not be oriented towards transforming reality, but towards those superior beings responsible for the problematical situation, or towards that presumed incapacity" (CAF:63).

Freire states that semi-intransitive consciousness is characteristic of people trapped in the "culture of silence," unable to discover and articulate their view of the world and therefore unable to act to change it. He defines the culture of silence as "a superstructural expression which conditions a special form of consciousness [. . .] born in the relationship between the Third World and the metropolis" (CAF:57). This relationship is one of Third World dependence on the metropolis. Describing Brazil as a dependent society, Freire says:

The dependent society is by definition a silent society. Its voice is not an authentic voice but merely an echo of the voice of the metropolis—in every way, the metropolis speaks, the dependent society listens. (Freire quoted in Hawthorn 1980:30)

Freire sees the culture of silence as characteristic also of "those areas in the metropolises which identify themselves with the Third World as 'areas of silence'" (CAF:57). For Freire, the "Third World" denotes any groups of people who have experienced cultural invasion (PO:121). It is on the basis of statements such as this that some educators claim that his approach is generalizable and applicable to the education of poor and oppressed people in countries such as Britain or the United States.[10]

As people emerge from the semi-intransitive state of consciousness, they enter what Freire terms the "naive transitive" stage. Naive transitivity is characterized by

*an over-simplification of problems; by a strong tendency to gregarious-
ness; by a lack of interest in investigation, accompanied by an accentu-
ated taste for fanciful explanations; by fragility of argument; by a strongly
emotional style; by the practice of polemics rather than dialogue; by
magical explanations. (EPF:18)*

Freire states that progress from the semi-intransitive stage to the stage
of naive transitivity is a natural result of the pressures and stimulation of urbanization on increasing numbers of people (EPF:19). This
implies that there is no role for education per se during this transition: the environment is the educator.

At the next stage of the process, however, Freire warns that there
is a danger that people will proceed from the naive transitive stage,
not to critical transitivity of consciousness but to fanaticized consciousness, because there is "a close potential relationship between
naive transitivity and massification" (EPF:19). People with a fanaticized consciousness are irrational, defeated, debased and dehumanized, dominated and directed by others while believing themselves
to be free, though at the same time fearing freedom. If the descent
into fanaticism is to be avoided, what is required is "an active, dialogical educational program concerned with social and political responsibility" (EPF:19). Freire claims that "an explicit relationship
has been established between cultural action for freedom" with
"conscientization as its chief enterprise" and "the transcendence of
semi-intransitive and naive-transitive states of critical consciousness"
(CAF:78). The goal of conscientization, critically transitive consciousness, is characterized by

*depth in the interpretation of problems; by the substitution of causal
principles for magical explanations; by the testing of one's "findings" and
by openness to revision; by the attempt to avoid distortion when perceiv-
ing problems and to avoid preconceived notions when analysing them;
by refusing to transfer responsibility; by rejecting passive positions; by
soundness of argumentation; by the practice of dialogue rather than polemics; by receptivity to the new for reasons beyond mere novelty and by
the good sense not to reject the old just because it is old—by accepting
what is valid in both old and new. (EPF:18)*

Critically transitive consciousness is accordingly typical of "authentically democratic regimes and corresponds to highly permeable, interrogative, restless and dialogical forms of life" (EPF:18–9).

Freire's subsequent references to conscientization are characterized by attempts to correct misconceptions about its meaning. For example, attempting to counter accusations that conscientization is "a falsely intellectual attitude towards reality," Freire asserted in 1970 *"Conscientização* cannot exist without or outside praxis, that is, outside action-reflection" (Freire 1976a:224).

The tension within his concept of conscientization between reflection and action remained problematic for Freire, triggering a shift in the mid-1970s toward a greater emphasis on the importance of action. Criticizing his earlier view of conscientization, encapsulated in his assertion in *Pedagogy of the Oppressed* that "to speak a true word is to transform the world" (PO:60), Freire commented:

My mistake was not that I recognised the fundamental importance of a knowledge of reality in the process of its change, but rather that I did not take these two different moments—the knowledge of reality and the work of transforming that reality—in their dialectical relationship. It was as if I were saying that to discover reality already meant to transform it. (Freire 1975:15)

The distinction between the two moments is recognized by Cynthia Brown in her account of Freire's literacy process. She describes conscientization as "a process in which people are encouraged to analyze their reality, to become more aware of the constraints on their lives, and to take action to transform their situation" (C. Brown 1975:20). Freire makes the same point in *Pedagogy of Hope:* "The revelatory, gnosiological practice of education does not of itself effect the transformation of the world: but it implies it" (PH:31).

After a while, all Freire's efforts to communicate the meaning of conscientization seem to have struck him as inadequate. In 1979, during a visit to India, Freire stated that he had not used the word for seven years because it was so corrupted in Latin America and the United States (Freire 1979:1). In *Pedagogy of the City* he explained that he stopped using the term because people treated conscientization as a "magical pill" which would change the world. Instead, he tried to clarify what he meant in interviews, seminars and articles (Freire 1993:111).

Why is the concept of conscientization, at once so significant for Freire and so important for anyone seeking to understand his work, at the same time so elusive? Part of the problem is undoubtedly Freire's prolix writing style. Difficulties of translation may have compounded the problem, although Freire emphatically denied this with respect to *Pedagogy of the Oppressed* (PH:74). Freire's own use of the term changed, and his undeclared decision to stop using it can only have added to the confusion. It is likely, also, that Freire began by assuming a shared understanding of *conscientização* among his readers. Since 1964 Freire came increasingly to address an international audience which cannot be assumed to share the experience, the worldview or the terminology of Catholic radicals in South America. But there are serious problems with his staged theory of consciousness which may point to underlying reasons for Freire's difficulties in communicating what he means by conscientization; these are discussed below.

However hard Freire found it to convey the real meaning of conscientization, he never abandoned the concept, which remains a key motif in his recent writings. For Freire, conscientization is still "the deepening of the coming of consciousness" (Freire 1993:109) and he endorses the term again in *Pedagogy of Hope*, quoting a passage originally published in 1975 (PH:103). He insists that "in not using the word for a time, I did not refute its signification [. . .] I was always involved with the most profound comprehension of this concept in my theoretical and practical activities" (Freire 1993:109, 110).

Praxis and Dialogue

If conscientization is the aim of the education process, then Freire's concepts of praxis and dialogue are the two interrelated principles on which the process rests. Writing in *Pedagogy of the Oppressed,* Freire states that by praxis he means, "the action and reflection of men upon their world in order to transform it" (PO:52). For Freire, action and reflection should occur simultaneously (PO:99) and he elaborates the concept of praxis as follows:

Action   } word = work = praxis

Reflection   }

Sacrifice of action = verbalism

Sacrifice of reflection = activism (PO:60 n1)

Praxis alone is not enough, however, without dialogue, by which Freire means "the encounter between men, mediated by the world, in order to name the world" (PO:61). Dialogue is more than mere communication, it has an almost mystical significance for Freire. In a passage redolent with biblical overtones, Freire affirms that dialogue involves communion between leaders and people, teachers and students, a communion which is only possible when there is love, hope, faith, trust and humility: "Love is at the same time the foundation of dialogue and dialogue itself" (PO:62). Freire has reaffirmed his commitment to dialogue in *Pedagogy of Hope* (PH:116–7), stressing its democratic nature: "Dialogue between teachers and students does not place them on the same footing professionally; but it does mark the democratic position between them."

Given that conscientization is the aim of Freire's educational project, and that praxis and dialogue are the two fundamental principles informing it, what kind of education process does Freire propose? In *Pedagogy of the Oppressed* Freire answers this question by using a device that recurs throughout his writing: presenting two sets of statements as bipolarities, with the preferred position identified in terms of its antithesis. He counterposes "banking education" and "problem-posing education" in terms that leave no room for doubt as to which is the favored approach.

"Banking Education" and "Problem-Posing Education"

While banking education "anaesthetizes and inhibits creative power," attempting "to maintain the *submersion* of consciousness," problem-posing education involves a constant unveiling of reality" and "strives for the *emergence* of consciousness and critical intervention in reality" (PO:54). For Freire, banking education

attempts, by mythicising reality, to conceal certain facts which explain the way men exist in the world; problem-posing education sets itself the task of de-mythologizing. Banking education resists dialogue; problem-posing education regards dialogue as indispensable to the act of cogni-

tion which unveils reality. Banking education treats students as objects of assistance; problem-posing education makes them critical thinkers. Banking education inhibits creativity and domesticates (although it cannot completely destroy) the intentionality of consciousness by isolating consciousness from the world, thereby denying men their ontological and historical vocation of becoming more fully human. Problem-posing education bases itself on creativity and stimulates true reflection and action upon reality, thereby responding to the vocation of men as beings who are authentic only when engaged in inquiry and creative transformation. In sum: banking theory and practice, as immobilizing and fixating forces, fail to acknowledge men as historical beings; problem-posing theory and practice take man's historicity as their starting point. (PO:56)

Education in the banking mode is narrative rather than dialogical in character. By contrast, problem-posing education dissolves the distance between the roles of teacher and student, and merges them together into a new entity. Problem-posing education demands a resolution of the teacher-student contradiction so that "through dialogue, the teacher-of-the-students and the students-of-the-teacher cease to exist and a new term emerges: teacher–student with students-teachers" (PO:53). This means that "the teacher is no longer merely the one who teaches, but one who is himself taught in dialogue with the students, who in their turn while being taught also teach" (PO:53).

For Freire, "problem-posing education does not and cannot serve the interests of the oppressor" (PO:58–59). The issue is disarmingly simple: the education process mirrors society as a whole, so that banking education mirrors oppressing society and dialogical, problem-solving, conscientizing education is characteristic of a humane society based on libertarian values. But what does this mean in terms of what actually happens in the education process? Here we turn to examine the educational method which bears Freire's name and which is designed to make problem-posing education a reality.

The "Psycho-social" Method
The *"método Paulo Freire"* (a designation that Freire disliked, Freire 1993:55), known also as the "psycho-social method" of problem-posing education (Sanders 1973; McGinn 1973) was first described

in *Education: The Practice of Freedom* (EPF) and subsequently elaborated in *Pedagogy of the Oppressed* (PO). It consists of two stages, a literacy campaign and a postliteracy phase, designed to bring about conscientization. Both are informed by the anthropological concept of culture, the fundamental distinction between the natural world and the world of human agency. The starting point must always be with people "in the 'here and now', which constitutes the situation within which they are submerged, from which they emerge, and in which they intervene" (PO:57). It is only by starting from this situation "which determines their perception of it" that they can begin to move through the stages of consciousness outlined above. Freire states that "to do this authentically they must perceive their state not as fated and unalterable, but merely as limiting—and therefore challenging" (PO:57).

Against this background, Freire's literacy method eschews primers and instead exploits the fact that Portuguese words are composed syllabically. This means that all Portuguese words of more than one syllable can be "generative" in the technical sense of yielding syllables which can be reassembled to generate new words. However, some words are more generative than others in the sense that they are particularly significant—they generate meaning—for the people concerned. Such generative words are identified through an investigation of the learners' vocabulary and the circumstances of their lives. A selection is made by the investigators on the basis both of the phonemic complexity and semantic power of the words for the people concerned. These generative words are then re-presented in the form of "codifications," visual images on slides prepared by the investigators showing typical existential situations of the learners. The codifications are intended to challenge the learners to "decode" elements of their own reality. Cards are prepared showing the breakdown of the phonemic families corresponding to the generative words. These are then made into slides.

Freire describes how the process works with the Portuguese word *favela* (slum):

After analysing the existential situation (a photograph showing a slum), in which the group discusses the problems of housing, food, clothing, health and education in a slum and in which the group further perceives

*the slum as a problem situation, the coordinator proceeds to present the
word favela with its semantic links visually.*

a) First a slide appears showing only the word: FAVELA
*b) Immediately afterward, another slide appears with the word sepa-
rated into syllables: FA-VE-LA*
c) Afterwards the phonemic family: FA-FE-FI-FO-FU
d) On another slide: VA-VE-VI-VO-VU
e) Then: LA-LE-LI-LO-LU
f) Now the three families together:
FA-FE-FI-FO-FU   }
VA-VE-VI-VO-VU   } Discovery card
LA-LE-LI-LO-LU   }
*The group then begins to create words with the various combinations.
(EPF:82).*

Using this method, Freire claims that in six weeks to two months, a
group of twenty-five people would be reading newspapers, writing
notes and simple letters, and discussing problems of local and national interest (EPF:53 n16).

The postliteracy phase involves the selection of "generative
themes" (PO:81) through a similar process of investigation. All aspects of the life of the area are observed and recorded. These observations are then the subject of evaluation meetings of the investigators, designed to bring them closer to a perception of the
contradictions with which the lives of the inhabitants are enmeshed.

The second stage of the investigation involves the investigators
in selecting some of these contradictions to develop the codifications to be used in the thematic investigation. The investigators then
return to the area to initiate decoding dialogues in "thematic investigation circles," each of a maximum of twenty people. Freire recommends that there should be enough circles to involve 10 percent
of those living in the area under study. Discussions (during which
material prepared in the previous stage is decoded) are taped and
subsequently analyzed by the interdisciplinary team.

The last stage begins as the decoding is completed, when the
investigators undertake a systematic interdisciplinary study of their
findings, listing the themes explicit or implicit in the affirmations

made during decoding sessions. These themes are then classified in a process Freire terms "thematic demarcation" (PO:91). When the thematic demarcation is completed each specialist (a sociologist or a psychologist) presents to the team a project breaking down the theme into "the fundamental nuclei which, comprising learning units and establishing a sequence, give a general view of the theme" (PO:91). During the discussions the other specialists add their suggestions, which may be incorporated into the project or included in essays written on the themes. Freire acknowledges the need to include what he calls "hinged themes" (PO:92). These are themes which, though not suggested by the participants in the circles of investigation, are nevertheless felt by the investigators to be necessary, perhaps to fill a gap or to show a general connection.

Codification follows the thematic breakdown. Freire stresses that the codifications must pose questions and not suggest answers. Didactic material, including photographs, slides, filmstrips, posters, reading texts, and small introductory manuals are produced after the thematics have been codified (PO:93). Examples of such codifications are reprinted in *Education: The Practice of Freedom* (EPF:62–84). The end of the process occurs when "the thematics which have come from the people return to them—not as contents to be deposited, but as problems to be posed" (PO:94).

The problem is that the process of collection, selection and presentation of thematics and codifications is far from being a straightforward matter. It raises fundamental questions, such as who selects images, on what grounds, how are the images presented and how are they read? For example, the question of the selection of an aspect of the people's reality is a crucial issue and once selected it will inevitably be susceptible to multiple readings. The codified images that Freire presents in *Education: The Practice of Freedom* (EPF:62–84) exemplify the problem. The first situation shows a barefoot man in the foreground with a book in one hand and a hoe in the other, standing on the edge of what looks like cultivated land. There are trees in the picture and in the background there is a house, a well, and a woman walking toward the house, holding a small child by the hand. The text states: "Through the discussion of this situation—man as a being of relationships—the participants arrive at a distinction between two worlds: that of nature and that of culture"

(EPF:63). This is one reading of the picture but hardly the only one. It could equally well be seen as illustrating the idea that a woman's place is in the home looking after children, or that the family members (assuming they are a nuclear family) have everything they need (with the possible exception of a pair of shoes for the man). The situation was presumably selected for the reasons set out in the text but another political agenda might have produced a very different reading.

Taylor's analysis of this problem in relation to the same image is illuminating (Taylor 1993:86–92). He points out that the image endows the book with a totemic significance and thus sets the agenda for the literacy program as: "*The individual who is Subject cannot live without the book*" (Taylor 1993:88). Meanwhile the hidden agenda is to ensure that the participants arrive at an understanding of the distinction between nature and culture. As Taylor (1993:88) notes, this requires "a deft use of manipulation to achieve the objectives of the session." Thus, the image of the enlightened peasant shown in this drawing

is important precisely because he or she is the model of the ideal student. By definition, their enlightenment means that they already know what it is that they are supposed to know, except only that they do not know it in the way that the teacher knows it. In what is really an example of pedagogic bad faith, the peasant is enlightened because he or she has been judged to be "in the image and likeness of" the teacher. (Taylor 1993:89)

Taylor deconstructs "the dialectical relationship between the Power of Literacy and the Literacy of Power" in Freire's literacy work, revealing a contradiction at the heart of his method (Taylor 1993:147).

Freire does not appear to recognize this problem, which strikes at the heart of his methodology. Nor is the problem confined to Freire's own writing. It extends to at least one of his followers: Weiler (1996:365 n21) draws attention to similar problems in the codification of a photograph in Gadotti's reverential *Reading Paulo Freire* (Gadotti 1994).

Freire does, however, recognize the difficulty of creating a new attitude of dialogue which he finds "so absent in our own upbringing and education" (EPF:52). Accordingly, while teaching the technical aspects of the method is straightforward, Freire recommends that "the period of instruction must be followed by dialogical supervision, to avoid the temptation of anti-dialogue on the part of the coordinators" (EPF:52). Freire accepts that usually the educators/coordinators will be drawn from the middle class (which he sees as allied to and identified with the oppressors of the poor). In order to become dialogical educators, they must commit "class suicide" (LGB:15). Through this effort of moral will they may then be reborn, in what Freire terms an "Easter experience," newly committed to the interests of the poor and oppressed (PO:37). The expression "class suicide" is attributed to Amílcar Cabral, but the concept is Frantz Fanon's, in his classic anticolonialist text, *The Wretched of the Earth:*

The historical vocation of an authentic national middle class in an under-developed country is to repudiate its own nature in so far as it is bourgeois, that is to say in so far as it is the tool of capitalism, and to make itself the willing slave of that revolutionary capital which is the people. (Fanon 1967:120)

Freire recognized the difficulties that this entails and later modified his position to some extent. Accordingly, in a letter to the team of educators to which he was consultant in Guinea-Bissau, he writes

I am convinced that it is easier to create a new type of intellectual—forged in the unity between practice and theory, manual and intellectual work—than to reeducate an elitist intellectual. [. . .] The challenge [. . .] is not to continue creating elitist intellectuals so that they can commit class suicide, but rather to prevent their formation in the first place. (LGB:104)

Similarly, in an earlier letter to Mário Cabral, Commissioner of State for Education and Culture in Guinea-Bissau, Freire writes:

If it were not possible either to count on peasants who can be rapidly trained in literacy work, as in Chile, nor on urban youths capable of committing "class suicide" and of "knowing how to become integrated

into their country and with their people," then I would rather dedicate the necessary longer time to train peasants who might become authentic educators of their comrades, than to use middle-class youth. The latter may be trained more rapidly, but their commitment is less trustworthy. (LGB:82)

However, this only takes the problem one stage further back: the teachers may be peasants, but the organizers of the education process are still likely to be the self-sacrificing middle-class intellectuals of his earlier formulations. The question of who should supervise the supervisors is not addressed, although the participation of representatives of the inhabitants in all activities of the investigating team (PO:84) is presumably intended as a safeguard against antidialogical attitudes.

Freire has also modified his position on the teaching process itself, acknowledging that under certain circumstances elements of both traditional and democratic teaching may be appropriate, for example, in the initial stages of working with adults who are accustomed to traditional approaches (Freire in Horton and Freire 1990:160). In "The People Speak Their Word: Literacy in Action," published in his talking book with Macedo, Freire gives an account of his literacy method in São Tomé and Príncipe (Freire and Macedo 1987:63–9). It is strikingly different from his descriptions of the equivalent process in Brazil in the early 1960s. The Popular Culture Notebooks developed for the campaign sound perilously close to the primers that Freire abhors in all but their choice of themes. The themes of the literacy campaign are all concerned with production and the work process, technical training and the role of culture in national reconstruction.

The postliteracy phase (never reached in Brazil because of the coup) deals with the act of studying, national reconstruction and work and transformation. These themes sound to me as if they have come from the government rather than the people, as Freire insists they should in his earlier work. The key words in one of the Notebooks illustrate the point: they are "unity," "discipline," "work" and "vigilance." Nor are the themes and the key words the only things to change: in the literacy campaign Freire emphasizes for the first time the importance of writing as well as reading and the postliteracy phase aims to increase the students' knowledge of grammar.

In a talk given in 1982 Freire elaborated a further set of polarities around the role of the educator, distinguishing between the "critical practice and understanding of literacy, as opposed to the naive and so-called 'astute' practice and understanding" (Freire and Macedo 1987:37–8). In this formulation, critical literacy educators eschew the myth of the neutrality of education; they accept the impossibility of separating education from politics and questions of power and they recognize the need to "respect the levels of understanding that those becoming educated have of their own reality" (Freire and Macedo 1987:41). By contrast, "naive" educators see education as a neutral matter of pure task; they identify with the consciously reactionary educators whom Freire designates the "astute." But although "both the naive and the astute find themselves marked by the dominant, elitist ideology, [. . .] only the astute consciously assume this ideology as their own" (Freire and Macedo 1987:42). Freire then further elaborates this idea with the concept of the "astutely naive" educator who, while aware that education is not neutral, does not affirm that this is so. He differentiates between the "non-malicious naive person and the astute or tactical naive person" on the grounds that the former are able to learn from their own practice and so come to renounce naivete and assume a new critical posture (Freire and Macedo 1987:43).

But in order to be critical, the educator must be politically aware and Freire constantly asserts that his is a political pedagogy. His writing is also shot through with theological terms and concepts. It is therefore necessary to examine the warp and the weft of Freire's theoretical fabric: his politics and his theology.

Freire's Politics and Theology

Freire does not claim to be a theologian, any more than he claims to be a political theorist, but I believe that an understanding of his theology as well as his politics is necessary in order to reach a fair evaluation of his thought. Freire's theology has been less thoroughly explored than his politics, but as Taylor emphasizes, in Freire's writing:

*the language of the Christian faith is more than the mere clothes for
dressing and presentation: it is actually the skeleton or underpinning of
his philosophical and social analysis. (Taylor 1993:56)*

Freire himself insists that theology has "a vital function to perform"
(Freire 1972b:8). Elias, who writes authoritatively on Freire's theology from a liberal Catholic perspective, states that Freire considers
two articles of his on the church, written in the early 1970s, to be
important for understanding his more mature thought (Elias
1994:143). These are "Education, Liberation, and the Church" (reprinted in PE:Chapter 10) and "The Educational Role of the
Churches in Latin America" (Freire 1972a). As well as the theological references that recur throughout his published work, Freire has
published "A Letter to a Theology Student" (Freire 1972b) and a
passionate endorsement of James Cone's *Black Theology of Liberation* (reprinted in PE:Chapter 11).

Elias identifies Freire with that eminently political theology, the
Theology of Liberation. This he characterizes in the following ways.
It speaks to involvement with the liberation of the oppressed, calling
upon Christians, especially those in the Third World, to be revolutionaries in society. It deals realistically with the issue of political
involvement, even to the point of proposing revolutionary violence,
and it stresses some neglected elements in the Christian tradition:
politics; utopia; the liberator God; the prophetic church (Elias
1994:136). Elias sees Freire's theology as a theology of hope, utopian in its denunciation of injustice and annunciation of freedom
and justice, imbued with a vision of a God who empowers people to
make history through their efforts at liberation (Elias 1994:138).
The starting point for Freire's theology is humanity: "just as the Word
became flesh, so the Word can be approached only through man"
(Freire, quoted in Elias 1994:141). Thus, Freire's insistence on dialogue as an educational technique is born of his insistence that "*the
very nature of human life is characterized by dialogical communication
with God, nature and other persons*"(Elias 1994:140, emphasis in the
original).

Elias stresses Freire's emphasis on death and resurrection and
the necessity for every Christian to have an "Easter experience" (Elias
1994:141). He stresses also that Freire sees the church as an institu-

tion involved in history and outlines Freire's designation of three types of churches—traditionalist, modernizing and prophetic—as exemplars of different levels of consciousness, respectively: semi-intransitive; naive; and critical. The Basic Church Communities (CEBs) and the churches in Cone's *Black Theology of Liberation* (PE:Chapter 11) are, for Freire, examples of the critically conscious church (Elias 1994:143–5).

As well as discussing the influence of Liberation Theology on Freire, Elias outlines Freire's influence on Liberation Theology, citing favorable references to Freire's pedagogy by leading liberation theologians Gustavo Gutierrez and Juan Segundo (Elias 1994:145–7). While he is critical of some aspects of Freire's theology, such as his failure to take account of original sin, Elias's verdict is that Freire is a "Christian-existentialist-Marxist educator" (Elias 1994:44).

Gillian Cooper's (1995) article is also timely. She argues convincingly that one reason why Freire is so commonly misunderstood is that Marxist or socialist Freirean educators miss his theology and Christian Freirean educators downplay his Marxism and simplify his Christianity (Cooper 1995:66). She argues that there is "a potential match between Freire's ontology and Christian theology" such that "Freire's optimism about human nature, and his faith in its worth, are thus not only Marxist but Christian" (Cooper 1995:71). Freire's utopian optimism is important, since, as Cooper points out:

Many of those working in adult education [. . .] would recognise Freire's description of education which has ceased to be utopian. Rather it is characterised by pessimism and pragmatism. It has become caught in the ideology of capitalism, and resounds with the language of the market and a fearful pragmatism. (Cooper 1995:72)

Cooper cites several contributors to Jarvis and Walters's (1993) useful edited collection, *Adult Education and Theological Interpretations*, including Welton, who argues compellingly that Freire's understanding of the conscientization process as a "'conversion of the oppressed' transposes explicitly biblical themes into historic pedagogical practice" (Welton 1993:74). Cooper concludes that a "continuing conversation between Freirean educators and the educators of the church could be fruitful for both" (Cooper 1995:78).

I have argued above that Freire is best understood as a radical Catholic, emerging from the milieu that produced Liberation Theology and identifying with its tenets. Freire's pedagogy of liberation may thus be seen as the pedagogical analogue of Liberation Theology. Liberation Theology defines itself in opposition to the traditional and modernizing church and, as Giroux affirms, Freire is "a harsh critic of the reactionary church" (Giroux in PE:xvii). Against that background, Freire's role is prophetic, in the sense discussed by Cooper, who points out that, rather than foretelling the future, "the main tasks of an Old Testament prophet were to challenge thinking and expose ideology" (Cooper 1995:75). Freire's prophetic optimism is a beacon of inspiration to many adult educators who may be unaware that its source of power is Christian theology.

So what of Freire's politics? Here the picture is more complex. Although Freire was clearly identified with the Left, he did not stand still politically. At the time that his literacy work in Brazil was developing under the auspices of a populist government, Freire was convinced that the Brazilian people "could be helped to learn democracy through the exercise of democracy" (EPF:36). Education in this context was, he believed, an important adjunct of democratic nationalism because

Nothing threatened the correct development of popular emergence more than an educational practice which failed to offer opportunities for the analysis and debate of problems, or for genuine participation; one which not only did not identify with the trend toward democratization but reinforced our lack of democratic experience. (EPF:36)

As it turned out, the populist government and Freire's democratic nationalism fell victim to a threat far greater than an inadequate educational practice in the form of the coup of 1964.

As we shall see, Freire is still accused of being a populist, but most observers date his shift to a more overtly radical, ostensibly Marxist, political stance from the coup and his subsequent exile. Freire himself insisted that the shift is reflected in his writings from *Pedagogy of the Oppressed* (written in 1968) onward (PH:88–89). Not everyone agrees on when—or whether—the shift took place; however, Frank Youngman (1986:Chapter 5), in his careful assessment of Freire's pedagogy, discerns a not altogether satisfactory shift from radical humanism toward a more explicitly Marxist position in the 1970s (i.e., after *Pedagogy of the Oppressed*) exemplified in his *Pedagogy in Process: The Letters to Guinea-Bissau* (LGB). Youngman contends that at this time Freire became more concerned with the role of the revolutionary party. However, as will be seen in the discussion below, I do not find this an entirely convincing argument, partly because I see Freire's commitment to the revolutionary party in Guinea-Bissau as insufficiently critical: more an act of faith than a political commitment. It could also be seen as a continuation, in a different political context, of his uncritical acceptance of the government line in Brazil before the coup.

Freire's own account of his experience of exile in Chile in *Pedagogy of Hope* is couched in terms of a movement leftward, but one in which he avoided the sectarianism which he found to be endemic on the Marxist Left. He writes sympathetically of the *Movimento Independente Revolucionário* (MIR), which he describes as

constituted of revolutionary youth who disagreed with what seemed to them to be a deviation on the part of the Communist party—that of "coexistence" with elements of "bourgeois democracy." (PH:36)

Freire distances himself from MIR's politics by his use of the phrase "what seemed to them to be a deviation." Nonetheless, he recounts with approval his impression of an education project run by the MIR in Nueba Habana, Chile, which he visited in 1973: "Nueba Habana had a future, then, if an uncertain one, and the climate surrounding it and the experimental pedagogy being plied within it was one of hope" (PH:37). In fact, Freire's approval of the MIR may stem as much from its enthusiasm for popular education initiatives as from its politics, which Freire describes as "constantly to the Left of the Communist party" (PH:36).

Freire clearly deplores left sectarianism. His verdict on the splintering of the left groups in Chile is uncompromising:

At this distance, it is easy to see that only a radical politics—not a sectarian one, however, but one that seeks a unity in diversity among progres-

*sive forces—could ever have won the battle for a democracy that could
stand up to the power and virulence of the Right. (PH:37)*

As well as numerous mini-schisms, in much of Latin America a major
sectarian schism in the Left was that between Marxist-Leninist and
Maoist positions. Freire avoided committing himself to either camp,
and I suspect that his efforts to remain nonaligned in the face of left
sectarianism may account for much of the elusiveness of his political
writing. Nevertheless, there are persistent resonances of Maoism in
Freire's writing, as becomes clear in the discussion below of Freire's
concept of revolutionary leadership. There is also an ambivalence
about class, explored below in the context of my discussion of Freire's
concept of oppression.

Since 1980, however, Freire identified himself with the politics
of the party he helped to found, the Workers' Party (PT), described
by Torres in his conversation with Freire (in McLaren and Lankshear
eds. 1994:101) as "a democratic socialist party." His statement of
his present political position in *Pedagogy of Hope* is couched unequivocally in class terms:

*The progressive postmodern, democratic outlook in which I take my po-
sition acknowledges the right of the working class to be trained in such a
way that they will know how their society functions, know their rights
and duties, know the history of the working class and the role of the
popular movements in remaking society in a more democratic mold. The
working class has a right to know its geography, and its language—or
rather, a critical understanding of language in its dialectical relationship with thought and world: the dialectical interrelations of language,
ideology, social classes, and education. (PH:132)*

Elsewhere in the same book he writes of the opportunity, as he sees
it, offered by the collapse of soviet-style "realistic socialism" to "continue fighting for the socialist *dream*, purified of its authoritarian
distortions, its totalitarian repulsiveness, its sectarian blindness"
(PH:96).

So is Freire no longer *Marxisante*, but rather a fully-fledged
Marxist? I think not: the PT is not a revolutionary Marxist party.
Freire's relationship to Marxism remained ambiguous—but no more

so than that of many other left intellectuals of his generation. In his recent writing, Freire dismisses the suggestion that Marx is a "has-been," maintaining that "to me, he continues to be, needing only to be reseen" (PH:88). Freire's thought and his faith are syncretic; for him Marxism and Christianity are complementary. As he said in an interview in 1974, "When I met Marx, I continued to meet Christ on the corners of the street—by meeting the people" (Freire quoted in Walker 1980:126). More recently, he affirmed that he enjoyed "a certain camaraderie with Christ and with Marx, which surprises certain Christians and makes naive Marxists suspicious" (Freire 1993:55).

Debates about Freire's political orientation continued throughout his career from a variety of perspectives, overshadowing those about his theology. Thus far, my discussion of Freire's politics has been couched in terms of his allegiance (or lack of it) to a political party and his espousal of (or refusal to espouse) a political "line." But Freire's politics have come under fire from quarters which defy such categorization, in particular from feminists. These critiques are considered below.

The question is whether Freire's political and theological fabric is strong enough to bear the weight of the claims he makes for it. In order to test it I shall look at some of the ways in which Freire's politics and theology are conceptualized: in his concept of oppression; in his model of revolutionary leadership; and in his formulation of the pedagogical process.

Freire's Concept of Oppression

Freire describes himself as a product of a highly racist and *machista* society and affirms that in his early life he was "first and foremost struck by class and racial oppression" (Freire and Macedo in McLaren and Leonard eds. 1993:171). Nevertheless, one of the commonly voiced criticisms of Freire is that he lacks that essential tool for a Marxist: a class analysis. Freire has vehemently denied this (PH:88*ff.*) and it is certainly possible to find many passages in his writing where he expounds Marxist ideas of class oppression and resistance. For example, in *Pedagogy of the Oppressed* Freire writes of "those who buy and those who are obliged to sell their labour" and of the "unconcealable antagonism which exists between the two classes"

(PO:113). In a dialogue with Macedo (Freire and Macedo 1993:172), Freire states that his major preoccupation at the time of writing *Pedagogy of the Oppressed* was a Marxist understanding of class oppression, pointing to "thirty-three references to social class analysis" in the text to support his case. In *Pedagogy of Hope* Freire reaffirms that:

relationships between classes are a political fact, which generates a class knowledge, and that class knowledge has the most urgent need of lucidity and discernment when choosing the best tactics to be used. These tactics vary in concrete history, but must be in consonance with strategic objectives. (PH:92)

Freire avers that the class struggle is but one mover of history, rather than *the* mover of history (PH:90). However, he maintains that "you still have to pass through class analysis" even "when a pedagogy tries to influence other factors that could not be strictly explained by a theory of class" (Freire and Macedo 1987:52). More typically, however, Freire writes of "the oppressed," the "popular masses" or "the people," a usage he has maintained in the new edition of *Pedagogy of the Oppressed* despite making other textual changes, and which he continues in *Pedagogy of Hope* alongside class-based referents such as "peasants" and "workers."

But it is not simply a question of whether, or how often, Freire uses the word "class." Freire's concept of class is problematic on several grounds. First, as Walker (1980:136–8) argues, the concept of class is a material and not a moral or religious one, as Freire's insistence on "class suicide" and the necessity of an "Easter experience" implies. Robbed of its materiality, class is reduced to a moral choice, analogous to that made by Freire in attempting to identify with the poor and oppressed. Furthermore, Freire's model of revolution as a national struggle for "socialism in one country" means that he regards "the class divisions inherent in class society as obliterated by the nationalist revolution, so that what remains in the struggle is almost entirely cultural" (Walker 1980:131). Freire has acknowledged that his concept of class in his early work, including *Pedagogy of the Oppressed*, is too abstract (Freire and Faundez 1989:101) and some of his later references to class are noticeably more concrete, as, for example in his statement about his "progressive postmodern, democratic outlook," quoted above (PH:132). But given Freire's avowed eclecticism, it is hard to see this as more than the appropriation of another set of influences, an addition to his stock, rather than a distinct change of direction. Overall, Freire's concept of class appears abstract and mechanistic. Walker's verdict on Freire's vision of the class struggle holds true: it is "determined mainly mechanically by consciousness of oppression" (Walker 1980:138).

There is a paucity of reference, also, to racial oppression in Freire's pre-1990s writing, an odd omission for one for whom education cannot be politically neutral and whose formative work took place in Brazil, a former slavocracy with a history of allowing the dispossession and even genocide of indigenous peoples. However, if Freire's outrage at the process of colonization is considered in that light, as I think it should be, this criticism loses some of its bite. When he does mention racism per se, Freire is clearly appalled by it, as for example, in *Pedagogy of Hope*: "The brutality of racism is something beyond what a minimum of human sensitivity can encounter without *trembling*, and saying, 'Horrible!'" (PH:144).

But while Freire clearly recognizes the problem of racism in his later writings, he rarely addresses it specifically and his pronouncements on the subject are superficial. For example, his solution to the divisions between oppressed groups created by racism is to urge "so-called minorities" to recognize that together they constitute the majority and to concentrate on similarities between themselves, "thus creating *unity in diversity*" without which they cannot "improve themselves, or even build a substantial, radical democracy" (PH:153). A laudable objective in my view, but as the long, painful birth of the "rainbow nation" of post-apartheid South Africa shows, not an easy thing to accomplish in practice.

What is missing is an understanding of the stuff of politics: power. Being in a majority is not enough, even in a democracy, where majorities are supposed to count. The problem is that power is not located simply on one side of a Freirean oppositional pair, it permeates and mediates relationships between individuals and between groups. Despite his presentation of himself as a "man of the South," Freire's exhortations are directed to a racialized, oppressed other. By positioning himself above racism, Freire constructs himself as free of its stain, instead of recognizing that racism degrades us all, whatever our views of it and however scrupulously we try to avoid racially oppressing others. This is not to say that all members of racial majorities are, knowingly or unknowingly, guilty of perpetrating racist oppression. It is to say that, however innocent we may be, racism concerns and affects us all. By constructing the problem of racism as a problem for the "so-called minorities," Freire distances himself from it. He then compounds the problem by presuming to name the correct pedagogical strategy for those suffering racist oppression.

Freire has also been criticized by feminists from the early 1970s on, for his sexist language and, as bell hooks puts it, his "phallocentric paradigm of liberation—wherein freedom and the experience of patriarchal manhood are always linked as though they are one and the same" (hooks 1993:148). Freire acknowledged that such criticism was "not only valid but very timely" (Freire and Macedo 1993:170) and his revision of the sexist language of *Pedagogy of the Oppressed* in the new edition (Freire 1995) is one response to it. In conversation with Macedo (Freire and Macedo 1993:171) he states that he has consciously avoided sexist language in his later work, citing as examples *The Politics of Education* (PE) and *Literacy: Reading the Word and the World* (Freire and Macedo 1987).

But avoiding sexist language, while necessary, is not sufficient. There are other ways in which Freire's insensitivity to the politics of gender manifests itself. The gender of the parties in Freirean dialogue is generally left unstated in Freire's writing, or given as "he"; for example, the "ex-illiterate of Angicos" who "declared that he was no longer part of the *mass*, but one of the *people*" (EPF:56). Nor is this only a feature of his early writings, it occurs also in *Pedagogy of Hope* (PH *passim*). Mayo (1994:18; 1991), who is generally sympathetic to Freire, points out that none of Freire's talking books involved a sustained conversation between Freire and either a woman or a person of color. The juxtaposition of Freire's dialogue with Macedo on the subject of his treatment of gender and hooks's "playful dialogue" with herself (as Gloria Watkins) on the same subject in McLaren and Leonard's book (1993), makes this point most poignantly.

In his contributions to McLaren and Leonard's book Freire addresses the "recurring challenge" from feminists. In the Foreword,

Freire avers that since the 1970s he has learned much from feminism and has come to define his work as feminist (Freire in McLaren and Leonard eds. 1993:x). Lest this should seem like a late conversion, Freire reminds Macedo that in the 1970s he shocked an audience at the University of London by declaring "I am too a woman" (Freire and Macedo 1993:175) and he states in the Foreword:

I have always maintained that a pedagogy of liberation must be structured as a partnership among groups of men and women devoid of hierarchical control and free of patriarchal assumptions [. . .] a critical pedagogy works best when it is coalitional and attentive to the role of power in experience. (Freire in McLaren and Leonard eds. 1993:x)

It is not clear whether Freire's and Macedo's dialogue took place after they had read bell hooks's chapter—presumably not, as it is not cited. Kathleen Weiler (1996:368 n23) states that there is some evidence that the dialogue took place in 1991, in which case Freire could not have read any of the essays in the McLaren and Leonard collection. Weiler's critique of "Freire and a Feminist Pedagogy of Difference" is cited in the interview, however, by Macedo, and listed as in press in an edited collection by McLaren and Lankshear. Weiler considers that this constitutes an undeclared framing of the interview with her later critique, "thus providing a more sophisticated meaning to Freire's statements" and implying "that Freire has read feminist analyses of his work, when it is not at all clear that this is the case" (Weiler 1996:368 n23). Weiler's failure to give detailed evidence for her contention that the Macedo/Freire dialogue actually took place in 1991 weakens her case, but, given the welter of bibliographical and biographical confusions surrounding Freire, it would not be altogether surprising if this were what happened.

Whatever the facts of that particular matter, in his dialogue with Macedo, Freire insists that he *does* recognize the specificities of oppression, including the oppression of women by men. However, he contends that it is not enough for women to liberate themselves; men and women should "simultaneously move toward cutting the chains of oppression" (Freire and Macedo 1993:174). He maintains that *the correct pedagogical practice is for feminists to understand the different levels of male oppression, while at the same time creating pedagogical structures in which men will have to confront their oppressive position. (Freire and Macedo 1993:174)*

Finally, he insists that his work should be seen within its historical context, reminding us that he "wrote *Pedagogy of the Oppressed* twenty years ago" (Freire and Macedo 1993:176).

In her chapter, bell hooks (1993), while acknowledging her "profound solidarity" with Freire, nevertheless regretfully concludes that gender remains a "blind spot" in his work. Weiler makes a similar point, arguing that Freire sets out his "goals of liberation and social transformation as universal claims, without exploring his own privileged position or existing conflicts among oppressed groups themselves" (Weiler 1994:34). In her examination of "theoretical lacunae" in Freire's work, Jeanne Brady sums up this criticism of Freire:

underpinning Freire's emphasis on a totalizing narrative of domination, his support of a unified subject, and a unified historical agent, we find a creeping essentialism in which gendered differences seem frozen in a pseudo-universal language that subsumes experience and cultural practice within a patriarchal discourse. (Brady 1994:143)

This seems to me the nub of the problem: Freire's inclusive, universalistic concept of oppression, expressed in his binary model of the oppressor–oppressed relationship. He never substantially modified this view, despite later statements with a distinctly postmodernist tinge, such as: "Oppression must always be understood in its multiple and contradictory instances" (Freire in McLaren and Lankshear, eds. 1993:x). As Giroux (1993:181) points out in a statement about colonialism which could equally well apply to Freire's struggles against all forms of oppression, Freire's "recourse to binarisms" means that "he often reverses rather than ruptures" the basic problematic. Likewise, Freire's strategy for overcoming gender oppression as part of a general totalized category of oppression seems to bear out the charge of universalism:

If the oppressed women choose to fight exclusively against the oppressed men when they are both in the category of the oppressed, *they may rupture the oppressor-oppressed relations specific to both women and men. If this is done,* the struggle will only be partial *and perhaps tactically incorrect. (Freire and Macedo 1993:174; my emphasis)*

As Weiler points out, Freire assumes that he can name "correct pedagogical practice" for women: "the most important focus for women [. . .] should be to understand men, and their second goal should be to 'help' men confront their own sexism" (Weiler 1996:369).

Lacking an understanding of power, his model of oppression is just too simple and indiscriminate to accommodate the multifaceted and contradictory nature of differential power relationships in terms of gender, class or any other social category. Arguably, in his later writing, Freire simply substituted an explicitly gendered, male, universal subject for an implicitly gendered, male, universal subject. The oppressed, in Freire's formulation, remain a generic other. Freire's model cannot account for oppression *within* a social category. Neither does his concept of oppression give a purchase on the question of the criteria by which judgments might be made to distinguish between the oppressive and the humane in any given situation, except in general terms. Again, I see continuity here between Freire before the 1964 coup in Brazil, in exile, and after his return to Brazil. As de Kadt (1970:99) points out in his discussion of *Ação Popular,* "the central tool for the dissection of Brazilian reality became the conceptual pair, *pólo dominante* and *pólo dominado* (dominant and dominated pole)." Surely this is the same central tool that Freire continued to employ.

The Concept of Revolutionary Leadership in Freire's Pedagogy

For Freire, the archetypal oppressive regime is colonialist and the archetypal revolution is an anticolonial movement of national liberation. He distinguishes between prerevolutionary and postrevolutionary politics. The struggle for liberation, which he calls "cultural action for freedom," is "carried out in opposition to the dominating power elite" and the struggle to maintain the postrevolutionary independent state ("cultural revolution") "takes place in harmony with the revolutionary regime" (CAF:82).

Freire draws parallels between his notion of cultural revolution and the Chinese Cultural Revolution of 1966–77 (CAF:83 n28 and PO:31 n9) and states that permanent cultural revolution is necessary lest "the revolution becomes stagnant and turns against the people" (PO:33 n10). Freire was not alone in holding this view—many on the left (at least outside China) in the late 1960s and early 1970s praised Mao for his bold move in revitalizing the revolution and indeed saw him as the archetypal Third World revolutionary. However, the revelations of its excesses make it appear, with hindsight, that the Cultural Revolution was precisely a case of the revolution turning against the people, yet Freire did not alter his favorable reference to it in the new edition of *Pedagogy of the Oppressed* (Freire 1995:36 n10).

Freire's rapprochement with Maoism extends beyond his support for the Cultural Revolution: he shares with Mao a conviction that consciousness is the key to the dialectic resolution of contradictions, what Mao calls "man's conscious dynamic role" (Mao, quoted in Gorman ed. 1986:151). Freire also allies his problem-posing pedagogy with the Maoist principle of the "mass line," as he acknowledges in a footnote in *Pedagogy of the Oppressed* (retained in the new edition), quoting Mao Zedong's dictum: "We must teach the masses clearly what we have received from them confusedly" (PO:66 n6; Freire 1995:74 n7). The same quote, in a slightly different translation, is given as a footnote in *Pedagogy in Process: The Letters to Guinea-Bissau* (LGB:25n), and Freire expressly underlines the importance of the "mass line" in his Introduction to that book (LGB:62*ff*.). In both editions of *Pedagogy of the Oppressed*, Freire quotes Mao extensively in support of his polemic against the banking mode in education and in revolution (PO:67 n8; Freire 1995:75 n10).

There are other affinities between Freire and Mao. Gary MacEoin (1973:70) points to the "striking similarity" between Mao's theory of revolution and Freire's, in that "there is no absolute 'before' and 'after', with the taking of power as the dividing line" (a point that could also be made about Gramsci's theory of revolution). The influence may not all have been in one direction, either: MacEoin cites the sinologist Paul Lin as stressing the importance of Freire's thought for "China's efforts to reorder education in conformity with the philosophy of an awakened people" (MacEoin 1973:70). Also, the masses, especially in Freire's early work, are likely to be peasants (or former peasants living in urban slums) rather than proletarians, just as they are for Mao—indeed, this is a major reason for Mao's popularity among revolutionaries in Third World countries with no significant proletariat. Walker argues that this is because Freire distrusts the urban proletariat and, like Mao, regards the peasantry as having greater revolutionary potential, "that is, more likelihood that they will follow the lead of the petit bourgeoisie" (Walker 1980:137–8).

In his later work, Freire has espoused the proletariat's cause as he sees it and his party, the PT, is the Workers' Party. However, it may be that the important issue for Freire is not so much whether the people are proletarians or peasants, but that they are oppressed. For Freire, the people's potential for revolutionary agency is not the issue—they are not the agents. Agency is vested in the leader. What matters is that the people are oppressed and consequently redeemable through the conscientization process. The people cannot become leaders in their own right and cannot themselves construct a theory of liberating action, since they are victims of cultural invasion "crushed and oppressed, internalizing the image of the oppressor" (PO:150), an image retained in Freire's revision of *Pedagogy of the Oppressed* (1995:164).

The moral integrity of the leader in this situation is vital. Freire states that "leaders who deny praxis to the oppressed thereby invalidate their own praxis" (PO:97) and refers with approval to "authentic revolutionaries" such as Guevara, Castro, Cabral and Mao. For example, Guevara is described as "an example of the unceasing witness revolutionary leadership gives to dialogue with the people" (CAF:74). Indeed, Freire maintains, following Guevara (PO:62 n4), that love must be the motivating force: "true revolutionaries must perceive the revolution, because of its creative and liberating nature, as an act of love."

Freire's vision of the authentic revolutionary leader is deeply patriarchal, consistent with his "phallocentric paradigm of liberation in which freedom and the experience of patriarchal manhood are conflated," as da Silva and McLaren put it (McLaren and Leonard eds. 1993:70). The authentic leader knows what is best for the people, he acts on their behalf and in their best interests, motivated, as we have seen, by love. Ultimately, his task is to redeem the people and lead them to salvation, through the realization of their vocation to become more fully human.

In his *Pedagogy in Process: The Letters to Guinea-Bissau* (LGB) Freire gives the clearest indication in his published work of the kind of revolution, and the kind of leader, of which he approves. Guinea-Bissau is a former Portuguese colony in northwest Africa, abandoned by Portugal in 1974. The African Party for the Independence of Guinea and Cape Verde Islands (PAIGC), led by Amílcar Cabral until his assassination by the Portuguese in 1973, waged an armed liberation struggle and formed the first government after independence. One of Amílcar Cabral's brothers, Luiz, became president of Guinea-Bissau, and he is eulogized in Freire's Introduction to the letters (LGB:35–7). Luiz Cabral subsequently survived a coup attempt in 1978, which he brutally suppressed, only to be overthrown by his former military commander, Nino Vieira, in a further coup in 1980. Luiz Cabral's overthrow was widely interpreted as a black nationalist strike against the influence in the economy and in government of Cape-Verdians, the former educated elite in colonial times, with Cabral, as the son of a Cape-Verdian father and a Portuguese mother, being seen as the embodiment of the Cape-Verdian influence (Joliffe 1983).

Amílcar Cabral was already dead when Freire began work in Guinea-Bissau in 1975. Regarded as "Africa's leading Marxist theoretician" (Hadjor 1993:58), he is mentioned frequently and with reverence by Freire:

Like Guevara and like Fidel, Cabral was in constant communion with the people, whose past he knew so well and in whose present he was so deeply rooted, a present filled with struggle, to which he gave himself without restriction. [. . .] In each of the days that he lived so intensely, there was always a possible dream, a viable history that could begin to be forged on that very day. (LGB:18)

Freire's admiration for Amílcar Cabral is carried over into identification with the cause of the PAIGC, even to the point of suppressing his disagreement with the party over its literacy campaign strategy. In his review of the literacy campaign in Guinea-Bissau, Freire reveals that the decision to use Portuguese was one of which he strongly disapproved, since Portuguese was the language of the erstwhile colonizers and was not spoken by the majority of the population, especially outside the towns. Freire's reason for not making his position known publicly at the time was, he says, that "the timing was not appropriate with respect to greater political concerns" (Freire and Macedo 1987:112). Having revealed that he had compromised himself in this way, Freire nevertheless defends his method:

With or without Paulo Freire it was impossible in Guinea-Bissau to conduct a literacy campaign in a language that was not part of the social practice of the people. My method did not fail, as has been claimed. Nor did it fail in Cape Verde or São Tomé. (Freire and Macedo 1987: 112–3)

In an effort to set the record straight, Freire includes as an Appendix in his book with Macedo (Freire and Macedo 1987:160–9) and in his spoken book with Faundez (Freire and Faundez 1989:110–6) the text of a previously unpublished letter to Mário Cabral, Guinea-Bissau's Minister of Education, written in July 1977, in which he makes clear his objections to the use of Portuguese in the literacy campaign. He advocates instead developing a written form of Creole, the "language of national unity," and using that in literacy work (Freire and Faundez 1989:114). While the Creole language is being transcribed, literacy education in Portuguese should be confined to areas where "reading and writing Portuguese can be of great importance to those who learn and for the effort of national reconstruction" (Freire and Faundez 1989:114). The reasons for using Portuguese should be discussed with the students and those populations which do not fall into the categories selected for literacy in Portuguese should be helped

to "read" the reality of their situation in association with projects to act on it, such as collective vegetable gardens and production cooperatives, closely linked with health education campaigns, without the need for the population to read words [. . .] not every programme to act on reality initially involves actually learning to read and write words (Freire and Faundez 1989:114–5)

Although publication of this letter does go some way to answering Freire's critics, he does not go so far as to acknowledge that the letter should have been included in *The Letters to Guinea-Bissau* and reiterates, "I believe that the broad lines of the proposals I made in Guinea-Bissau still stand" (Freire and Faundez 1989:118).

A textual note reveals Freire's disenchantment with his hero Amílcar Cabral over the nature of language:

In stating that "language is nothing more than a tool for human beings to communicate with each other," Amílcar Cabral failed lamentably to perceive the ideological nature of language, which is not something neutral. [. . .] This is one of the rare statements in Cabral's work which Paulo has never been able to accept. (Freire and Faundez 1989:142 n22)

However, perhaps Cabral, and after him his party, the PAIGC, realized very well the ideological nature of language and preferred the use of Portuguese for ideological as well as practical reasons—because it was the language of the revolutionary group and their power base, the Cape-Verdians and the petit bourgeoisie living in the towns, and because it was a more effective tool for communication with the outside world than Creole.

Freire reaffirmed the importance of the language issue in a recent statement:

colonized persons and colonized nations never seal their liberation, conquer or reconquer their cultural identity, without assuming their language and discourse and being assumed by it. (PH:179)

Nevertheless, such important concerns would probably not have seen the light of day in the book that Freire planned to write analyzing Amílcar Cabral's role as a "pedagogue of the revolution," since he has stated that he "would not have published the book without the party's approval" (Freire and Macedo 1987:104).

Whatever his misgivings on the issue of language, Freire remains in agreement with Cabral's (and Fanon's) model of revolutionary change, in which the colonial situation "offers the petit bourgeoisie the historical opportunity of leading the struggle against foreign domination" (Cabral quoted in Walker 1980:135). Despite Cabral's Marxist credentials, Freire's support for such views laid him open to the charge of being a populist, a charge which he vigorously denied (Freire 1993:118). He regarded populism as a political style characteristic of regimes challenged by the people and responding to some of their demands in order to stay in power, a reactive and insufficiently revolutionary stance for his liking. Characterizing Brazil's governments of the 1950s and 1960s as populist, Freire states that it is the ambiguity of populist alliances that makes them interesting:

The populist leader stimulates people to political participation and, simultaneously, sustains a political option to that of oppression. This contradiction is well represented by the popular saying: to light a candle to God and another to the devil. (Freire in de Figueiredo-Cowen and Gastaldo 1995:66)

He was prepared to work with such regimes up to a point, as he did in Brazil before the coup, stressing that "one is not necessarily populist because one makes certain contributions to a regime that is regarded as populist" (Freire and Macedo 1987:102).

However, Freire would qualify as a populist in de Kadt's terms. De Kadt describes movements as populist in the Brazilian context insofar as:

1. They are made up of intellectuals (and students), concerned with the life-situation of the down-trodden masses in society, the "people," who apparently cannot assert their interests;
2. these intellectuals have a deep-seated horror of the manipulation of the people: their central credo is that solutions to the problems lived by the people must ultimately come from the people themselves, that their own ideas and visions, developed in a wholly different milieu, may at most serve as a sounding board for, but never as signposts to the people. (de Kadt 1970:98)

As a corollary of the first point, de Kadt notes that an exploited people cannot take its destiny into its own hands until it has become aware of its exploitation: "Such awareness constitutes the basis for action. Hence the importance Brazil's radical Catholics attached to *conscientização"* (de Kadt 1970:98). Freire's pedagogy of the oppressed fits both de Kadt's criteria of populism, although with regard to the second, perhaps the problem with Freire's writing is that, rather than rejecting signposts, he sets up too many, pointing in different directions, with the result that some of his readers may get hopelessly lost. A standard definition of populism states that it:

mobilizes masses of the poorer sectors of society against the existing institutions of the state, but under the very firm psychological control of a charismatic leader. (Robertson 1986:268–9)

There are clear similarities here with Brazil before the 1964 coup as well as with Guinea-Bissau in the struggle for liberation. Freire's defence of his record on the language issue misses the point that it is unease about the idealized relationship of leader to led in his work which is at the crux of the accusation of populism. As Walker (1980:137) points out, this model of leadership is profoundly problematic and certainly not Marxist: "For Freire, if the petit bourgeoisie ends up on the side of the oppressed it is a result of dialogics: for Marx, of dialectics." Freire's petit bourgeois leaders "remain pedagogues, but dialogical pedagogues, not monological" (Walker 1980:139). It may be significant here that messianic movements were fairly common in Brazil in Freire's youth, as de Kadt (1967:197) describes. Freire has stated that he rejects the messianic attitude on the grounds that it is elitist (Freire and Faundez 1989:81), but it is difficult to know how else to describe his attitude to "authentic" leaders such as Cabral, Castro and Guevara.

Freire maintains that literacy can only "have genuine meaning in a country which is going through revolutionary change" (Freire quoted in Cardenal and Miller 1981:17). But notwithstanding his advocacy of revolutionary change, Freire's work in Brazil and in Guinea-Bissau was possible only because the political agenda had been set by the governments concerned (although the government in Guinea-Bissau was certainly revolutionary in the sense that it was made up of leaders of the party of liberation which had replaced the colonial regime). His period of office as Secretary for Education in São Paulo was also under the auspices of the city's PT administration. His first-hand experience was thus, in his terms, of "cultural revolution," rather than "cultural action for freedom."

In his consultancy work in the service of such cultural revolutions Freire's concern was that he should not be used as part of a process of cultural invasion. Consequently, when asked to collaborate on a government-sponsored literacy campaign, he always made sure "as a prerequisite [. . .] that the government and I share common ground" (Freire and Macedo 1987:64). Perhaps Freire was being wise after the event here, but having presumably established that common ground existed, his record in Guinea-Bissau indicates that he was prepared to hand over responsibility to the government. Far from being an aberration, Freire's action in Guinea-Bissau is consistent with his model of revolutionary leadership, in which a potentially dangerous mixture of power, admiration and trust are vested in the leader/patriarch. In the final analysis, Freire's concept of leadership calls for an act of faith on the part of the led analogous to that required from religious devotees. The relationship between leader and led in Freire's work reveals his politics as compromised by his theology.

The Pedagogical Process in Freire's Work

In Freire's pedagogy agency and authority is vested in the educator. Throughout his career (see for example, Freire 1974, Freire in Horton and Freire 1990:181, Freire in de Figueiredo-Cowen and Gastaldo 1995:21), Freire distinguishes between the educator's authority, which he sees as necessary, and authoritarianism, which he deplores. Dialogue, as a moral commitment to a mode of being, is the sole safeguard against the abuse of authority, against manipulation of the learners by the educators. As Taylor points out (1993:55), Freire draws little distinction between epistemology and ontology, between knowing and being. This leaves him trapped in a circular argument: if the educators engage in "authentic" dialogue with the learners they will know what the learners' problems are; if they do not engage in "authentic" dialogue, their knowledge of the learners' problems will be flawed. For a pedagogy based on problem-posing, this closed circle is a serious weakness.

Freire's distinction between banking education (oppressive) and problem-posing education (humane) exemplifies the problem. Freire is locked into a dualism that disallows the very thing he claims to stand for—dialogue. One is either for or against, no other position is possible if one accepts the terms in which Freire sets out his argument. In every case in Freire's juxtaposition of banking and problem-posing education the preferred option is presented as the only reasonable option. To prefer narration to dialogue; to advocate the inhibition of creativity; to aim to "conceal certain facts which explain the way men exist in the world"—to identify with this pole of the argument would be to brand oneself as inhumane, immoral, authoritarian. After all, who would wish to be described as at worst malicious or at best naive, in thrall, knowingly or unknowingly, to "the dominant, elitist ideology" (Freire and Macedo 1987:42)? Each proposition presupposes its opposite, so that problem-posing education logically presupposes banking education and vice versa, begging the question, as Taylor (1993:54) points out, of whether, ontologically, the new, proposed polarity can actually exist. Accordingly, Freire's "'middle terms', in the few cases where he gives them, serve primarily as rhetorical pointers to the preferred direction" (Taylor 1993:54).

Even given an educator who wholeheartedly identifies with the banking mode, to what extent is banking education actually possible? Take, for example, one of Freire's pairs of statements: "Banking education treats students as objects of assistance; problem-posing education makes them critical thinkers." Assuming all the objectivity of the archetypal fly on the classroom wall, how would one tell which form of education was underway in any particular instance? Granted that the teacher might be treating students, intentionally, as "objects of assistance," what if the students are resisting his or her attempts to do so? Whose agenda counts? Is banking education to be defined in terms of the teacher's intention or the students' experience? Furthermore, how would one identify whether students had been made into critical thinkers by problem-posing education? Perhaps they were critical thinkers before the process started, and in any case, how is critical thinking to be defined and recognized?

The dichotomy to which Freire draws attention in banking education between the teacher's presentation of the "cognizable object" so that he is "cognitive" at one point and "narrative" at another

(PO:53–4) may be hard to avoid in problem-posing education also, given that selection remains the responsibility of the educator. Freire insists on the need to engage in dialogue with the oppressed, but he does not address the question of who the other party to the dialogue is. Put simply, if the world is divided into oppressed and oppressors, to which camp does the liberator belong? The oppressed are seen as at least initially separate from their liberators, although Freire says that they must become involved in the struggle for their liberation (PO:40) and do so as subjects not as objects (PO:44). This fundamental problem is glossed over in Freire's formulation which identifies subject with process: "men are praxis—the praxis which, as the reflection and action which truly transform reality, is the source of knowledge and creation" (PO:73). His solution, class suicide, is ultimately unconvincing and it is hard to see how 'suicide' is an option in other types of oppression, such as gender and race. Freire's failure to address such problems leaves him trapped in a closed binary system of logic. His distinction between banking and problem-posing education thus emerges as ideological in nature. Taylor's verdict is that "Freire's approach differs only in degree, but not in kind, from the system which he so eloquently criticizes" (Taylor 1993:148). Taylor contends that Freire has converted the "banking system" into a "co-operative banking system," but affirms that he remains "at heart a very traditional pedagogue" (Taylor 1993:148–9).

Freire's staged theory of consciousness is also problematic. As we have seen, Freire presents a linear, guided progression through a hierarchy of stages of consciousness from ignorance to enlightenment, defined in advance by the educator. Freire equates the lower, semi-intransitive and naive-transitive states of consciousness with "false consciousness," a term often erroneously attributed to Marx.[11] As Freire states in *Cultural Action for Freedom*, conscientization implies overcoming "false consciousness" but "it implies further the critical insertion of the conscientized person into a demythologised reality" (CAF:75). The problems with false consciousness identified by David McLellan (1986) apply also to Freire's use of the concept. McLellan states that the concept of false consciousness is too clear-cut, in that Marx does not operate with a true/false dichotomy, and too general to encompass Marx's meaning because it is essential to know what kind of falsity is involved; "indeed, Marx's point is often that ideology is not a question of logical or empirical falsity but of the superficial or misleading way in which truth is asserted" (McLellan 1986:18).

Freire does operate with a true/false dichotomy; he is concerned with logical or empirical truth and falsity, but as moral categories rather than material ones. He seems to believe that a demythologized reality exists which is initially visible only to the educator and which the false consciousness of oppressed people prevents them from seeing. He further implies that educators have a moral imperative to determine and to expunge the false consciousness of the oppressed. Freire's two-stage model, with its literacy and postliteracy phases, involves educators in prior research among those who are to be members of the circles of culture and the construction of a teaching program based on the research. Freire stresses the need for the investigators and those whose world is to be investigated to come to share a "critical perception of the world, which implies a correct method of approaching reality in order to unveil it [. . .] critical perception cannot be imposed" (PO:82–3).

In this respect, Freire treats as one and the same two rather different concepts: reality and the perception or experience of reality. When he writes of reality he assumes the presence of a human being who experiences that reality. Freire's concept of the education process as a constant unveiling and demythologizing of reality assumes that reality is an absolute, reified entity, capable in the final analysis of only one correct interpretation: an ultimate unveiling. Also, if by reality he means the whole of the experience of reality (even if only that of one individual) there must inevitably be a selection process employed by the educator to determine which aspects of reality are more or less significant and worth demythologizing. Whose experience of reality counts, and who determines what is and what is not false consciousness? The answer seems to be the Freirean educator in each case. False consciousness may not be a Marxist concept, but it is certainly a Freirean one.

Another problem with Freire's staged theory of consciousness as a rationale for educational intervention is that at crucial points in the process education has no part to play. Freire indicates a role for education in the transition from naive-transitive to critically transitive consciousness, and possibly in the transition from semi-intran-

sitive to naive-transitive consciousness, yet not in tackling the fanaticized stage of consciousness, only in avoiding it. Does this mean
that the fanaticized stage of consciousness is a final stage, irredeem-
able through educational action?

Further questions are raised by the fact that Freire does not make
clear whether the stages of consciousness are to be understood as
mutually exclusive. Can elements of semi-intransitive consciousness
persist in the critically transitive stage? Can elements of different
stages of consciousness exist simultaneously in one person? Are the
stages of consciousness to be understood as stages through which an
individual passes, given appropriate education at the crucial stages,
or are they stages of mass consciousness characteristic of a whole
society—or both? Is semi-intransitive consciousness characteristic
of childhood or do some people never experience it? Once a society
or an individual has achieved the higher stages of consciousness, is it
possible to revert to an earlier stage of the process, or, worse, to lapse
into fanaticized consciousness?

Leach draws attention to another difficulty with Freire's concept of semi-intransitivity:

*If this is an "historical" state of consciousness—a starting line from which
historical progression is made—rather than a conceptualised abstraction
(a kind of extrapolation "backwards" in time from the more fluid state
of "naive transitivity" in which inertia and movement towards human-
ization co-exist), then where is the fertile ground for the first seeds of
critical consciousness? Is Freire in fact saying that there are numbers of
people who are no better than animals, for their critical faculties are, for
all intents and purposes, dormant? (Leach 1982:195)*

Leach thinks not, but the fact remains that Freire's formulation of
conscientization raises such fundamental questions. Here it may be
noted that the designation of the situation of the rural poor as "subhuman" was strongly associated with Bishop Helder Câmara in the
mid- and late 1960s (de Kadt 1970:72 n48). While this is not the
same as designating the people themselves as subhuman, it is easy to
see how some conceptual slippage might occur, especially if the educators are drawn from more privileged social strata.

Similarly, Freire's powerful idea of a culture of silence is also problematic. On one level it may be seen as a reworking of the image of ignorance associated with darkness, familiar from Christian teaching. On another level it may be seen as a version of false consciousness. The vision of the education process as one of liberation from ignorance and false consciousness is exhilarating and endows a certain glamor on the role of educator. Indeed since the conscientization process renders those participating in it more fully human, it may be seen as a reworking of the myth of creation, with God, through the medium of the educator, imparting the gift of speech-with-understanding to those who had been trapped in the culture of silence.

However, might not the culture of silence which Freire so eloquently evokes, equally well be a culture of deafness on the part of the oppressors? Are the oppressed silent, or are they not being heard? Are they being silenced, as Freire indicates on at least one occasion? For example, linking Cone's Black Theology of Liberation with the theology of liberation in Latin America, Freire states:

The prophetic nature of both these theologies lies not in their merely speaking for those who are forbidden to speak, but, most important, in their side-by-side struggle with those silenced so that they can effectively speak the word by revolutionarily transforming the society that reduces them to silence. (PE:146)

But in Freire's formulation of semi-intransitive consciousness, as we have seen, the culture of silence signifies the passivity of the oppressed. It is as if Freire were saying that the oppressed have no voice rather than (as here) that they are forbidden to speak.

Freire writes with delight of the often profound and moving statements made by peasants in the circles of culture. Statements such as "I want to learn to read and write so that I can stop being the shadow of other people" and "I have the school of the world" (EPF:50) have the force of discoveries newly made. An educational process which calls forth and celebrates such powerfully poetic affirmation has much to recommend it. However, how does Freire know that similarly profound statements were not made by the peasants before the investigators were there to record them? If so, the process Freire describes would be one of discovery of the peasants' words by the investigators, rather than discovery by the peasants of the truth of their own insights.

The problem remains that since people are manifestly unequal, by definition, in oppressive societies, the implication is that Freire's educative process is necessary to enable them to become more fully human, more equal, of greater intrinsic worth. The corollary is that without the educative process people are less than fully human, less equal, of less intrinsic worth, a point Leach himself makes (1982:195). It is this which makes Freire's concept of dialogue contradictory, for it envisages dialogue as both the means and the end of the educational process. If this is so, it is necessary to be able to discriminate between these two types of dialogue: dialogue-as-means or technique and dialogue-as-ends or goal. Are they qualitatively different or different only in degree? Freire nowhere acknowledges the problem exists, or indicates the criteria by which such discrimination might be made.

There are also more mundane contradictions. Freire's emphasis on dialogue implies a quasi-conversational, discussion-based mode of teaching and learning belied by his highly structured methodology of literacy and postliteracy teaching. Similarly, Freire's habit of quoting members of the culture circles in Brazil without naming them, (for example, "a man from the backlands of Rio Grande do Norte," "an illiterate from Recife"), while naming the professionals involved in the educational program (for example, Professor Jomard de Brito, Professor Jarbas Marciel) (EPF:50–1) is paradoxical. Surely this does not indicate the equality in dialogue that Freire advocates throughout his work?

Taylor (1993:80–1) points out a further fundamental contradiction in Freire's method, all the more devastating since it comes from a sympathetic critic. Taylor cites Bernstein's argument that nominal forms lead to universalist statements, while pronomial forms are particular, personal and situation specific. Only the latter form of expression supports a process which is intended to be deeply personalizing. Freire's process of naming the world is quite literally nominal, therefore, Taylor argues, literacy acquired in terms of his lists of nouns can be only subliteracy. Freire's pedagogy

proposes naming the world as a means of conscientization, yet it can never realize its objective of praxis, *that process of active reflection* and *reflective* action. *The nominalist discerning of the world cannot turn to action because, by definition, it can never go beyond the passivity of a "reading" of a word. As such, the use of nominative word lists is fundamentally anti-dialogic, for it never allows the learner to* personalize *the processes of reading and writing. (Taylor 1993:80)*

Freire lays himself open to the charge of naivete for failing to address these problems. More seriously, he lays his methodology open to abuse, as some sympathetic commentators argue has happened (see, for example, Archer and Costello 1990; Kidd and Byram 1982; Kidd and Kumar 1981). Without a clear exposition of the grounds for the selection of aspects of reality it is naive to assume that the posing of problems will, of itself, lead oppressed people to identify the causes of their oppression in such a way as to enable them then to act to change their circumstances, as Freire intends should happen, and to do so in ways of which he would approve. Even if, in Freire's terms, they identify the causes of their oppression correctly, they are risking a great deal if they attempt to mount a revolution founded on consciousness without organization.

In lieu of organization, Freire posits his notion of pedagogical leadership, raising further questions about the relationship between the problem-posing Freirean teacher and students, and their analogue, the revolutionary leader and people. In this relationship the Freirean educators hold all the cards; they design, initiate and control the education process; they identify the potential students as oppressed; they investigate the potential students' reality; they select the elements of reality to be re-presented to the learners; they pose the problems; they formulate the codifications. The students are consulted only once the process has been initiated and only on terms set by the educators. Their oppression and their state of consciousness are not defined by themselves but designated by the educators. The learners are heavily reliant on the good will and good faith of the educators and subject to the educators' definition of their interests, rather than their own. The relationship of educator to learner, far from being democratic, as Freire insists it should be (PH:79), is profoundly dependent.

The pedagogical relationship is one in which the learner is con-

structed at the outset as passive, silent, ignorant, unaware, inexperi-
enced, possibly fearful but acquiescent. By contrast, from the outset
the educator is active, in control, free, aware, experienced, wise, fear-
less and self-sacrificing. Through the education process, the learner
is deemed to undergo an awakening, leading to fulfilment as a more
complete human being. The educational encounter is thus revealed
as a sexualized one in which the roles of the protagonists are
stereotypically gendered, with the educator cast as the "male lover"
and the learner as the "female virginal beloved," the object of desire.
This feminization and, to an extent, also, infantilization of the learner
is the nub of the inequality at the heart of the Freirean pedagogical
relationship. Conscientization, which Freire conceives as an act of
love, is revealed as at best a consensual but unequal coupling, at
worst an invasion, a rape.

Conclusion

In his books, consultancies and personal appearances, Freire reported
on the world of the silent to the metropolitan world which, for him,
had monopolized the word. He seemed unable to resolve the contradiction between reporting and dialogue. Even in his later work,
where his style is noticeably less opaque, he falls into the error, for
one committed to dialogue, of publishing only one side (his own) of
the correspondence with Guinea-Bissau.

Freire's rhetoric is seductive, yet his pedagogy of liberation remains a romantic ideal, and like other romantic ideals it has its dark
side. Ultimately, I do not accept Freire's inconsistent class analysis,
his universalist concept of oppression, his idealism and his bizarre
notion of a revolutionary leadership composed of patriarchal, charismatic, indeed messianic, members of the petit bourgeoisie. It is
not enough to say that political leaders, or educators, must commit
class suicide and devote their lives to the people. Without a clear
political framework such action is a sacrifice, but to what end?

One is left with the vision of relatively privileged individuals
driven by guilt to atone for the sins of their class through service to
the poor and oppressed, and in the process either silencing themselves or silencing those they have imposed themselves on, unbid-
den, as leaders. In either case, such action is ameliorative at best, and
invasive and incorporative at worst. Freire may not have moved very

far after all from the Catholic Action movement of his youth. It may be that Christianity and Marxism are capable of synthesis, Freire did not achieve this synthesis in his work; neither has his response to his feminist critics, or his treatment of racism, been at all adequate. Nonetheless, his influence on radical adult educators is undeniable and will be explored in Chapter 5. Meanwhile, the next chapter considers the affinities and tensions between Freire's ideas and those of Gramsci.

Notes

1.   Information for this section has been drawn from a variety of sources, principally Taylor (1993) and Gerhardt (1993). I have noted inconsistencies and contradictions in the biographical literature on Freire in the text.

2.   Taylor (1993) gives a detailed account of the problems associated with the convoluted publication history of Freire's writings. Torres (1993:140 n2) states that a bibliography of Freire's writings is in preparation by Henry Giroux and Donaldo Macedo.

3.   Taylor (1993:14) states that a number of informed commentators report that Freire was considered by some of his teachers to be mentally retarded; Elias (1994:2) makes the same point.

4.   See Fernandes (1985) and Bruneau (1980) for discussions of the *Comunidades Eclesiales de Base* (CEBs).

5.   Taylor (1993:22) describes Câmara as Bishop of Recife at this time, but according to de Kadt (1970:73 n49) and Skidmore (1973:109), Câmara became Archbishop of Recife much later, in 1964.

6.   Speaking in 1993 about the pitfalls associated with international financial aid which Freire experienced when he was Secretary of Education for São Paulo, Freire stated:

> I am always open to discussion. But, if we need money to implement educational projects and programmes, we must be the owners of the destiny of the money. No country or international agencies can ever impose conditions on anyone, on any country. (Freire in de Figueiredo-Cowen and Gastaldo 1995:75)

7.   See Gutiérrez (1973) for the classic Liberation Theology text; see also Boff (1985) and Gheebrant (1974).

8.   Freire's references are to Fanon's anticolonialist classic: *The Wretched of the Earth* (1967), and to Guevara's declaration: "Christians must definitely decide for revolution, particularly in our continent, where the Christian faith is so important among the masses of the people" (quoted in McLellan 1987:155).

9.   In his survey of Catholic radicals in Brazil, de Kadt (1970:142) lists Lebret, Mounier, Marx, Sartre, Teilhard de Chardin and Vaz as the most important intellectual sources of radical ideas in the years immediately preceding the 1964 coup. De Kadt's study is authoritative, however, it is important to remember that he is focusing on *Catholic* radicals—as he points out, he does not refer to the radical views "which were developing—though on a far smaller scale—within Brazil's Protestant Churches" (De Kadt 1970:5). MacEoin's observation (1973:68) that the importance of Protestantism in Latin America is much greater than is

generally realized should be borne in mind. MacEoin states that progressive and radical Protestants made a tactical alliance with Catholic radicals and that Freire contributed to *Cristianismo y Sociedad*, a quarterly journal of theology, philosophy and political science, published by the progressive Protestant organization, ISAL (*Iglesia y Sociedad en América Latina*); ISAL was founded in 1962 in Uruguay (MacEoin 1973:68–9). Also, I do not mean to suggest that Freire necessarily read all the authors cited here before his exile from Brazil—he has said, for example, that he read Gramsci for the first time when he was in exile (Freire in de Figueiredo-Cowen and Gastaldo 1995:63). Taylor (1993:43) locates Freire's exposure to neo-Marxist ideas as well as to "a wide spectrum of classical and Marxist pedagogy and philosophy," including Gramsci, in his period of exile in Chile. See Chapter 4 for a discussion of Gramsci's influence on Freire.

10.   See for example, Giroux (1985) and Kirkwood and Kirkwood (1989).

11.   Although often considered a Marxist concept, false consciousness was never used by Marx, originating instead from Engels. As McLellan (1986) has shown, attempts to equate false consciousness with ideology in Marx are ill-founded, since any such attempt must rely heavily on *The German Ideology* and ignore Marx's later writings.

Chapter 4
Gramsci and Freire: Points of Contact and Divergence

Having considered Gramsci's and Freire's work in turn, in this chapter I shall explore the points of contact and divergence between them, beginning with a review of references to Gramsci in Freire's writing and going on to a comparison of their work in relation to the politics and purposes of the education of adults, the role of the educator, the educative process and the curriculum.

Freire's References to Gramsci

Freire has said that he first read Gramsci when he was in exile:

I read Gramsci and I discovered that I had been greatly influenced by Gramsci long before I had read him. It is fantastic when we discover that we had been influenced by someone's thought without even being introduced to their intellectual production. (Freire in de Figueiredo-Cowen and Gastaldo 1995:63)

As a result, Gramsci's influence is pervasive rather than specific. Freire cites Gramsci approvingly, together with many other writers. He does not claim that his ideas are founded exclusively, or even predominantly, on Gramsci's. Freire's purpose is not academic but pragmatic: he is interested in ideas which seem to him useful; he does not attempt theoretical purity. For example, in discussing the Gramscian topic of the role of intellectuals (Freire and Faundez 1989:54), Freire remarks to the Gramscian philosopher Faundez that it is important that Latin American intellectuals have a critical understanding of their role, "even independently of whether, as we examine the issue, we are, or are not, following closely the undeniably valuable thought of Gramsci."

One measure of the extent of Gramsci's influence on Freire may be judged from the following references to Gramsci that appear in a selection of Freire's books published in English. There are some direct references, although none appear in Freire's best-known book, *Pedagogy of the Oppressed* (PO), or in *Education the Practice of Freedom* (EPF) or *Pedagogy in Process: The Letters to Guinea-Bissau* (LGB). Gramsci's name appears alongside others as one of Freire's influences in *Pedagogy of Hope* (PH:18) and he is cited once in *Cultural Action for Freedom* (CAF), in a footnote in which Freire applauds Gramsci's insistence on the impossibility of entirely separating manual from intellectual work:

Action is work not because of the greater or lesser physical effort expended in it by the acting organism, but because of the consciousness the subject has of his own effort, the possibility of programming action, of creating tools and using them to mediate between himself and the object of his actions, of having purposes, of anticipating results. Still more for action to be work, it must result in significant products, which while distinct from the active agent, at the same time condition him and become the object of his reflection. (CAF:56 n10)

Freire gives no page reference to the Spanish edition of Gramsci's *Cultura y Literatura* but he is presumably referring to Gramsci's well-known insistence that *"homo faber* cannot be separated from *homo sapiens"* (SPN:9). However, if this is the reference, then Freire is placing a slightly different interpretation on it. Gramsci's point, made earlier in the same passage, is that "all men are intellectuals [. . .] but not all men have in society the function of intellectuals" (SPN:9). Certainly the predominance of mental to manual effort varies, but the crucial point for Gramsci is the social function of the effort, not whether it is primarily mental or manual. Freire reiterates this point in his talking book with Macedo, *Literacy: Reading the Word and the World,* in which he states that practical activity never lacks a "technical intellectual dimension," however simple (Freire and Macedo 1987:78).

Another reference to Gramsci, this time his distinction between "common sense" and "good sense," comes in Freire's talking book with Shor, *A Pedagogy for Liberation* (Shor 1987). Here Freire states that he does not dichotomize "common sense from philosophical sense, in the expression of Gramsci." Instead,

Scientific rigor comes from an effort to overcome a naive understanding of the world. Science is super-posing critical thought on what we observe in reality, after the starting point of common sense. (Shor 1987:106)

An endnote to the chapter (Shor 1987:119 n2, presumably by Shor) picks up the reference, quoting Gramsci in the prison notebooks: "it is not a question of introducing from scratch a scientific form of thought into everyone's individual life, but of renovating and making 'critical' an already existing activity." Again, in his talking book with Macedo (Freire and Macedo 1987:78–9), Freire quotes Gramsci (in a passage from the prison notebooks) in support of his argument that people should be challenged and stimulated to exercise their "right to know better what they already know," an idea he earlier attributed (correctly) to Mao (PO:66 n6; LGB:25n) but a legitimate reading of Gramsci also, as we have just seen.

More problematic is Freire's linking of his notion of conscientization with Gramsci's theory of hegemony, as when he affirms that a "critical reading of reality [. . .] constitutes an instrument of what Antonio Gramsci calls 'counterhegemony'" (Freire and Macedo 1987:36). Elsewhere in the same book he speaks of "antihegemonic movements" (Freire and Macedo 1987:62). This is problematic not only because Gramsci did not, as far as I am aware, use the term "counterhegemony" (or "antihegemony") but more importantly because it impoverishes Gramsci's subtle concept of hegemony, turning it into one half of one of Freire's binary opposites. This reading of Gramsci has been influential in the education literature, as we shall see in Chapter 5.

In an earlier conversation with Macedo, recorded in *The Politics of Education* (PE:182), Freire recounts an incident in Tanzania which made him reflect on the *machismo* of his own culture. He cites Cabral and Gramsci as important in increasing his cultural awareness, remarking that "Gramsci has profoundly influenced me with his keen insights into other cultures." Similarly, Giroux, in his Introduction

(Freire and Macedo 1987:1–2 and 8), presumably approved by Freire, states that Freire extends and affirms Gramsci's notion of the politicized nature of the language issue in his contention that literacy can be both hegemonic and counterhegemonic: both an instrument by which people are silenced and a terrain of struggle for empowerment.

The issue of the language in which literacy campaigns should be conducted (a problem, as we have seen, for Freire in Guinea-Bissau) is also discussed with reference to Gramsci in a chapter later in his book with Macedo. Stating that the issue is still unresolved, they illuminate their point with a quotation from Gramsci (the same quote opens Giroux's Introduction to the book) in which he writes that the fact of the language issue coming to the fore is a sign of a reorganization of cultural hegemony (Freire and Macedo 1987:150). Referring to former Portuguese colonies in Africa, they state:

What is hidden in the language debate in these countries is possibly a resistance to re-Africanization, or perhaps a subtle refusal on the part of the assimilated Africans to commit "class suicide." (Freire and Macedo 1987:150)

The most explicit and sustained association of Gramsci's ideas with Freire's own comes in his talking book with Faundez (Freire and Faundez 1989). Gramsci is frequently mentioned in the course of the conversation, although mostly by Faundez rather than by Freire. Freire's direct references to Gramsci are brief, as in their discussion of "national popular culture," in which Freire refers in passing to Gramsci's treatment of the topic "in the light of Marxist internationalism" (Freire and Faundez 1989:80). Nevertheless, Freire makes clear his agreement with points for which Faundez cites Gramsci's authority and reiterates his proscription of intellectuals acting for, rather than with, the people.

Freire's and Faundez's discussion of language is conducted in Gramscian terms in the context of class relationships, economic conditions and power. Where there are two languages, that of the rulers and that of the ruled, Freire advocates "a dialectical synthesis of the two, a transcending of the dominion of one language over the other and of one syntax over the other, in short, a rediscovery of language"

(Freire and Faundez 1989:81). This is interesting in relation to Gramsci's discussion of the language issue in Italy (see SCW:164–95; SPN *passim*), in particular his criticisms of the Gentile Education Act of 1923 in which no provision was made for the teaching of "normative grammar." As Forgacs points out (SCW:166), Gramsci objected to this because it put working class and peasant children, who did not speak educated Italian, at an even greater disadvantage. Gramsci argues for measures to expedite the formation of a common national language "centralizing what already exists in a diffused, scattered but inorganic and incoherent state," including organized interventions in the struggle against illiteracy (SCW:182), but he does not advocate a dialectical mixture of linguistic forms, such as Freire proposes. Here it should be remembered that Gramsci's concept of hegemony probably owed much to his early study of the spread and development of languages, as noted in Chapter 2. For Gramsci, the development of a common language may be part of the formation of a new "common society." He analyzes the history of Latin and Italian and its dialect forms and concludes that a common language cannot be created artificially—forced into existence ahead of the conditions which would bring it into being. Instead,

One will obtain a unified language, if it is a necessity, and the organized intervention will speed up the already existing process. What this language will be, one cannot foresee or establish: in any case if the intervention is "rational," it will be organically tied to tradition. (SCW:183)

By contrast, Freire's approach is ideological and prescriptive: he describes what he considers ought to happen. Freire's unhappiness with the use of Portuguese in the Guinea-Bissau literacy campaign and his belief that the campaign with Miskito people in Nicaragua should be conducted in their English-based Creole rather than in Spanish (the majority language in other parts of Nicaragua) (Freire and Faundez 1989:75), indicate that while he and Gramsci would agree that literacy campaigns could be used to expedite the development of a common language, they would disagree on whether they *should* be used for that purpose.

Given that Freire, while generally sympathetic to Gramsci's ideas, was not a disciple of Gramsci per se, what are the points of contact and divergence between them on the politics and purposes of the education of adults?

Politics and Purposes of the Education of Adults

At first glance Gramsci's and Freire's political orientations appear similar. Both are on the left of the political spectrum. For both, their work has an overt social and political purpose: that of bringing about and sustaining revolutionary change in society, and their writings on education must be seen in that context. Both are broadly in the humanist tradition. Both regard the education process as politically committed rather than politically neutral. For both, the education of adults transcends strictly educational concerns and is a vehicle for wider political ends. While this is on one hand an expansion of the educational task, it is also, paradoxically, a diminution of it, subordinating education to the greater good represented by the hoped-for changes in society.

In their conceptions of the revolution itself an intriguing parallel emerges in that for both Gramsci and Freire revolution is not just a matter of the seizure of power, so that it is not possible to draw clear lines between pre- and postrevolution. Whether Freire takes this idea from Mao or from Gramsci is a moot point (see Chapter 2 for a discussion of the influence on Freire of Mao's theory of revolution and the possible influence on Mao of Freire's pedagogy). Certainly both Mao and Gramsci have featured in the heady mixture of radicalisms current on the Left since 1956, important as alternatives to Stalinism as well as for any intrinsic value they may have. Both were therefore available to Freire.

Both Gramsci and Freire contend that the role of revolutionaries in bringing about social, economic and political change is an educative one. For Gramsci, the relationship between education and politics is integral. As Green comments (1990:99), Gramsci's work is a sustained meditation on "the way in which the dominant and the subordinate classes seek to educate society into their own conceptions of the world." The educative process is, for Gramsci, a broad-based and highly differentiated process of the creation and maintenance of hegemony, undertaken by the state or its deputies, seeking to maintain control, and by revolutionaries seeking to gain control of society.

Gramsci emphasizes agency, with the working class and its political party the agents of revolutionary change. Education in the widest sense is a vehicle for the promulgation of revolutionary agency and plays an important role in generating and maintaining support for the party and thus for the revolution, among subordinate groups. For Freire, at least in some of his writings, the actual mechanism of social change is a critical educational effort based on favorable historical conditions. Unlike Freire (although Freire is ambivalent on this point), Gramsci does not propose that the liberation of the protagonists will occur as a result of the education process itself, rather as a result of education in the context of a political process which is in itself educative.

Gramsci sees education, in the broad sense in which he uses the term, as a means of equipping everyone to run society. The question for Gramsci is whether the education process helps the individual and the group to take a directive role in the revolutionary struggle. Gramsci identifies a key task of education as

the problem of assimilating the entire grouping to its most advanced fraction; it is a problem of education of the masses, of their "adaptation" in accordance with the requirements of the goal to be achieved (SPN:195).

For Gramsci the "goal to be achieved," Marxist revolution, is paramount. This is why, in both the pre- and postrevolutionary contexts, adult education cannot be objective or value-free but must have "the character of impassioned militancy" (Gramsci, quoted in Davidson 1977:224). Freire's goal is that the participants should become more fully human through the conscientization process and in so doing, transform the world. Freire would certainly agree that education cannot be objective or value-free and that it can be an instrument of liberation. However, to Gramsci education is an instrument of class liberation, that is, liberation by the working class as leaders in a revolutionary process with the potential to liberate all oppressed groups and ultimately all society. By contrast, class is an ambivalent concept in Freire's writing and I have argued that he does not have a clear vision of the nature of the revolution. Freire's thesis is that social and political change results, in the right circumstances, from changes in the consciousness of oppressed individuals, leading to the development in those individuals of "critically transitive consciousness." He aims to bring about such changes through cultural action with the masses.

Marx and Engels (in McLellan ed. 1977:164) however, pointed out that "life is not determined by consciousness, but consciousness by life." Gramsci concurs; warning, for example, of the danger of the revolution lapsing into mechanism, he argues that "a revision must take place in modes of thinking because a change has taken place in the social mode of existence" (SPN:336). Geoffrey Nowell Smith, in a footnote to *Selections from the Prison Notebooks*, points out that this conception is very important to Gramsci and constantly recurs in his prison writings (SPN:336 n25). Freire's contrary view limits the applicability of his method to situations in which people's "social being" is already determining their consciousness along lines of which Freire approves. As a result, Freire's educational method is not so much revolutionary as consensual. Not only is his approach dependent on favorable political and economic circumstances but, for example in the postcolonial situation of Guinea-Bissau or the populist regime in Brazil in the early 1960s, it also seeks to generate support for the status quo.

While consent is one feature of hegemony, it is a somewhat one-dimensional concept implying passive acquiescence by the many to the rule of the few and is not synonymous with Gramsci's multi-faceted concept of hegemony, which encompasses and subsumes consent. Hegemony is exercised by a class or alliance of classes forming a "historical bloc," not an individual leader, as in Freire's model, although an individual, such as Croce, may be a significant organizer of hegemony. Nevertheless, the notion of popular consent is important to Freire and it is the closest parallel in his work to Gramsci's concept of hegemony. His emphasis on the importance of popular consent partly accounts for the resonances of Gramsci's work in Freire's writing, despite the paucity of direct references. Freire here employs his own version of one of Gramsci's key insights in the service of his project, as he does also with the insights of many thinkers, including Marx.

Although he is often considered to be a Marxist, Freire does not explicitly make this claim, any more than he claims to be a Gramscian, so a divergence of view from Marx should not surprise us. Meanwhile, Gramsci's work constitutes a major contribution to Marxism, not least in his conceptualization of the revolutionary process. Gramsci's political vision is highly differentiated: he is concerned with the agency and interrelationships of workers, peasants and party members in the context of the attempt to create and sustain a communist revolution through a sustained attack on the hegemony of the ruling "historical bloc" and the establishment of revolutionary working class hegemony. Whether the Gramscian intellectual is conceived as male is a moot point (discussed in Chapter 2), but certainly a sophisticated, materialist, Marxist concept of class is fundamental to Gramsci's analysis. Green (1990:91) rightly praises his "exceptional grasp of the role of different class fractions and their competing ideologies in the maintenance of class domination."

By contrast, Freire's vision is universal and humanistic, strongly imbued with the Christian values of Liberation Theology. Although he does refer to classes and he refutes the charge of sexism leveled against him by some feminists, Freire typically writes of the oppressed, subsuming workers, peasants and the landless poor, male and female, into a theoretically undifferentiated mass, oppressed by an equally undifferentiated oppressor. In his later work Freire utilizes a more differentiated concept of oppression but his writing is patchy in this respect and his vision remains overwhelmingly utopian,[1] religious and universalist.

Unlike Freire, Gramsci was certainly not religious, but he was very interested in the role of the Roman Catholic church in particular, and organized religion generally, devoting many of his prison notes to this subject (FSPN:1–137; SPN *passim*). He denoted Catholic Action, the organization through which Freire and Elza first worked with the poor, as one of the "twin apples of the Society of Jesus's eye" (FSPN:101). However, Gramsci did not regard the Church as an institution to be conquered or destroyed. Instead, he maintained that "While Marxist socialists are not religious, neither are they anti-religious and a future workers' state, like the liberal state before it, must find a system of equilibrium [with] the spiritual power of the Church" (FSPN:xxi).

Freire, like Gramsci, conceives of revolution as a process rather than a single dramatic event. For Gramsci, the process of the establishment of a new revolutionary hegemony continues through and beyond the takeover of the state: it is "a continuous process, a never-ending development towards a realm of freedom that is organised and controlled by the majority of the citizens—the proletariat" (SPWI:55). While his vision is always historically and geographically specific and situated, Gramsci conceives of national revolution in an international context, as his work for the Comintern shows. Rather than proletarian revolution, Freire's model of revolution is an anticolonial war of liberation leading to a kind of socialism in one country. Education for conscientization remains essential after the revolution as a means of keeping the revolution on track, but it does this through keeping the people in touch with their leaders in a state of mutual trust, respect and communion.

Freire is primarily concerned with the quality of the communion between leader and led, rather than with the direction of leadership, or the nature of power, both of which are central concerns for Gramsci. Freire is ambivalent, also, about the nature of the political changes he and his work support, whether Marxist and revolutionary or nationalist, reformist and populist. His professed "camaraderie" with Christ and Marx may be seen as an expression of Catholic syncretism. In fact, this last association represents a link, albeit indirect, between Gramsci and Freire, since some Liberation Theologists claim Gramsci as an important influence (Boff 1985; Gutiérrez 1973). Gramsci, together with Marx and Lenin, was also an important influence on the Peruvian "Dean of Latin American Marxists," José Carlos Mariátegui. Mariátegui was a contemporary of Gramsci's, and spent three of the momentous years 1919–23 in Italy, where he was exposed to Gramsci's ideas. Mariátegui was one of the first Latin Americans to employ the concept of dependent development and to understand the revolutionary potential of the peasantry, both ideas that underpin Freire's thought (Gorman ed. 1986:216–7).

Freire's work includes strong echoes of Marxism, particularly in his insistence on the need to unite theory and practice in "praxis." Gramsci uses the term "praxis" in a similar way: he denotes Marxism the "philosophy of praxis," a term he borrowed from the Italian Marxist, Labriola, and used in the prison notebooks partly for its connotations of the "unique nexus [. . .] between theoretical and practical activity" and partly as a device to deceive the censor (SPN:xxi).

However, Freire's formulation of action in relation to reflection and man in relation to the world treats the world and human agency as antithetical and thus falls within an idealist framework. Indeed, Freire seems close to making a religion of the education process when he says that "to speak a true word is to transform the world" (PO:60). Instead of identifying theory with practice as he insists is necessary, Freire dichotomizes action and reflection and then stresses the need for coincidence between the two in the educational or political process (PO:99). He rejects both "mindless activism" and "empty verbalism" and posits instead the somewhat obscure notion that "word=work=praxis" (PO:60 n1). Even when rejecting one, Freire thinks in dichotomies, consistent with his emphasis on dialogue as an educational and political technique. Although Freire later dropped this coincidental view in favor of a staged approach, this does not entirely solve the problem. He remained convinced of the power of the "true word" to transform the world, the difference is that in his later work he acknowledges that this will only happen under the right circumstances.

Gramsci's work also contains dichotomies and dualities, detailed by Anderson in his "The Antinomies of Antonio Gramsci" (Anderson 1976–7), but he treats these dialectically, placing one element of a paradox in relation to another in a process of mutual transformation to a new condition. Throughout his work, Gramsci urges that theory and practice must be dialectically related, with political action informed by analysis. Gramsci criticizes as primitive the "insistence on the practical element of the theory-practice nexus" (SPN:335). Instead, for Gramsci, the dialectical unity of theory and practice "is a critical act, through which practice is demonstrated rational and necessary, and theory realistic and rational" (SPN:365).

The agent through which the identification of theory and practice is brought about is, for Gramsci, the revolutionary political party, and in their attitude to the role of the party a further significant difference is revealed between Gramsci and Freire. Gramsci worked to create a revolutionary organization based on first the Socialist Party (PSI) and then the Communist Party of Italy (PCd'I). His focus is always on how to *organize* change and the instrument of this organization is the revolutionary political party. Gramsci's political work in the PCd'I in Italy, and then in Moscow and Vienna, was part of a wider international movement. Even after his arrest, he tried to continue his political work through his writing and through organizing classes for his fellow political prisoners. Gramsci's position was thus that of a leader of a revolutionary political party, part of the international Communist movement, in opposition to the Italian state and to international capitalism. His position is strikingly unlike that of Freire, whose own political party, the PT, is, as has been noted, a democratic rather than a revolutionary organization. Freire's record of office in São Paulo was of "drastic" (Torres and Freire 1994:102) rather than revolutionary change. Freire often repeats his condemnation of "sectarianism" on the left and, especially in his pre-1990s writing, he does not usually engage with party politics. When he does do so, as in the case of his fulsome praise of the PAIGC in Guinea-Bissau, he reveals a certain naivete.

Gramsci and Freire appear to have little in common in their conceptions of the relationship between education and the state. This seems to stem from a crucial difference in their conceptions of the state itself. Indeed, Freire does not elucidate a conception of the state as such, although he acknowledges that the attitude of the government has a major bearing on the possibility of education for liberation (LGB:110–7). Consequently, Freire does not articulate political and educational strategies in relation to different forms of the state or governments of different political complexions. This, while unexceptional in an educational theorist per se, is an odd omission for one for whom education is political.

By contrast, Gramsci's concept of the educative state allows him to differentiate between state formations and to analyze the relationship of institutions to each other and to the state. This is particularly significant in relation to adult education in many countries, including the United Kingdom with its strong voluntarist tradition, and in Third World countries where adult education is part of the work of aid programs coordinated by nongovernmental organizations (NGOs). In both these cases, adult education takes place in quasi-autonomous or relatively independent institutions of civil society whose relationship to the state is ambiguous.

On a biographical level, Gramsci's and Freire's backgrounds have intriguing parallels. For example, they could be said to share a "southern" background in the sense in which Gramsci uses the term in his ground-breaking essay on the "Southern Question" (SPWII:441–62); in Freire's terms, both are men of the "Third World." Although his family was relatively privileged, Freire originated from the "southern" setting (in Gramscian terms) of northeast Brazil, arguably the equivalent of the poor, feudal south of Italy, in its relationship with the richer and more industrial southeast of Brazil. Gramsci, as a Sardinian, grew up in a similarly poor and remote region. He and his family, too, were better off than their neighbors, at least until Gramsci's father's imprisonment. Both Gramsci and Freire were clearly influenced by their early environments. However, while Freire went on to do his formative work in the region in which he grew up, Gramsci, like thousands of Italians from the south and the islands before and since, went to Turin, and it is in the very different environment of industrial northern Italy that his life's work developed.

Accordingly, their constituencies of learners are significantly different. Freire worked first with illiterate peasants and the urban poor of the northeast of Brazil, for whom becoming literate entailed the right to vote. In exile he worked with similar groups, typically in the context of consultancies with the governments of newly independent former colonies with high rates of illiteracy. In this context the eradication of illiteracy was seen as a political and economic imperative, part of the process of nation-building in which Freire played an important supporting role.

By contrast, Gramsci's early political work in Turin was with a relatively literate, politically organized industrial proletariat, with whom he worked as a political activist and journalist, to foment a Marxist revolution—albeit one that entailed forging links between the proletariat, peasants and other groups in the creation of a new hegemony. However, as he acknowledged, the occupation of the factories in Turin failed to trigger a revolution precisely because of the PCd'I's failure to forge those links. After 1920 his attempts to put right this failure were overshadowed by the rise of Fascism, to which ultimately he fell victim. Gramsci's imprisonment was a period of prolonged personal and political isolation, illness and censorship of his writing; his recognition as a major twentieth-century Marxist has been achieved posthumously.

Freire's experience was as a teacher, writer, consultant and organizer of education. His early work was variously sponsored by the

Catholic Church, by the employers' organization, SESI, and then by the university and the regional and national government, with grant aid from the home of international capitalism, the United States. In his prolonged exile, an experience Freire undoubtedly found painful and difficult, as he relates in his talking book with Faundez (Freire and Faundez 1989:21–4), he was employed first by the Chilean government and UNESCO, then, briefly, by Harvard University, before moving to the World Council of Churches and IDAC. On his return to Brazil he worked as a university professor and then as Secretary for Education in the PT administration of São Paulo, his first and only period as a political appointee. He achieved international recognition during his lifetime and he is venerated by many adult educators.

While Gramsci was a revolutionary, Freire's position was that of a committed professional adult educator concerned to expound and propagate the political nature of his task in the service of progressive but not necessarily revolutionary change. Freire's is thus a secondary involvement in a supporting role, while Gramsci writes as a prime mover in the revolutionary process. Accordingly, while both stress the interrelationship of education and politics, they do so in different ways and from different starting points: for Gramsci, politics is educative, whereas for Freire, education is political, although he, too, stresses the "pedagogical nature of the revolution" (PO:43).

On the economic and political fronts, also, there are congruences. Wynia's (1990:216) description of the Doctrine of National Security, which prevailed in Brazil during Freire's period of exile, as resembling the Fascist ideology of Italy, indicates a political parallel. In his monograph on the "Southern Question" and its Brazilian parallels, Timothy Ireland (1987) argues convincingly that the uneven economic development that he discerns in contemporary Brazil closely mirrors that in Italy in Gramsci's time. The economic parallel is not exact, however, since Brazil's industrial development in the 1950s and early 1960s relied heavily on finance from abroad to fund the manufacture of goods to substitute for imports, whereas Italy's industrial development in the period around 1919 was controlled by a powerful local bourgeoisie and its products sold on the expanding European and home markets.

It is important, also, not to elide Gramsci's analysis of the relationship between the south and north of Italy with the later (and simpler) concept of the "Third World" which suffuses Freire's work. This is what Ireland tends to do in his otherwise careful analysis of the Popular Education movement in Brazil. For Freire, the relationship between the First World and the Third is a dependent relationship between center and periphery, metropolis and margins, between powerful north and dependent south in the world context, between powerful southeast and dependent northeast in Brazil. The relationship between south and north Italy, for Gramsci, is specific, contingent and reciprocal, rather than general and schematic, as the corresponding relationship is for Freire. Although in both cases the relationships are based on exploitation, Gramsci explores the contradictory nature of that exploitation while Freire asserts and deplores the fact of it.

One particularly telling example of the contradictory nature of the relationship between north and south, for Gramsci, is in the cultural field. Although Ireland contends (1987:26) that cultural domination plays a similar role in the relationship between southeast and northeast Brazil as it did in Gramsci's Italy, citing the "dearth of periodicals, reviews, newspapers, publishing houses, etc. of truly national circulation" emanating from northeast Brazil, Gramsci's point is the opposite. In an extract from "Some Aspects of the Southern Question" quoted by Ireland, Gramsci states that an influential publishing house and review, great intellectuals, academies and cultural bodies of the greatest erudition do exist in the south. What is missing is "any organization of middle culture" around which dissenting intellectuals might group themselves: such intellectuals had instead grouped themselves around reviews outside the south (as Gramsci himself had done) (SPWI:459). Gramsci is precisely interested in the contradictory way that southern intellectuals such as Croce act as hegemonic forces in a state in which economic strength is located in the north.

The Educative Process

The educative process for Gramsci and Freire reflects the similarities and differences in purpose outlined above. For Gramsci, the educative process in the context of proletarian revolution is molded by his conception of revolution as a process rather than a single event. In keeping with his highly articulated conception of the revolutionary process, Gramsci differentiates between types of education appropriate at different historical moments in the revolutionary struggle, and for different groups in society. However, whether it is for the population as a whole, or for workers or party members, it is always the party that directs the educational process.

The precise nature of the educational task depends on the historical circumstances pertaining at any given moment and encompasses political activity, personal teaching in formal and informal groups, journalism and political education in the factories, as well as the educative activities of the state. Mass ideological preparation is "a necessity of revolutionary struggle and one of the indispensable conditions for victory" (SPWII:290). Gramsci also describes the form of education that should be organized by and for party members in his "Introduction to the First Course of the Party School" (SPWII:285–92). The education of party members and activists is of particular concern in the period of revolutionary struggle, as their leadership is crucial. Gramsci recognizes that political activity is highly educative and that education also has a role in developing activists' powers of analysis in order to help them to develop appropriate strategies. Once working class hegemony is established, Gramsci prefigures a form of education appropriate for society as a whole in his notes on education in the prison notebooks (SPN:26–43). For Gramsci education is broad-based and contingent. The institutional base, mode of organization and content appropriate in one educational context are not necessarily appropriate in all other contexts.

Unlike Gramsci, Freire is closely identified with a specific *modus operandi* and methodology. For Freire, the culture circle, wherever it takes place, is the favored model; his base is both narrower and more specific. His work has typically involved the initiation of national literacy and postliteracy campaigns, financed and controlled by governments, as in Brazil and Guinea-Bissau. His conscientization process is intended to enable people to perceive the economic, social and political contradictions in society and to put them into a state of mind in which they are capable of taking action in order to transform reality. Through conscientization, individuals may achieve the highest form of consciousness, which Freire calls critically transitive consciousness, and to recognize themselves as cultured and therefore potential agents of change in society, given the presence of good (i.e., trustworthy) leadership. It is for this reason that education should be dialogical rather than narrative, problem-posing rather than didactic. However, while Freire emphasizes the active and equal participation of the learners in the educative process, nevertheless agency is primarily vested in the educator. Moreover, Freire's concepts of dialogue and praxis, reflection and action, problematization and codification, all involve individual rather than group responses. He does not make clear how individual reflection might be translated into political action.

That political action should be in a leftward direction, for Freire, is clear, although exactly what that means is less so. For Freire, "the authentic Left cannot fail to stimulate the overcoming of the people's false consciousness, on whatever level it exists, just as the Right is incapable of doing so" (CAF:78). Freire appears to believe that critical thought is bound to lead leftward, perhaps because he sees the political and philosophical views of the Right as without foundation in logic and therefore as incapable of standing up to reasoned critical argument. His elaboration of the stages of consciousness through which the education process should lead appears to bear this out, since his description of "fanaticised consciousness," a state in which people are irrational, debased and dehumanized, dominated by others while believing themselves to be free, though at the same time fearing freedom, is strongly reminiscent of the state of mind induced in followers of a Hitler or Mussolini. It is the descent into fanaticized consciousness that Freire's education process seeks to avoid.

By contrast, Gramsci never dismisses his opponent's argument, recognizing that one needs to know what the arguments are in order to combat them effectively. His concepts of good sense and common sense are tools for the analysis of the ideas that inform actions, whereas Freire is concerned rather with the process of thinking itself and the way in which different ways of thinking, characteristic of different stages of consciousness, predispose people to certain ways of acting and are expressed in their praxis. There is nothing inherently active in the process of change of consciousness itself, although action may result from it. When that happens, the change of consciousness becomes transcendant: it becomes conscientization.

The aim of a shared critical perception of the world, the need for a correct method and the notion of there being one reality susceptible to unveiling, all belie Freire's assertion that "critical perception cannot be imposed." While it cannot be imposed, Freire seems to be saying, it can be contrived. Freire's is a "pedagogy of the question" (Bruss and Macedo 1985), but the question is scripted and ultimately there is only one correct answer. So where does this leave the educator?

The Role of the Educator

Gramsci's intellectual embodies the organizing, educating principle, encompassing the state in its educative, hegemonic role, the political party and the individual. Thus the ISEB intellectuals in the late 1950s were organizers of a project to modernize Brazil along democratic nationalist lines. Unlike Croce, who, in Gramsci's assessment of his role, detached the radical intellectuals from the peasant masses, forcing them to take part in national and European culture (SPWII:460), ISEB fulfilled its "extremely important 'national' function" by doing the opposite. ISEB acted as a conduit, a filter, an interpreter and a disseminator through which aspects of radical, mainly European thought could be applied to the Brazilian context. Radical intellectuals, including Freire, attached themselves to the peasant masses as part of the democratic nationalist project, inspired also by religious conviction. The parallel and interconnected project of Liberation Theology could be seen as a modernizing project within the Catholic Church, with its own organic intellectuals (principally Padre Vaz) filtering the ideas of Pierre Teilhard de Chardin and Christian existentialists like Emmanuel Mounier into the Brazilian context, and, in the process, producing a new theology, just as the ISEB intellectuals produced a new social science. That new theology was a regional rather than a strictly national phenomenon, appropriately enough for a supranational organization such as the Catholic Church. The conjunction of imperatives from Liberation Theology and the democratizing project articulated by ISEB, both directed at the poor, (particularly in the case of Liberation Theology) must have had a powerful effect on Catholic radicals like Freire. But it does not make them, in Gramsci's terms, organic intellectuals of the masses, still less of the proletariat. Rather, from a secular point of view, they were organic intellectuals of the bourgeoisie, organizing the incorporation of the masses into the democratic, nationalist, modernizing project. It is in this context that Freire's literacy work was so significant—being literate meant being able to vote. In religious terms, they were lay people with a mission to bring the neglected poor and ignorant masses closer to God, and (given that Christian radicalism in Brazil was strongly imbued with humanist ideas) in so doing enable them to realize their humanity more fully. For a time in Brazil before the coup of 1964, it seemed to Freire and others that these two aims could coincide.

For Gramsci, the modernizing class is not the bourgeoisie but the proletariat. His organic intellectuals of the working class must work out and make coherent the principles and problems raised by the masses in their practical activity: they are the revolutionary "educators." For Gramsci, education in the broad sense is the means by which the interchangeability of intellectuals and those who are not intellectuals by social function is ensured. The aim is to get everyone to the point where they can "lead," meaning that they can operate and make decisions in the sphere of production and politics which are informed by and coherent with the general direction of revolutionary hegemony. Gramsci's organic intellectuals of the working class are not identical with those who have attained Freire's critically transitive stage of consciousness unless and until such individuals put their organizing abilities at the service of the revolution in the creation of proletarian hegemony. Even then, would they be revolutionary organic intellectuals in the Gramscian sense? Would they not then be making a Freirean moral choice to work with the oppressed, acting as Gramscian intellectual defectors rather than revolutionary organic intellectuals?

In keeping with his more restricted concept of the educative process, Freire conceives of the educator in narrower, more specific terms than Gramsci. Freire does not conceive of the state as educator and the political party does not necessarily figure in his educational process. He endorses Gramsci's rejection of the distinction between manual and intellectual labor, but otherwise his adherence to Gramsci's theory of the intellectuals is not sustained. In the most directly comparable case, that of the teacher, Gramsci defines the role of teacher and the teacher/student relationship in relation to the type, stage and setting of the education concerned and the level of maturity of the student, whereas Freire conceives of an archetypal dialogical teacher/student common to all situations.

The relationship between the teacher and the student symbolizes Freire's ideal of the relationship between leader and led in society. In Freire's early work the roles merge and interchange in a kind of mystical communion involving the class suicide of the middle class (oppressor) teacher prior to his or her "resurrection" through identification with the oppressed. However, in his later work Freire acknowledges that this is not always practicable and advocates using as educators people from the local community. In either case, Freire's aim is for the teacher to identify with the student, either because they share the same background or because the teacher has deliberately renounced his or her privileged background in an act of self-sacrifice. Freire's focus is always on the quality of the relationship between teacher and student, which, he believes, should be characterized by humility, tolerance, trust and love (de Figueiredo-Cowen and Gastaldo 1995:20).

Gramsci's aim is different: every citizen should be educated so that she or he is formed "as a person capable of thinking, studying and ruling—or controlling those who rule" (SPN:40). Trust in the leader is not enough, as Gramsci makes clear (SCW:21); it is what people fall back on when they cannot work out for themselves what direction to take. The notion of the citizenry controlling their rulers or becoming rulers themselves is alien to Freire, for whom the role of the people is to support rather than to replace or direct the leader.

Curriculum

In the area of curriculum Gramsci and Freire appear to come together to some extent, although, as before, some of the similarities are superficial. For example, both Gramsci and Freire stress the importance of curricula linked to the productive process. Thus, as Cammett (1967:81) points out, in the factory councils, the commissars organized schools within the factory, aimed at increasing the workers' skills in their own trades or industrial functions and at preparing workers to become autonomous producers. The factory was a fertile ground for the development of a new proletarian hegemony because, as Gramsci remarked, "The more the proletarian is specialised in a job, the more he feels the need for order, method, precision" so that society comes to appear as "one immense factory, organized with the same precision, method, order that he sees as vital in the factory where he works" (Gramsci quoted in Cammett 1967:79).

Similarly, Freire describes a curriculum in which education is integrated with and indistinguishable from production, when he puts forward the outline of a proposed education system for the newly independent Guinea-Bissau. He contends that, as the country moves toward socialism, it needs

to structure its education in close relation to production, both from the point of view of the understanding of the productive process and also the technical training of the learners. (LGB:105)

This is in the context of the need to overcome the division between manual and mental labor in the new society, something which Gramsci also stresses.

Assuming the success of the revolution, something Gramsci by no means takes for granted, especially in his later writings, education as a function of leadership and working class support for the revolution would change as the role of the party and the working class changed. In the postrevolutionary society, working class hegemony in education would be underwritten by "a common basic education" followed by vocational training or productive work (SPN:27). Adults would continue their vocational and political education through the trade unions and the factory councils to enable them to run their factories and other enterprises.

Gramsci stresses the need for political education such as that undertaken at *l'Ordine Nuovo*'s School of Culture and Socialist Propaganda, where the idea of a new "State of the Councils" was explored. *L'Ordine Nuovo* was itself a vehicle for political and cultural education with regular features on a wide range of subjects. In his notes on the study of philosophy in the prison notebooks (SPN:331), Gramsci outlines an appropriate curriculum for the political education of adults, based on a criticism of "common sense": "an introduction to the study of philosophy must expound in synthetic form the problems that have grown up in the process of development of culture as a whole."

For Freire, "the basic challenge is not simply to substitute a new program for an old one that was adequate to the interests of the colonizers" (LGB:102). Instead, the curriculum must be worked out anew in each situation in order to establish a coherence between the revolutionary society and the education that is to serve it. The starting point is an exploration of people's awareness of the contradictions affecting their lives. Accordingly, Freire proposes an open-ended, research-based curriculum, without the backing of doctrine of any kind, in the belief that critical education will inevitably lead to liberation.

In their sharply divergent responses to the new educational ideas developed in France and Germany in the 1920s the difference between Freire's and Gramsci's approaches to education is most stark. These were the ideas behind the Gentile reforms of Italian education, and Gramsci was deeply critical of them in that incarnation. More generally, he regarded the active school as still in its "romantic phase," he critiqued it, he did not reject it altogether. Instead Gramsci looked forward to a new form of the active school, which would "find in the ends to be attained the natural source for developing the appropriate methods and forms" (SPN:33). By contrast, Taylor (1993:37) shows the pervasive influence on Freire of the French *éducation nouvelle*.

Both Gramsci and Freire decry what Freire calls the "banking" approach to education, in which culture is regarded as a commodity to be acquired and "men as mere receptacles to be stuffed full of empirical data and a mass of unconnected raw facts to be filed in the brain as in the columns of a dictionary," as Gramsci wrote in 1916 (SPWI:10–1). Gramsci contrasts this spurious approach to culture with culture as

organization and discipline of one's inner self, a coming to terms with one's own personality; it is the attainment of a higher awareness with the aid of which one succeeds in understanding one's own historical value, one's own function in life, one's own rights and obligations. (SPWI:11)

This sounds very like Freire's critically transitive stage of consciousness. However, the reference to "rights and obligations" is a reminder that, for Gramsci, unlike Freire, the attainment of higher awareness leads to the recognition of one's historical role in the furtherance of the communist revolution rather than to an unspecified "liberation."

Freire sees banking education as the negation of dialogue. In his detailed exposition of what is meant by the term, quoted in Chapter 3, Freire describes banking education as mirroring society as a whole. Dialogue prefigures a future society where there is "love, hope, faith, trust and humility between people" (PO:62). Under these circumstances, education will be a matter of dialogue, not of "narration" (PO:45). However, Freire's distinction between banking and problem-posing education could be likened to the distinction drawn by idealist educationists in Italy (Croce, Gentile and their followers) between instruction and education. As Gramsci points out, excessive emphasis on this distinction has been a serious error of educational idealists

For instruction to be wholly distinct from education the pupil would have to be pure passivity, a mechanical receiver of abstract notions—which is absurd and is anyway "abstractly" denied by the supporters of pure educativity precisely in their opposition to mere mechanistic instruction. (SPN:35)

This is precisely the claim that Freire makes: that banking education, by treating students as passive, turns them into "pure passivity," whereas problem-posing education enrolls students as active participants in the education process.

Accordingly, while both Freire and Gramsci regard what Freire calls a banking approach to education and culture as incorrect, they do so for different reasons. For Freire banking education is manipulative and stultifying, serving the interests of oppressors opposed to the liberation of the people. For Gramsci, the distinction between education and instruction is a false dichotomy: education should include instruction. He argues that for the overwhelming majority of children who are living in an environment steeped in folklore, their individual consciousness "reflects social and cultural relations which are different from and antagonistic to those which are represented in the school curricula" (SPN:35). Under these circumstances there is no unity between school and life, and it is for this reason that there is no automatic unity between instruction and education. He contends,

For the teacher to be able to unite instruction and education he must be aware of the contrast between the type of culture and society which he represents and the type of culture and society represented by his pupils, and conscious of his obligation to accelerate and regulate the child's formation in conformity with the former and in conflict with the latter. (SPN:36)

For Gramsci "a mediocre teacher may manage to see to it that his pupils become more informed, although he will not succeed in making them better educated" (SPN:36). Nevertheless, this is still preferable to the subjective and rhetorical nature of the education system brought in by the Gentile Reform of the old Italian education system, because "a date is always a date, whoever the examiner is, and a definition always a definition. But an aesthetic judgement or a philosophical analysis?" (SPN:36). Gramsci contends,

The more the new curricula nominally affirm and theorize the pupil's activity and working collaboration with the teacher, the more they are actually designed as if the pupil were purely passive. (SPN:37)

The pupil will be sold short, receiving an empty, rhetorical education.

Freire's formulation of the culture of silence may appear at first sight reminiscent of Gramsci's description of the condition of the "subaltern element" in the prison notebooks:

If yesterday the subaltern element was a thing, today it is no longer a thing but an historical person, a protagonist; if yesterday it was not responsible, because "resisting" a will external to itself, now it feels itself to be responsible because it is no longer resisting but an agent, necessarily active and taking the initiative. (SPN:337)

The "subaltern element" of "yesterday" sounds very much like the submerged "object" of the oppressor's reality of whom Freire writes. Gramsci's analysis is more subtle, however; he asks,

But even yesterday was it ever mere "resistance," a mere "thing," mere "non-responsibility"? Certainly not. Indeed one should emphasize how fatalism is nothing other than the clothing worn by real and active will when in a weak position [. . .] In fact [. . .] some part of even a subaltern mass is always directive and responsible, and the philosophy of the part always precedes the philosophy of the whole, not only as its theoretical anticipation but as a necessity of real life. (SPN:337)

The implications for the education process in a revolutionary context are far-reaching: the seeds of revolution are inherent in the "subaltern mass" itself, nurtured by the conditions in which it finds itself. What is needed, according to Gramsci, is for the situation to be correctly analyzed and action taken on the basis of a thorough understanding of contemporary conditions viewed from within the revolutionary movement, in line with an ongoing development of Marxist theory.

Both Freire and Gramsci make use of the anthropological concept of culture, drawing a fundamental distinction between that which is produced by human beings and transmitted to their successors by other than biological means and that which is the result of the action of natural forces. This distinction enables both Freire and Gramsci to differentiate between that which can be changed by human agency and that which cannot. For Gramsci, the insight predates his commitment to socialism: in an essay written probably in 1911, he states that "social privileges and differences, being products of society and not of nature, can be overcome" (SPWI:5). He makes the same point in an article written six years later, where he argues that "above all, man is mind, i.e. he is a product of history, not nature" (SPWI:11). Also in 1916, in an *Avanti* article, he writes that "events should be seen to be the intelligent work of men, and not the products of chance, of fatality" (SPWI:18).

For Freire, the anthropological concept of culture informs the curriculum: it is "the first dimension of our new programme content" (EPF:46). Like Gramsci, Freire defines the anthropological concept of culture as "the distinction between the world of nature and the world of culture" and stresses the importance of culture as historical, as "a systematic acquisition of human experience (but as creative assimilation, not as information-storing)" (EPF:46). The anthropological concept of culture is important to Freire because it forms the basis of the desired change of consciousness. He states,

From that point of departure, the illiterate would begin to effect a change in his former attitudes, by discovering that he, as well as the literate person, has a creative and re-creative impulse. (EPF:47)

Freire's educational process accordingly seeks to unlock that which is already within individuals but hidden, both from themselves and from others. Culture is therefore a condition of humanity, but one which is unrecognized by individuals in certain stages of consciousness. For Freire, the consciousness of being cultured is the casualty of oppression. The education process, by developing the consciousness of being cultured in oppressed people, enrolls them as equal members of the human race with their oppressors, and thereby puts them in a position to challenge their oppression. The overt moral dimension here is in keeping with the essentially religious quality of Freire's ideas.

Similarly, both Gramsci and Freire recognize the importance of overcoming superstition. Freire gives an example of Amílcar Cabral discussing the magical powers of amulets with some soldiers and remarking that future generations will say, "Our fathers struggled hard but they believed in some very strange things" (LGB:19). Gramsci was acutely aware of the prevalence of superstition and the need to overcome it through his childhood in Sardinia. He contends,

The discovery that the relations between the social and natural orders are mediated by work, by man's theoretical and practical activity, creates the first elements of an intuition of the world free from all magic and superstition. It provides a basis for the subsequent development of an historical dialectical conception of the world, which understands movement and change, which appreciates the sum of effort and sacrifice which the present has cost the past and which the future is costing the present, and which conceives the contemporary world as a synthesis of the past, of all past generations, which projects itself into the future. (SPN:34–5)

For Gramsci, oppressed people achieve consciousness of their oppression through political struggle, which is itself educative, and through an educational process geared to their advancement as a class. The fact that they are cultured is not in doubt; what is important is to judge which elements of their culture constitute good sense and tend toward progressive historical aims.

Both Freire and Gramsci agree that education must be a critical process. Gramsci's political and educational methodology is rooted in a critique of opposing viewpoints, as in his critique of Croce. However, the educative process does not begin and end with criticism, as it tends to do with Freire. To Gramsci, "to criticize one's own conception of the world means therefore to make it a coherent unity and to raise it to the level reached by the most advanced thought in the world" (SPN:324). Through such a critical process one may become politically conscious, that is, conscious of being "part of a particular hegemonic force" which is "the first stage towards a further progressive self-consciousness in which theory and practice will finally be one" (SPN:333). For Gramsci, it is the role of the party to "represent this higher consciousness" (SPWII:288). Accordingly, at least one element of the curriculum is compulsory: it is "a duty for the militant to know Marxist–Leninist doctrine, at least in the most general terms" (SPWII:289).

As we have seen in Chapter 3, for Freire, as for the MEB, the curriculum should be developed from the learner's perception of the world rather than imposed by the educator. However, since the learner is initially trapped in the culture of silence, the catalyst for that development can only come from outside and the investigation process, and hence the curriculum content is ultimately controlled by the educator. Furthermore, educators' vision of reality is privileged because they have presumably already attained the higher level of consciousness that the conscientization process is designed to bring about. The aim is to unveil a reality hidden, at the outset, from the learners but revealed, albeit dimly, to the educator. Freire's educative process, I would argue, is thus potentially more prescriptive than Gramsci's, precisely because it rests on a concept of revelation, whereas Gramsci's rests on reason. It is possible to disagree with Gramsci; Freire demands an act of faith.

Conclusion

In the absence of explicit developmental links, the assumption that Gramsci's and Freire's ideas are compatible remains unproven. Gramsci's and Freire's ideas are significantly different, despite some similarities. They do not complement each other, and are best understood as emerging from somewhat separate, although overlapping, intellectual and political traditions and, in Freire's case, from his religious faith. The echoes of Gramsci that occur in Freire's writing probably result as much from Gramsci's influence on Latin American left intellectuals, both directly and mediated by Mariátegui, and on Liberation Theology, as from any attempt by Freire to use Gramsci's ideas directly and systematically. Freire pays tribute to Gramsci, but does not claim to be a Gramscian. Nevertheless, there are some areas of congruence, particularly in Freire's later writing, where he adopts a more explicitly materialist stance, but these are outweighed by important areas of incongruency.

A final parallel is fortuitous, but may account to some extent for the linking of Gramsci's and Freire's ideas in the adult education literature. Gramsci's posthumous fame coincided with Freire's rise to international prominence as a guru of radical adult education. Both therefore emerged onto the international scene at a turbulent time, against the background of the Cold War. In the West it was a time of student unrest, the New Left, the civil rights and women's movements and protest against the United States' role in the Vietnam War; in the Soviet bloc, the invasion of Czechoslovakia by Soviet troops; in China, Mao Zedong's Cultural Revolution; in the Middle East, the Six Days War and its aftermath. In Africa, South and Central America and elsewhere, it was a time of guerrilla wars of liberation, proxy wars fought on behalf of the Cold War protagonists. Gramsci's and Freire's ideas thus entered the public domain at a time of unrest and profound political questioning, especially on the Left, in which debates about the nature of politics and the relationship between politics and education played a significant part.

Against this background, Gramsci's and Freire's ideas began to be associated in the construction of a radical adult education project and it is to a consideration of the ways in which they featured in that project that I now turn.

Notes

1.   De Kadt (1970:64) draws a distinction between

> "utopia," seen as an ideal construct based on certain political or philo-
> sophical notions, which can serve as a guide for purposeful social
> change, and "utopics," the belief in the actual possibility of the con-
> struction of an ideal society, free from evil, power, "contradictions,"
> etc.

I would cast Freire's thought as utopian rather than utopic in this sense.

Chapter 5
Gramsci and Freire: Apologias, Critiques and Interpretations

In this chapter I shall look first at some of the ways in which Gramsci's and Freire's ideas have featured as emblems of a radical project for adult education. This takes the form of a roughly chronological selective review of the English language literature on adult education in which Gramsci and Freire are cited, focusing first on Freire and then on Gramsci and picking up points where their ideas have been associated. The fact that other thinkers are not mentioned should not be taken to mean that *only* Freire and Gramsci are mentioned by these writers. Nor should this review be regarded as entirely comprehensive; there are doubtless omissions and others might bestow emphasis in different places. My reading of the balance of citations between Freire and Gramsci accords with the findings of John Field and his colleagues (Field et al. 1991), but I have not attempted to duplicate their painstaking statistical work. The focus on Gramsci and Freire as emblems of a radical project for adult education should not be understood, either, as meaning that the only radical adult education worthy of the name is that which draws inspiration from one or the other of them. Gramsci and Freire are cited in a particular—although wide—range of theoretical and practice-related contexts, outlined below; they are on the whole absent from debates in other areas.

The latter part of this chapter explores the explicit linkage of Gramsci's and Freire's ideas, focusing on the cases made by Peter Mayo and by Paula Allman and John Wallis. Finally, as a coda, I consider Peter Leonard's reflections on Freire's and Gramsci's place in his work in one area of the diverse field of the education and training of adults, that of social work education.

I shall begin with Freire, as he is more often cited in the literature and his ideas have undoubtedly been more directly influential.

Freire As a Radical Hero of Adult Education

I am tempted to head this section "Freire as *the* Radical Hero of
Adult Education." There can be few adult educators anywhere in
the world who have not heard of him, even if they have not read his
writings. His celebrity is reflected in the adult education literature,
not only in English (my focus here), but also in many other languages. His work is widely cited, often signaling a radical commitment on the part of the writer, or at least a discussion of the pros and
cons of a radical approach to the education of adults. Freire's partners in his talking books, including Ira Shor, Donaldo Macedo,
Antonio Faundez and the late Myles Horton, have also contributed
to his international standing through their collaborations with him.

Freire is a controversial as well as a celebrated figure; his pedagogy of the oppressed provokes strong reactions, both positive and
negative. Nonetheless, "a surprisingly wide range of writers," as Frank
Youngman (1986:152) points out, comment approvingly with only
"occasional reservations about the complexity of his writing style or
the political implications of his approach." That approach has been
widely adopted—and adapted—in (in his terms) the "Third World"
and his ideas have been influential internationally in various educational fields.

For example, in North America Freire was for a while associated
with the deschooling movement, and he is an acknowledged influence on Ivan Illich and Everett Reimer (Grabowski 1972:108). Radical educationists, including Henry Giroux, Jonathan Kozol and
Stanley Aronowitz, cite Freire's ideas in their attempts to go beyond
what Giroux (in Freire and Macedo 1987:23–4) calls the "polariz-
ing logic of reproduction versus resistance" to develop a critique of
mainstream education in relation to possibilities for social change.
Shor has advocated the application of Freire's ideas in the North
American context in job training education (Shor 1988) and in his
edited collection *Freire for the Classroom: A Sourcebook for Liberatory
Teaching* (Shor ed. 1987). The latter is intended to bring Freire'
ideas into North American schools, although his endeavor has been

criticized by Brady (1994:144) and others as depoliticizing and decontextualizing Freire's work.

Freire's influence has been greatest in the field in which his ideas developed, nonformal adult education. As Torres (1993:127) points out, Freire's pedagogy proposes a strategy for liberation in which the focus shifts from mainstream education systems to the nonformal, less structured field of adult education. Its main proponents, including Freire himself, work in universities or private institutions, often closely connected with churches. Torres suggests some "complementary arguments for this strategy," quoted here in full:

1. Freire and Liberation educators had originally developed their approach in this field in Brazil (1960–4), in Chile (1965–70), and in Africa.

2. The political implications of adult education vastly exceed those of formal schooling (e.g., using community needs for designing vocabulary for literacy programs).

3. Adult education programs from the point of view of this educational philosophy are better linked to community needs and more responsive to community pressures than the formal schooling system. Thus, this "popular education" should be understood more as a form of education developed by *the oppressed rather than* for *the oppressed.*

4. Adult education has the curricular and organizational flexibility that formal schooling lacks.

5. The results of adult education are more immediate than those of formal schooling. It is not necessary to wait 10–15 years, as in formal training, for the incorporation of the "graduate" into the labor market or into political activities as in the case of children.

6. The potential demanders of adult education in peripheral capitalist social formations are always the dispossessed. This testifies to their lack of power and, furthermore, shows that illiteracy, far from being a "social illness," is an outcome of hierarchical class structure or violent historical processes such as colonization.

7. Finally, adult education has shown great importance as an instrument for political mobilization and critical consciousness in some processes of transition to socialism, such as in Cuba and Nicaragua. (Torres 1993:127)

Against this background, many adult educationists seek to interpret and critique Freire's work for an international anglophone audience, including Torres himself, who has written extensively on Freire, particularly in relation to the Latin American context (1990a, 1991, 1993; Torres and Freire 1994).

Some would see themselves as working in an explicitly Freirean mode. For example, in the United Kingdom, Tom Lovett (1978, 1982) was one of the first to recognize Freire's significance in his work in adult community education. Freire features strongly in contributions to *Adult Education for a Change* (Thompson ed. 1980), a book published as a rallying cry to radical adult educators and focusing predominantly on adult community education. In the United States Marilyn Frankenstein makes innovative use of Freire's pedagogy in mathematics teaching to adults (Frankenstein 1987, 1989) and discusses Freire's epistemology in her paper with Arthur B. Powell (Frankenstein and Powell 1994). Wendy Ball (1992) reflects on her experience of adult education as a site for critical social research and antiracist feminist praxis, informed by Lather's (1986) partly Freirean concept of "research as praxis" and Freire's pedagogy of liberation. On the basis of her research into antiracist/antisexist programs in one local education authority in England, Ball concludes that a strategy which "seeks to develop a critical pedagogy, to link in with local community-based struggles and which remains reflexive is essential for ensuring a context in which the power differences" between the researcher/educator, other participants in adult education networks and members of local communities, can be addressed (Ball 1992:23). Paula Allman, both in her solo writing (1987, 1988, 1994) and in her collaborations with John Wallis (1988, 1990a, 1990b, 1995a 1995b), applauds Freire as an inspirational theorist of radical adult education.

Others, while not claiming to be working in a Freirean mode are nevertheless happy to associate their ideas with Freire's in some way. For example, the adult educationist Stephen Brookfield (1987 cites Freire, along with many others, in his book *Developing Critical Thinkers,* and the psychologist of personal freedom, Carl Rogers claims affinity with Freire. Jack Mezirow (1977:156–7) allies his concept of "perspective transformation" with Freire's "seminal writing" which extends "the possibilities of using education to trans form one's frame of reference [. . .] in fostering personal and social change."

In the field of adult literacy, Cynthia Brown's (1975) account of Freire's literacy method, *Literacy in 30 Hours,* has done much to make it accessible to anglophone readers. Other literacists, including Colin Lankshear (in Lankshear and McLaren eds., 1993; Lankshear 1987, 1993), Herbert Kohl (1973), Carol and Lars Berggren (1975), and Barbara Bee (1980, 1993) stress the importance of Freire's contribution to what Giroux rightly calls a "gravely undertheorized" field (in Freire and Macedo 1987:4).

Freire has not gone unchallenged. William S. Griffith (1974), argues that Freire's approach to adult literacy is neither new nor revolutionary, that his advocacy of revolution is unsound since he fails to provide effective strategies for its achievement, and that his popularity in North America reflects a widespread disillusion with public education. Peter Berger (1976), in a scathing attack on Freire, argues that his view of consciousness is hierarchical despite the fact that it is not possible to prove that any individual's consciousness is superior to anyone else's. Berger also takes issue with Freire's insistence that he is not elitist, while contending that his own political philosophy is superior to all others and particularly appropriate for the oppressed. Other commentators, including Boston (1972), Collins (1977:113), Griffith (1974) and Merriam (1977:198), complain of the obscure, rhetorical style of Freire's writing. For example, Boston (1972:86–7), in his "Notes of a Loving Critic," remarks on the contradiction between Freire's insistence on the "demythologising, demystifying and deobfuscation of society" and the mythologizing, mystifying and obfuscating qualities of his own writing.

Evaluative literature on Freire's literacy method in action is similarly polarized. Some commentators have reported outstanding success as a result of using Freire's literacy methods (for example: Lloyd 1972:10; Stanley 1973:41) but nonpartisan evaluation of his work is hampered by the lack of an agreed theoretical framework both for literacy work in particular and for adult education in general.

In Guinea-Bissau, where Freire was directly involved in the literacy campaign, Torres (citing Linda Harasim 1983, as his source) reports that there is no evidence of its efficacy in terms of increased literacy rates. He states that by 1980 *reports from Guinea-Bissau began to acknowledge that the goals of literacy for national reconstruction had failed to materialize: of the 26,000 students involved in literacy training practically none had become functionally literate. (Torres 1993:133)*

An earlier attempt at evaluation was made by Beverley Chain (1974), who examined three "Freire-inspired" literacy programs in Bolivia, Guatemala and Honduras in the early 1970s. She found that in all three countries, the benefits were greater for the teachers than for their students and that the "extent of [. . .] critical consciousness or politicization which results depends on the skills and insights of individual teachers rather than the approach itself" (Chain 1974:406).

Lankshear (1993:122) reports similarly profound effects on the young urban *brigadistas* in Nicaragua's National Literacy Crusade of 1980, following the 1979 Sandinista revolution. Freire's ideas permeated the crusade, although the use of a primer—described by Lankshear (1993:121) as "overtly and unapologetically 'ideological'"—departed from Freirean practice. Lankshear (1993:136) also reports the educators' unease about the Sandinista government's decision to use Standard English, rather than Creole English in the bilingual English/Spanish campaign among the Miskito and other peoples of the Nicaraguan Atlantic coast, echoing the language issue that beset Freire's work in Guinea-Bissau. But despite many difficulties, the Nicaraguan National Literacy Crusade seems to have been successful, at least in terms of increased literacy rates. Lankshear's article and Robert Arnove's (1986, 1987) studies of revolution and education in Nicaragua show a dramatic decrease in illiteracy from 50.3 percent in 1978 to under 15 percent in 1984 (see also Archer and Costello 1990; Hirshon 1983; Lankshear 1987:Chapter 5; Miller 1985; Torres 1991). Possibly the crusade was also successful in terms of increased political awareness and activity—conscientization, in Freire's terms—although the defeat of the Sandinistas in the 1990 elections inevitably raises doubts about this. Lankshear concludes that the effect of the crusade was mixed—for some people minimal and temporary, for others "integral to the experience of personal and collective empowerment and tangible material progress" (Lankshear 1993:137).

In Grenada in 1981–2, a literacy campaign was initiated by the revolutionary New Jewel movement, led by Maurice Bishop. Although Freire's approach was very influential at the beginning, Torres (1991:120 n34) reports that there were problems applying the method to the Grenadian context, with the result that it departed even further from Freirean principles on the primer issue. He quotes the organizer of the Grenadian literacy campaign, Valerie Cornwall, as stating,

English is not a syllabic language. Thus, when we saw that we could not construct the generative words, we tried other means. Finally, what we did was to adapt the text-book series "Lady Bird," that are the materials used traditionally in the anglophone Caribbean, although making changes, and naturally, with other contents, those of the Revolution. (Torres 1991:120 n34)

In 1983 the Grenadian revolution was cut short by a combination of internal pressures, leading to the murder of Maurice Bishop and the subsequent U.S. invasion. It was too short-lived for the literacy campaign to be properly evaluated, thus tragically underlining the political and logistical difficulties besetting both the operation and the evaluation of Freire's pedagogy of liberation.

There seems to be little conclusive evidence that Freire's political pedagogy works in the terms he sets for it. Taylor (1993:80) quotes MacEoin's devastating comment, published in the *National Catholic Reporter* in 1972:

For years I have been searching for an instance in which peasants have broken out of their oppression, even at a local level, but I have found none. When I asked Freire, he admitted that neither had he.

Freire has also been criticized by Brian Street, a leading British theoretician of adult literacy, for tending to believe that there is only one "Western-type literacy" without which people are unable to "read the world" (Street 1991). By contrast, as Street points out in his analysis of literacy in theory and practice, research has eschewed the theory of a "great divide" between literacy and illiteracy that dominates public rhetoric and is instead concerned with "literacies" rather

than a single, monolithic "literacy" (Street 1984:8). Street also points
to anthropological evidence showing that self-reflection and critical
thought are found in supposedly nonliterate societies, thus under-
mining Freire's assumption that the process of becoming literate is
necessarily part of the process of critical enlightenment.

Street differentiates between an "ideological" and an "autonomous" ostensibly politically neutral model of literacy (identified with
UNESCO), arguing that, although Freire's work represents in some
ways a shift towards an "ideological" model, he has not entirely
shrugged off the assumptions of the "autonomous" model. Street
points out that Freire's analyses often appear to be rooted in theories
of cognitive development which take no account of the social context in which literacy is embedded and questions how well his approach takes account of cultural and ethnic variations. He argues
that some applications of Freire's approach seem to show that his
work is less radical than is commonly thought (Street 1984:14).

Taylor (1993:Chapter 4), in a brilliant analysis of Freire's literacy method, outlined here in Chapter 3, comes to the conclusion
that its nominative focus is antipathetic to personal change and incapable of leading to the individual's engagement in social and political change.

Several sympathetic commentators focus not on weaknesses in
the method or approach itself, but instead express their fear that
Freire's ideas may be co-opted and stripped of their radical potential. Kidd and Kumar (1981) and Kidd and Byram (1982), for example, warn against pseudo-Freirean adult education, as practiced
in Botswana and Thailand as well as elsewhere in the Third World,
where an amelioratory concern with poverty is substituted for a
liberatory Freirean concern with oppression. These warnings seem
to have been vindicated. For example, M.D. James (1990:15–16)
deplores as illusory and idealistic "a pervasive tendency" in the United
States "toward literacy for adaptation" couched in Freirean language.
Literacy work in this mode is, he contends, regarded as "the sole
agent of social change by educators and activists" and "takes on an
almost mystical character, a capability of empowering people." Similarly, David Archer and Patrick Costello (1990:105), writing of the
National Institute of Adult Education (INEA) in Mexico, cite the
"bizarre belief" of INEA workers that "generative words have magi-

cal properties" through which "some miracle will take place, whereby illiterate people will become well-motivated and enabled to learn." They describe the co-option and perversion of Freire's ideas as

sometimes the product of a misreading or misunderstanding of Freire's work, but sometimes it appears as a deliberate attempt to hijack a set of radical ideas and methods. In both cases the effect is the same, giving reactionary literacy programmes a progressive gloss, and taming the methods themselves by inoculating people against Freirean language. (Archer and Costello 1990:105)

Commentators come to different conclusions about the political complexion of Freire's radicalism. For example, he is described by Robert Mackie (1980b:107) as formerly a liberal democrat, now a revolutionary socialist. By contrast, Jim Walker (1980:150) sees Freire, notwithstanding his generally approving references to Marxism, as a liberal populist who "stands clearly in the broad catholic tradition of syncretism." Frank Youngman (1986), reviewing Freire's work from a Marxist perspective, applauds his stress on the political nature of adult education, his anthropological concept of culture, his sensitivity to linguistic issues, and his concern with consciousness and cultural domination. Nonetheless, he identifies philosophical weaknesses, a neglect of the mode of production and political-economic analysis and class analysis, and lack of commitment to Marxist theory and socialist revolution. His verdict is that Freire's work does not provide a satisfactory basis for adult education for socialism (Youngman 1986:190–1).

The ambivalent relationship between Christianity (in the form of Catholicism) and Marxism in Freire's work is particularly problematic in this context, since his radical hero status depends, at least in part, on his left-wing, Marxist credentials. Some commentators see Freire's Christian theology as paramount (for example, Cooper 1995; Elias 1994), others, his politics—Marxist or otherwise (for example, Berger 1976; Walker 1980; Youngman 1986). Yet others see eclecticism as his defining characteristic (Mackie 1980b), allowing for the conjunction of disparate ideas, as, for example, in the description of Freire's ideal society as "Marxist in structure and Christian in ethics" (Carr quoted in Benseman 1978:29). Paula Allman

(1987) also sees Freire's Christianity and his Marxism as complementary, arguing that the "assumptions which underpin his approach, and the approach itself, are Marxist" but his language is that of the theologies of liberation (Allman 1987:215). In Allman's formulation it is Marxism which informs the substance and Christianity the expression of Freire's work.

Allman contends that Freire makes three Marxist assumptions. The first assumption concerns what it means to be fully human, a condition thwarted by alienation produced by "limiting social and economic formations" and "the relations that arise from them" (Allman 1987:216). The second assumption "locates education as a specific form of both pre- and post-revolutionary strategy": education must aim for liberation rather than domestication in either case (Allman 1987:217). The third assumption is that learners and teachers must struggle together to overcome the oppressive relations of banking education (Allman 1987:218). Here Allman contends (1987:219) that Freire's concept of critical thinking involves a "permanent critical approach to reality" which entails "the same method of logic or theorising developed by Marx in his later works, that is dialectic thinking." However, later in the same article she acknowledges that Marx does not describe this method in his writing (Allman 1987:224).

Allman develops her argument in her 1994 article "Paulo Freire's Contributions to Radical Adult Education," in which she states that Freire's educational philosophy is directly "based on Marx" (Allman 1994:146). She emphasizes the importance of Freire's

understanding of Marx's theory of consciousness, and his negative or critical concept of ideology in which ideology, or ideological, refers neither to a "system of beliefs" or "false consciousness" but to explanations, or actions and symbols based on such explanations, which are partial and fragmented and thereby distorted. (Allman 1994:148)

Against this background, Freire's "educational projects are based on a critical (dialectical) perception of reality amongst the participants" (Allman 1994:148). His approach "involves starting with 'where people are' but moving with them to an increasingly critical consciousness," which would enable them to "understand how their own experience of oppression, e.g. race, class, gender and so on, is linked to a total structure of oppression and to redefine their aspirations accordingly" (Allman 1994:152). Conscientization is achieved through analyzing and struggling to transform the relations which pertain in "traditional (bourgeois) cultural practices," and experiencing the transformations (Allman 1994:153). This involves transforming the teacher-learner relation through dialogue, at the same time as both teacher and learner transform their relation to knowledge, making it the object of critical thought.

In setting out Freire's ideas as she sees them, Allman is arguing against the depoliticization of Freire's ideas by commentators who reduce him to an educational methodologist. She sees his ideas as at risk from a postmodernist, eclectic, relativizing project "devoid of any coherent, theoretical 'guiding thread'" (Allman 1994:160). For Allman, the "guiding thread" should be provided by a correct reading of Freire, which means reading Freire in the light of (her reading of) Marx; this reading is discussed below in the context of her writing with Wallis, in which they argue for the linking of Freire, Gramsci and Marx in the creation of a radical theory of adult education.

Freire himself insists only on a "camaraderie" with Marx (Freire 1993:55) and remained a practicing Catholic. He is not alone in this conjunction, which he shares with liberation theologians and many Italian communists, but his influences are notably diverse both within and beyond Marxist and Christian thought. It is partly this that makes his omissions—for example of issues of racism and gender, noted with regret by Peter Mayo (1993), bell hooks (1993), Kathleen Weiler (1994) and Jeanne Brady (1994) and discussed in Chapter 3, more remarkable and more regrettable.

Some applications of Freire's ideas are far from Marxist, as with William Wilson's (1978) advocacy of "F Groups" (named in honor of Freire) to break down manager/worker conflict and establish interdependence and industrial democracy based on a functional understanding of work and its organization (Wilson 1978:v). For Wilson (1978:33), "Only when collective bargaining is linked to fully transitive consciousness i.e. critical consciousness arising out of dialogical education, is cultural revolution realised." Leach finds Wilson's idea "unconvincing" and I share his misgivings: it seems highly unlikely that Wilson's F Groups could form the basis of a transformed democratic society such as he envisages. Wilson fails to address the key issue of power: who has it, how to get it and what to use it for—a hiatus, as I have argued in Chapter 3, in Freire's work also. In the absence of an effective organization working for fundamental political change (something Wilson does not address), in whose interests would such an outbreak of industrial harmony be?

Given Freire's avowed eclecticism, it is not surprising that commentators view his work so differently and are able to point to contradictions in his thought, especially since he claims "the right to be contradictory" (Freire 1979:11). Taylor's comprehensive review of selected sources and influences shows just how complex are the interweavings between Freire's "backgrounds and borrowings" (Taylor 1993:Chapter 2).

The contributors to two recent edited books on Freire give an indication in their chapters of the extent and range of Freire's influence and the growing sophistication of the debate. McLaren and Lankshear's *Politics of Liberation: Paths from Freire* (1994) includes Kathleen Weiler on feminist pedagogy; Marguerite and Michael Rivage-Seul on peace education; Ian Lister on political literacy in Britain; Marilyn Frankenstein and Arthur B. Powell on ethno-mathematics; Carlos Alberto Torres in conversation with Freire, reviewing the twenty years since the publication of *Pedagogy of the Oppressed;* Edgar González Gaudiano and Alicia de Alba on the education of indigenous peoples in Mexico; Peter Findlay on conscientization and social movements in Canada; Michael Peters and Colin Lankshear on hermeneutics and education; Jeanne Brady on critical literacy, feminism and a politics of representation; Adriana Puiggrós on the politics of the personal, viewed from Argentina; Peter McLaren on postmodernism and the death of politics. McLaren's earlier edited book with Peter Leonard, *Paulo Freire: A Critical Encounter* (1993), covers an equally wide range of topics, including Tomaz Tadeu da Silva and Peter McLaren on Dermeval Saviani's critique of Freire's pedagogy, based partly in a reading of Gramsci, and Leonard's review of the influence of Freire and Gramsci on his work in social work education; these are discussed below. But although Freire is a major presence in both collections, he is perhaps more the figurehead than the captain of the ship: his pedagogy is not the major focus of each contribution. As Weiler (1996:354) points out, a number of the essays in both these collections "use a reference to Freire to stand in for a conception of progressive political education and then move to discuss their own concerns," while others "engage Freire's thought in a wider context."

Until his death in 1997, Freire was internationally known and widely revered, even if his approach is honored more in the breach than in the commission. I shall end this selective review of the literature on Freire with a brief look at accounts of two Freirean adult education projects, the Adult Learning Project (ALP) (Kirkwood and Kirkwood 1989), in Scotland and the Regenerated Freirean Literacy Through Empowering Community Techniques (REFLECT) (Archer and Cottingham 1996a, 1996b). While both read as honest accounts, neither account is—or claims to be—disinterested: the authors in each case were actively involved in establishing the projects about which they write.

ALP was established as "a systematic attempt to implement Freire's approach in Scotland" (Kirkwood and Kirkwood 1989:xii). According to Kirkwood and Kirkwood, it is an experiment that works and Freire, who visited the project in the 1980s, endorsed its work. The ALP project does not treat Freire's ideas as holy writ and there are other philosophical and practical influences on ALP which are outlined in the Kirkwoods' book. The Kirkwoods' commitment to an honest interpretation of Freire's ideas and methods is impressive—and strikingly unusual in a field noted more for its pragmatism than for rigorous testing of theory. While a full evaluation of the project, and their account of it, is outside the scope of this book, some elements which the Kirkwoods relate specifically to Freire may be considered here: these are the issues of authority, dialogue, and alienation.

On authority, the Kirkwoods (1989:135) state that "ALP struggles to restore the authority of the educator and of expert knowledge, while at the same time promoting the authority of the learner as co-educator." Their choice of the word "restore" is interesting here. It raises questions concerning the legitimacy of the educator's authority and of expert knowledge, which are addressed in Freire's writing in terms of his distinction between "authority" and "authoritarianism." It is often assumed that issues of authority and resistance do not arise in adult education because of its generally noncompulsory nature but this is an oversimplification. Adults manifestly do not always avoid situations in which authority is exercised over them—or even abused; examples abound of abusive relationships, both personal and institutional, which persist despite the apparent freedom of the victim to leave. There is also a widely held view in nonformal adult education circles that even to speak of authority is elitist, smacking of the worst excesses of traditional, didactic forms of education (Freire's banking mode). Thus the Kirkwoods' recognition that issues of authority are problematic in adult community education as well as in compulsory schooling is a refreshing insight. What is being addressed here is the problem of the power differential between educator and learner, between different kinds of knowledge and different ways of knowing. The Kirkwoods are rightly pointing to the fact that issues of authority may be just as acute in informal community adult education settings as in compulsory schooling. Much clearly depends on the educators' integrity in not abusing that authority, a problem, as I have argued above, which is distinctly Freirean.

Kirkwood and Kirkwood also problematize Freire's notion of dialogue, recognizing that although dialogue presupposes a shared language, this does not necessarily exist between parties to the educational process. As they put it, learners in ALP are situated "at a set of interfaces between different languages": Paulo Freire's abstract language, the ALP workers' translations of it, and the language of other group members. Dialogue in this context entails "issues of movement from concrete to abstract and from colloquial to formal, to say nothing of the different meanings individuals intend by the words and phrases they use" (Kirkwood and Kirkwood 1989:136). However, rather than seeing this multiplicity of languages as a problem, they see it, at least potentially, as a major source of learning for both parties to the educational enterprise. The notion of dialogue, thus problematized and removed from the confusions brought about by its association in Freire's work with dialectics, is, I believe, useful. Dialogue, thus conceived, does not just spontaneously occur, and it is in the structures and procedures for enabling it to take place that the ALP workers' commitment to Freire's ideas is most immediately obvious. Stressing that "structure in ALP does not mean rigidity" (Kirkwood and Kirkwood 1989:136), the ALP approach entails a sequence of stages with clear tasks, which, as they acknowledge, is unusual in the informal world of community education.

Rather than oppression, the Kirkwoods say that the groups they worked with identified alienation and the increasing privatization of people's lives as the fundamental theme (1989:137). This is significant because one of the difficulties adult educators in liberal democratic states have found in coming to terms with Freire's ideas has been that such states are not usually regarded as oppressive. This complacency has been vigorously challenged by Marxists, feminists, antiracists and others, but oppression is still largely seen as a problem of poorer, more backward nations, or as a residual problem situated at the margins of developed democracies. Alienation, in a sense close to Durkheim's "anomie,"[1] is rather more familiar, although use of the term is mainly restricted to academic circles: the concept is familiar even if the name for it is not. For Kirkwood and Kirkwood (1989:137), a major task implied by the prevalence of alienation is "to encourage people to contact, communicate and collaborate with each other, and begin to see the possibility of taking risks and contributing to change in society." This raises questions—which people, what kind of risks and what kind of change?

The Kirkwoods do not spell out the answers to these questions in detail. Instead they highlight the ethical and religious implications of the work of ALP. This is partly a deliberate attempt to redress the balance, since, as they say, "Much writing on Freire has stressed the political dimensions at the expense of the educational work" (Kirkwood and Kirkwood 1989:138). As a result, it is not clear what form of political organization of society is implied by their approach, but the form of morality with which it should be imbued is more clear. As they conclude,

Freire's pedagogy is about facilitating people's emergence from their isolated position in the crowd, and their struggle to help create the good society, founded on dialogue and respect for each person as a subject, where people take responsibility for themselves and for others, where being is recognised as more important than having, where the need to have enough is seen as a necessary precondition for being to the full, and where the attempt by the few to accumulate great power and wealth is recognized as a denial of participation to the many. (Kirkwood and Kirkwood 1989:138)

By contrast with ALP's inner-city Edinburgh, REFLECT operates in more typically Freirean Third World contexts. REFLECT is a program of the British nongovernmental organization (NGO) ACTIONAID, sponsored by the U.K. Overseas Development Administration (ODA). It seeks to build on Freire's theoretical framework through the use of techniques developed in Participatory Rural Appraisal (PRA), an approach to community development in poor rural areas influenced by Freire but primarily identified with the work of Robert Chambers (1983, 1993). Chambers cites Freire's "dialogics and conscientization" as one of a family of participatory approaches which PRA "belongs to, draws on and overlaps with," including also work in community development in the 1950s and 1960s, participatory action research, and the work of activist NGOs (Chambers, quoted in Archer and Cottingham 1996a:8).

REFLECT thus differs from ALP in that it is not attempting to test Freire's ideas but to go beyond them. In their action research report on three REFLECT pilot projects, David Archer and Sara Cottingham (1996a:6–7) point out theoretical and practical limitations and distortions of Freire's approach which the REFLECT program is designed to overcome. These include being prescriptive, reinventing the primer as the main tool of literacy tuition and laying his approach open to an undialogical "mechanical practice of literacy" in which learners become bored and disillusioned. Archer and Cottingham also agree with D. Brown (1994) that Freire elevates so-called rational knowledge over the existing knowledge and beliefs of the people, quoting Brown's view that this

can only reinforce whatever ideological biases exist within both the extension agency and the wider society, cutting the intervention off from any capacity to draw upon the positive elements in the claimed dual consciousness of the oppressed. (D. Brown, quoted in Archer and Cottingham 1996a:9)

As Brown points out, Freire's work runs directly counter to the ethos of Chambers and other exponents of PRA on this important issue, since PRA advocates an intervention process in partnership with local people, starting from their local knowledge, whereas Freire regards the people as initially trapped in the culture of silence and their lowly stages of consciousness. But Freire also advocates a more participatory approach on occasion. For example, he is quoted as stating, in 1982,

Our task is not to teach students to think—they can already think; but to exchange our ways of thinking with each other and look together for better ways of approaching the decodification of an object. (Freire, quoted in Frankenstein and Powell 1994:74)

Whatever the justification for it, Freire is often identified with concepts and practices of participatory research; for example, Patti Lather (1986) relates her concept of "research as praxis" to neo-Marxist critical ethnography, participatory research (which she identifies as Freirean) and feminist research.

Against this background, the REFLECT program is intended to make good what Archer and Cottingham regard as Freire's most serious shortcoming: his failure to formulate an effective literacy methodology. This is ironic in view of the fact that Freire is widely regarded as the originator of a radically innovative literacy technique. The aim of REFLECT is to "regenerate" Freirean literacy work in ways that are "ideological" in Brian Street's terms, and which are "rooted in a faith in people's existing knowledge and beliefs as a starting point"—something which Archer and Cottingham acknowledge owes more to Chambers than to Freire (1996a:9).

The REFLECT program aims to achieve this regeneration in the following ways: by emphasizing writing rather than passive reading of fixed texts; by emphasizing creative and active involvement of participants; by building on existing knowledge of participants, respecting oral traditions and other "literacies"; by focusing on learner-generated materials rather than prepackaged texts; by ensuring that the process is responsive and relevant to the local context (Archer and Cottingham 1996a:9). Accordingly, REFLECT participants undertake analyses of their situation and environment through a range of activities, such as constructing local maps, or calendars of their working year. These are techniques derived more from PRA than from Freire. For example, Chambers (1993:59) draws attention to the importance of what he calls "seasonal diagramming," a technique developed in agro-ecosystem analysis, in enabling rural people "to plan their own counterseasonal actions and to make demands for appropriate and timely services and support." Literacy and numeracy work arise naturally out of these activities, according to Archer and Cottingham (1996a:13–4).

The three REFLECT pilot projects (in Uganda, Bangladesh and El Salvador) have been hailed as successful by ACTIONAID on the basis of evaluation undertaken by ACTIONAID with the involvement of independent evaluators. Their claims for the program are that it is more effective in terms of increasing literacy and numeracy levels than conventional programs (and many Freirean programs also); that it is low-cost and cost-effective; and that it generates empowerment through the REFLECT process rather than through its outcome (literacy and numeracy). In fact, the claim of empowerment is noticeably low-key, by contrast with Freire: Archer and Cottingham (1996a:91) state only that "REFLECT could be used as a means to mildly improve the lot of the poor or to challenge overall power structures."

Fully independent evaluation will be required to test these claims. In the meantime, the program has been enthusiastically endorsed by Freire, who is quoted in the report as saying "This is exactly what I sought to do—but you give it more structure and stronger roots. [. . .] This is very exciting work" (Freire, quoted in Archer and Cottingham 1996a:92).

Gramsci As a Radical Hero of Adult Education

Gramsci's influence is harder to gauge than Freire's. I suspect that fewer adult educators would say they were inspired by Gramsci than would say the same of Freire. But although he may be less well-known among adult educators than Freire, Gramsci is widely cited in the literature, often in association with Freire, and he is a persistent presence in debates about the politics and purpose of the education of adults, as Peter Mayo's useful review of the turn to Gramsci in the adult education literature in English indicates (Mayo 1995).

Gramsci's ideas, like Freire's, have figured in the critique of theories of reproduction in education since the late 1970s. For example,

Michael W. Apple (1982:18), in his analysis of the relationship be-tween schools and the surrounding social order, cites Gramsci as important in his own "painstaking movement away from a focus on simple reproduction" in education toward an exploration of the scope for agency in the process of resistance. Similarly, Henry Giroux (1992, 1993) applauds Gramsci's dialectical concepts of culture and ideol-ogy in his project of moving from the question of how society gets reproduced in the interests of capital and its institutions to the ques-tion of how the "excluded majorities" have and can develop institu-tions, values, and practices that serve their autonomous interests. In his impressive exercise in "border crossings," Giroux (1992) explores cultural politics and education in his book of that name, citing both Freire and, more extensively, Gramsci. Giroux highlights Gramsci's importance:

In substituting hegemonic struggle for the concept of domination, Gramsci points to the complex ways in which consent is organized as part of an active pedagogical process on the terrain of everyday life. In Gramsci's view such a process must work and rework the cultural and ideological terrain of subordinate groups in order to legitimate the interests and authority of the ruling bloc. (Giroux 1992:186)

On this Gramscian basis, Giroux argues for "a view of democracy and learning in which multiplicity, plurality, and struggle become the raison d'etre of democratic public life" (Giroux 1992:134). The educator should be a combination of Gramsci's organic intellectual, "who connects his or her work to broad social concerns that deeply affect how people live, work and survive" with Foucault's specific intellectual, who takes up "struggles connected to particular issues and contexts" (Giroux 1992:82). The possibilities of such a combi-nation are discussed in Chapter 6 of this volume. Giroux's voice is an important one, both for the breadth and depth of his analysis and for his position on the border between the discourse of educa-tion and the wider fields of cultural politics and critical theory.

Gramsci has also featured in related debates about the relation-ship between education and the state. For example, Andy Green uses a penetrating Gramscian analysis of the development of state systems of education in his book *Education and State Formation*

(1990). Green's analysis focuses on education systems in general and thus on initial, rather than adult, education. Torres, who, as we have seen, also writes extensively on Freire (1990b), uses Gramsci's theory of the state in his analysis of the politics of nonformal education in Latin America. Martin Carnoy (1982) uses Gramsci's concept of hegemony (or rather a version of it in the form of counterhegemony) in his essay on "Education, Economy and the State." He argues that "the key to a Gramscian educational strategy, then, is the creation of counter-hegemony *outside* the state schools" (Carnoy 1982:91).

One group of voices in debates drawing on Gramsci has been that of adult educators committed to participatory research. In participatory research educators join with those to be educated to research matters of concern to them and construct an educational program on the basis of those concerns. Participatory research is one of the "family of approaches" (including Freire's and PRA) cited by Chambers (in Archer and Cottingham 1996a:8). A leading advocate of participatory research, Ted Jackson (1981), traces the influence of Gramsci on adult education around the world, highlighting the role of the participatory research movement in attempting to link Gramsci's work to the theory and practice of adult education. For example, Budd Hall (quoted in T. Jackson 1981:82), writing in 1978, uses Gramsci's distinction between traditional and organic intellectuals to argue for the need for organizers of working class politics "to make the links between the intellectuals of both types and foster the recognition of workers' right to create philosophy." Hall argues that this should be achieved by a democratic process of knowledge creation, and advocates participatory research as an appropriate model.

Ted Jackson (1981:83) describes the International Forum on Participatory Research convened in Yugoslavia in 1980, at which delegates discussed various aspects of Gramsci's work, including the construction of a "hegemonic proletarian science" and the process of the creation of organic intellectuals of the working class. Jackson ends by pointing to a growing interest in Gramsci among adult educators in Latin America, Asia and throughout Europe and identifies the International Council for Adult Education (ICAE) and its journal, *Convergence*, as important in facilitating the exploration of Gramsci's work internationally (T. Jackson 1981:85). Here again, there is a link between Gramsci and Freire: Freire is a past honorary president of ICAE and the Council has been instrumental in advocating Freirean ideals and approaches to the education of adults. Arguably, also, the investigation stage in Freire's educational process could be seen as a form of participatory research, but D. Brown's (1994) objection to the linking of PRA with Freire's approach, cited above, holds true also for participatory research. Neither sit comfortably with Freire's hierarchical concept of knowledge and his staged theory of consciousness.

Thomas J. La Belle draws on Gramsci's writings on the factory council movement in his analysis of nonformal education in Latin America and the Caribbean, stating that Gramsci is the most frequently cited Marxist theorist in the field (La Belle 1986:185). In a later article tracing the development from consciousness raising to Popular Education (*Educación Popular*) in Latin America and the Caribbean, La Belle sees participatory investigation as the typical first step beyond Freirean conscientization toward a potentially more effective politico-educational strategy, involving the organization of the masses (La Belle 1987). This he sees as central to Gramsci's conception of change and "the key element in moving beyond Freire's praxis of everyday life and intellectual praxis" (La Belle 1987:208). Although La Belle's article is describing a process he discerns in Latin America and the Caribbean, rather than evaluating the effectiveness of a Freirean or Gramscian approach per se, nonetheless the implication is clear: Gramsci is being used to make up for perceived inadequacies in Freire's approach.

Jackson (1981) traces the beginnings of the literature linking Gramsci to issues in adult education back to an article by Lovett (1978) entitled "The Challenge of Community Education in Social and Political Change," published in *Convergence* in 1978. In this article, Lovett stresses the need for progressive adult education to be linked to the social movements of working class people. Socially committed adult educators must be aware of working people's culture, he writes, paraphrasing Gramsci, because "in such knowledge, and in contact with the everyday lives of people, can be found the source of the problems, the contradictions" which they seek to resolve (Lovett 1978:48). In this way, Lovett argues in Gramscian terms, adult education may renovate and make critical the "common sense" of working people, so that they come to constitute a "cultural and social bloc." Lovett notes that such an approach also characterized the work of Highlander Education and Research Center in the United States and the Antigonish Movement in Canada in the 1930s.

The year 1979 saw the publication of the first book in English to explore the relationship between Gramsci's ideas and issues in adult education (although only 19 of its 179 pages are directly concerned with adult education). This was Harold Entwistle's *Antonio Gramsci: Conservative Schooling for Radical Politics* (1979), the title of which encapsulates the problem, as Entwistle sees it, with Gramsci's ideas on education. Entwistle's thesis is controversial: he argues that Gramsci's writing on the education of children is profoundly conservative, whereas his writing on the political education of adult workers advocates a radical pedagogy in which political education is integrated with technical education. Entwistle is not alone in this view, which is shared, for example, by Guy B. Senese (1991) and the Brazilian philosopher Dermeval Saviani (whose argument is discussed in Da Silva and McLaren, 1993). Entwistle's book sets out to explain this apparent paradox, while Entwistle's subtext is to use Gramsci in a polemic against the "new sociology of education."

On this somewhat questionable basis, Entwistle nevertheless presents some aspects of Gramsci's thinking accurately. For example, he correctly emphasizes the centrality of the adult world of work in Gramsci's thinking on education, arguing that "the key to his theory of political education lies in the education of adults, especially as workers in an occupational context" (Entwistle 1979:111). Accordingly, workers must be educated "with reference both to the technical aspects of work and to its political and cultural implications" and these must be tackled together: "Political activity is not a chronological outcome of political education. The two are concurrent" (Entwistle 1979:112). Through this process, organic intellectuals of the working class will develop

contingent upon the performance of an economic role as an adult worker. In this sense, as well as being necessary in the field of adult education, political education is intrinsic to vocational education, widely conceived. (Entwistle 1979:113)

Entwistle also welcomes Gramsci's broad conception of education as a lifelong process, which he likens to *education permanente* (Entwistle 1979:112).

Entwistle also correctly points out that "in denying that an intellectual can be 'socially unattached', [Gramsci] was focusing upon function rather than on social origins," thus the terms "organic" and "traditional" are not mutually exclusive: in this sense "all intellectuals are organic to some hegemonic class" (Entwistle 1979:115). The intellectual's function and commitment is more important than the type of intellectual skill he or she happens to possess and Entwistle concludes that the defining factor is the "general, directive function which every intellectual performs within the complex of social relationships" (Entwistle 1979:117). It follows that since intellectuality is defined by function, it is possible for erstwhile traditional intellectuals to change their allegiance and espouse the working class cause, although ultimately "organic intellectuals should be generated from within the working class itself" (Entwistle 1979:117).

Entwistle's book met with a mixed reception, with reviewers united in taking exception to the book as a polemic against the "new sociology" and several taking him to task for misunderstanding Gramsci (Alden 1981; Apple 1980; Giroux 1980; Hoare 1980; Holly 1980). One reviewer, Harold Alden (1981), rightly criticizes Entwistle for presenting Gramsci's doctrine of hegemony as a strategy replacing, rather than complementing, that of violent revolution. As he points out, this reduces Gramsci's notion of the "war of position" to a tamely educational affair, a matter of raising the workers' consciousness in order to combat the hold over them of capitalist hegemony. Alden also takes issue with Entwistle's belief that Gramsci advocated a neutral education for children, arguing that, for Gramsci, education could never be neutral. Lastly, Alden points to Entwistle's fundamental omission in failing to recognize the crucial role of the revolutionary Communist Party in Gramsci's thought. Another reviewer, Apple (1980), argues that Entwistle has missed the point, failing to recognize the centrality of politics for Gramsci. While agreeing that Entwistle is right on some aspects of Gramsci's thought, for example in recognizing the importance Gramsci placed upon rigorous intellectual work, nevertheless Apple states that Entwistle fails to appreciate that such rigorous work

was not a commitment to this ethic in the abstract, but instead was part
of a larger commitment to gaining power in the economic, cultural, and
political spheres through concerted action on a variety of fronts. (Apple
1980:438)

Reviews by Giroux (1980), Douglas Holly (1980) and Quintin Hoare
(1980) were equally critical. Giroux, for example, accuses Entwistle
of using a reductionist methodology, imposing a positivistic, one-
dimensional reading on Gramsci and depoliticizing the relationship
between power and culture. Giroux acknowledges that Entwistle
advocates a much more radical program for adult education, but
points out that he says nothing new on the subject. Holly finds
Entwistle's whole enterprise extremely distasteful and accuses him
of a sustained misrepresentation of Gramsci's position, especially in
the major part of the book devoted to an undifferentiated concept
of "schooling." The section on adult education he finds at least rea-
sonably accurate with regard to Gramsci's theory of the intellectuals,
but Entwistle's use of Gramsci to support his contention that "schools
should be about *information:* critical engagement with that information is a matter for adults" he finds indefensible, because Gramsci
continuously argued that existing knowledge should be treated critically (Holly 1980:318). In fact, Gramsci himself pointed out that
separating "'instruction', the 'informative' moment" from "'education', the 'formative' moment, the crowning-point of the educational
process" was a feature of Gentile's (Fascist) pedagogy (FSPN:72).

Hoare takes a more sympathetic view of Entwistle's book, although he points out that Entwistle largely ignores the political context of contemporary educational controversies and misreads Gramsci
in thinking him in any respect a conservative.

Despite the critical tenor of these reviews, Entwistle's book may
have been influential in that it offers an introduction to Gramsci to
busy adult educators who might find the prison notebooks heavy
going, and it has been cited in the adult education literature in lieu
of, or alongside, Gramsci's own writing (*cf.* Jarvis 1987:108; 1989
passim; 1993:20; Nisi and Mascia in Thomas and Elsey eds.,
1985:210–2).

The Gramsci-as-educational-conservative theme has been taken
up by Guy B. Senese (1991), who uses Gramsci in this way in his

critique of Giroux, Aronowitz and McLaren as exponents of critical pedagogy. Dermeval Saviani's refutation of Freire's ideas rests on his conservative reading of Gramsci. Saviani's thesis, according to da Silva and McLaren (1993:39, 40–1) is that educational and political practice are distinct. Freire is thus wrong, according to Saviani, in his central contention that education is always political, an indictment all the more devastating in that Saviani is a researcher and professor in the universities in São Paulo in which Freire also worked after his return to Brazil. Saviani argues that education should be a preparation for politics rather than a site of political struggle, an argument which is hard to square with Gramsci's notion of hegemony, as da Silva and McLaren (1993:42) point out. Saviani is also an opponent of active pedagogies and emphasizes the transmission of relevant content rather than method in his polemic against Freire, a position for which he cites Gramsci's support. In my view this is to distort Gramsci's position on the active school, as I have argued in Chapter 4. Neither was Gramsci only concerned with content, although this is a common assumption, stemming perhaps from Entwistle's book and a selective reading of Gramsci. The simultaneous equation of Gramsci equals content and Freire equals method is far too simplistic.

Far from seeing Gramsci as in any way conservative, most commentators see him as an important figure in the development of a socialist theory and practice of adult education, citing him with approval on the formation of working class organic intellectuals and the struggle against bourgeois hegemony. For example, the editor of *Adult Education for a Change*, Jane Thompson (Thompson ed. 1980:26), uses Gramsci's concept of cultural hegemony to support her argument that the ruling class imposes its ideas on the rest of society, in particular the working class, to prevent them from thinking for themselves. As was seen from my discussion of hegemony in Chapter 2, this is an unduly reductionist version of Gramsci's concept in my view: Gramsci does not talk about an imposed class ideology. Thompson's thesis is also the thesis of the book: that adult education is party to this deception unless it sets out to be actively counterhegemonic. This too is problematic, as I have argued in Chapter 2: counterhegemony reduces Gramsci's concept of hegemony to a matter of "for" and "against." But individual contributors problematize this in different ways. Thus, the sociologist Sallie Westwood (1980:43) offers a Gramscian analysis in her argument that Gramsci's concept of hegemony shows how adult education maintains a middle class status quo, "engendering a state of consensus and contributing positively to the mechanisms whereby hegemony is maintained." She argues that adult educators should become "cultural workers" as a first step toward a redefinition of adult education (Westwood 1980:44). Martin Yarnit (1980:175) also welcomes Gramsci's recognition of the importance of wider cultural developments to which proletarian advance gives rise. Keith Jackson in his Foreword (Thompson ed. 1980:15), cites Gramsci's analysis of the educative role of the capitalist state as particularly useful. Thompson, Keith Jackson and Westwood all also cite Freire approvingly in their chapters. Jane Thompson also cites Gramsci in her passionate book, *Learning Liberation: Women's Response to Men's Education* (Thompson 1983). She states that Gramsci offers hope for women through his conviction that adult education could challenge the hegemony of ruling groups. She argues that this is important for women, affirming that "for women the opportunity of education can be enormously significant" (Thompson 1983:97).

Adult Education for a Change was criticized by Michael Barratt Brown (1980:92) for inflating the importance of community adult education at the expense of trade union education. He argues that the enthusiasm for Gramsci shown by contributors to the book is based on a misreading of Gramsci and that the book's assumptions are much more those of the antitrade unionist Frantz Fanon, who believed in the revolutionary potential of the wretched and unorganized masses (Barratt Brown 1980:91). In fact, I suspect the influence of Fanon is indirect, mediated by Freire. In any case, Gramsci was by no means an uncritical supporter of the trade unions, criticizing them as bureaucratic (SPWI:98). The factory councils deliberately cut across trade union organization and Gramsci was criticized for this by syndicalist elements in the Left (see SPWI:98–113). Gramsci was precisely concerned about the potential for hegemonic links to be forged between organized labor and Fanon's "wretched of the earth." However, Barratt Brown (1980:92) ends his review on a thoroughly Gramscian note, stressing the need to build links between workplace organizations "and organizations where people live, not to deflate one in order to inflate the other nor to set them up as rivals for the concern of adult educators."

Gramsci continues to feature in discussions of radical adult education in a range of fields. For example, Gramsci and Freire are both cited in Lovett, Clarke and Kilmurray (1983) in their discussions of adult education and community action, though not without criticism of Freire for his emphasis on method at the expense of content and purpose. They argue that "pedagogic method is secondary to the overall purpose of the education; second, education aiming to promote the eradication of class division must include, at the very least, some old-fashioned instruction, set into an ordered curriculum, which includes basic information and skills required to execute necessary management tasks" (Lovett, Clarke and Kilmurray 1983:144).

Will Cowburn (1986) joined the debate with a Gramscian critique of community education, arguing that initiatives such as residential adult self-education courses at Northern College and Sheffield Council's Community Work Apprenticeship Scheme are capable of producing organic intellectuals of the working class. Such organic intellectuals would be "capable of challenging taken-for-granted processes and institutions in society" (Cowburn 1986:198), including the education system, which, Cowburn (1986:209) contends, "systematically fails the working class as a class."

W. John Morgan also applauds Gramsci's "pedagogical politics," arguing that Gramsci attempts "to break the bourgeois hegemony over the consciousness of the working class" through emphasizing "the need of the workers, through the workers' party, to educate themselves towards a confident and decisive belief in the possibilities of socialism" (Morgan 1987:307). In a more recent article Morgan explores points of origin and cultural and political concern in common between Gramsci and Raymond Williams, suggesting that the work of both men "has its heuristic value, perhaps even especially so in the cold climate of socialist retreat" (Morgan 1996:71). Likewise, Youngman (1986:233–4) argues that research into this period of Gramsci's career is important for the development of a socialist theory of adult education.

Another commentator, Paul Armstrong, celebrates Gramsci's legacy of adult education as political education for socialism and his "construction of a revolutionary strategy, which could no longer be crudely seen as merely the need to seize the political apparatus of the state" (Armstrong 1988:259). He also stresses the importance of the factory councils as sites of informal political education (Armstrong 1988:258). Armstrong's reading of Gramsci stresses the central role of consciousness: he states that "the operation of hegemony is through consciousness." He conceives of adult education as counter-hegemonic, so,

A new hegemony can be created to replace the old one, a necessary preliminary for revolutionary transition—a counter-hegemony which would raise the consciousness of the proletariat to make them aware of common class interests. (Armstrong 1988:256)

He concludes that "adult education has a significant part to play in both the prefigurative work as well as the post-revolutionary consolidation" (Armstrong 1988:260).

Moving away from a primary focus on class and socialism, Thomas Pantham (1986) suggests that Gramsci and Gandhi offer a model of a type of leadership which is emancipatory "in that it can bring about a transformation of oppressive social systems and yet avoid the reproduction of the contradiction between leaders and led" (Pantham 1986:165). This paper is particularly interesting in the light of Gramsci's discussion of Gandhi and India in the prison notebooks (FSPN:117–24). Pantham draws parallels between Gramsci's pedagogical politics and Gandhi's principles of *satyagraha:* "the admission of truths as relative, non-violence and toleration, and the self-suffering of the *satyagrahis*" and his concern for the emancipation of the oppressor as well as the oppressed (Pantham 1986:177–8). The comparison is alluring, but falls down, it seems to me, in his attempt to link Gramsci with a strategy of nonviolence and self-suffering. Although the fact that Gramsci suffered horribly during his imprisonment is undeniable, he did not deliberately set out to be a martyr. Furthermore, Gramsci dismisses Gandhi's strategy of nonviolence as "a dismal and dilute form of resistance, the mattress up against the bullet" (FSPN:119).

Timothy Ireland (1987) uses Gramsci in his perceptive study of Popular Education in Brazil, which is especially interesting in this context because Popular Education in Latin America is strongly influenced by Freire. Writing at a time when political energies were being released after long years of military rule, Ireland uses Gramsci's theoretical constructs as analytical tools and undertakes his investigation in the spirit of Gramsci's writing, locating his discussion "within and with reference to a specific context or social formation," that of Brazil in the late 1980s (Ireland 1987:2).

Ireland focuses particularly on Gramsci's essays "Some Aspects of the Southern Question" (SPWII:441–62; Gramsci 1995) and the "Lyons Theses" (SPWII:340–75). He compares the political and economic divisions in Italian society in Gramsci's day with those of Brazil in the 1980s, where the division between the industrialized southeast and the poor, rural northeast "is symbolic of the Brazilian bourgeoisie's incapacity to achieve hegemony without an alliance incorporating the reactionary sectors of rural society" (Ireland 1987:13).

Ireland considers that, whereas the clergy's role as mediators between landlords and peasants is diminishing because of internal divisions within the Church, reflecting the rise of Liberation Theology, the Church still plays an important role in the production and formation of intellectuals through the schooling offered in Catholic seminaries. Ireland compares Gramsci's analysis of the reformist Modernism movement in the Roman Catholic Church in Italy with the role of the Radical Catholic movement in Brazil, contending that whereas in Gramsci's Italy the southern clergy were the reactionaries, in Brazil their modern counterparts in the northeast are the more progressive.

Ireland's contention is that Popular Education in Brazil should contribute to the formation of working class cadres capable of directing their own class and creating a new hegemonic force (Ireland 1987:27). However, to decide what this means in practice is no more simple in Brazil than for Gramsci in Italy. Ireland argues that a reading of Gramsci should lead educators to analyze the working classes in order to understand how Popular Education may best contribute to the creation of proletarian hegemony. His own analysis leads him ultimately to depart significantly from Gramsci on the question of the persistence of religious belief, and to propose an extension to Gramsci's concept of hegemony "in which Christian and 'secular' humanism fuse to form a new synthesis acceptable to believers and non-believers alike" (Ireland 1987:73).

Ireland (1987:66) outlines three positions in the debate within Popular Education centering on different interpretations of the political nature of education:

Should all facets of an issue be expounded and discussed and then those involved left to draw their own conclusions and act accordingly? Should we seek to find common ground, a line upon which all those involved agree? Should or can Popular Education programmes or processes be conducted through political parties or other autonomous organizations pertaining to the popular classes?

The last of these questions is particularly pertinent to adult educators seeking inspiration from Gramsci: as Ireland acknowledges (Ireland 1987:66), Gramsci sees adult education of the working class as an inherently political enterprise which must be given organizational force and direction by its expression in the party. Popular Education, with its fragmented form and lack of a unifying organization hardly fits this prescription. Furthermore, there is no consensus among Popular Educators as to whether the political dimension of their task, which most accept, should be interpreted in party political terms. According to Ireland, this ambiguity is often expressed "in the division of activities into the implicitly political and the explicitly political which frequently goes under the title of 'Political Education'" (Ireland 1987:70).

Ireland (1987:72) divides Popular Educators into two groups: those who favor the spontaneous approach and those who maintain the special function of the educator-agent. He counterposes the first position to that of Gramsci, who, in the prison notebooks, points out the limitations of spontaneity in the revolutionary project (SPN:196–7). Those Popular Educators who favor spontaneity deny the agency of the educator, something Gramsci, with his theory of the organic, revolutionary intellectual, never does. Furthermore, they idealize working class culture and thereby base their educational practice on an inappropriate foundation. Although Ireland considers the second position to be the more Gramscian, nevertheless he recognizes that in Gramsci's formulation the intellectual's intervention is informed by a clearly defined, though not rigid, framework of political ideas. By contrast, the conceptual parameters of Popular Education are more open-ended. Ireland follows Gramsci in contending that "the degree to which the two perspectives differ or converge will depend upon the concrete historical conditions to which Popular Education seeks to respond" (Ireland 1987:73). Ireland (1987:78) concludes in Gramscian mode that greater attention should be paid to the role of the educator or agent and to the need for some unifying organization, agency or institution: a "Modern Prince."

In a very different context, that of the industrial shopfloor, Sallie Westwood argues for a Gramscian New Times analysis on the grounds that it leads adult educators to an engagement with fundamental questions such as the relationship between knowledge and power in adult education and the relationship between adult education and forms of industrial organization. She points to the loss of an important role for adult education entailed in the demise of Fordist "powerful unions and vibrant shopfloor cultures with which adult education could connect" (Westwood 1990:15). However, she argues that post-Fordist industrial processes and working practices offer at least the possibility of a new role for adult educators, building on the adult education tradition of looking to locality and region in order to develop specific practices appropriate to local areas.

Paula Allman and John Wallis (1995b, 1990b) offer a challenge "on behalf of Gramsci" to the influence of New Times thinking in radical education, including "community development-action" and political practice on the left (1995b:120). They contend that New Times thinking is seriously flawed because it is based on a misreading of Gramsci and lacks understanding of his use of Marx's dialectic. They accuse New Times thinkers of locating the struggle "on the terrain of ideas" solely in the cultural domain (Allman and Wallis 1990b:240). This is the old accusation of culturalism, leveled not at Gramsci this time but at his New Times (which Allman and Wallis equate with post-Marxist) interpreters. Allman's and Wallis's solution, on the theoretical level, is to return Gramsci to his rightful place as an interpreter, rather than reviser, of Marx. Their "explicit goal" is "abolishing capitalism and creating a socialist-communist future." On the practical level, this requires the formation of "a Party of the Left capable, given an appropriate historical conjuncture, together with appropriate pre-figurative preparation, of realising epochal transformation" (Allman and Wallis 1995b:139–40). Against this background, they propose a three-point plan:

The first element is the philosophy of praxis, i.e. Marxism based on Marx; second—and utilising the first element—the vast majority of people must be enabled to understand their present circumstances; third to establish a reciprocal relation between party activists and the people that will enable this understanding—an understanding which will render the thinking of the people critical. (Allman and Wallis 1995b:140)

In an earlier paper Allman and Wallis (1990b:242) spell out the role this implies for radical adult educators: they must "help people acquire a dialectical perspective" to enable them to grasp "the dialectic truth of their real world." This, they contend, entails revolutionizing adult education practice, joining with others in the investigation of both local and global conditions, collaborating in "the mental penetration of the pseudo-concrete phenomena" of people's lives in order to grasp the dialectic contradictions that cause the world to move and develop as it does. They end by calling for not only "a celebration of difference" but also

a celebration of our common goals and humanity, and the beginning of human history that is critically and creatively shaped by the mass of humankind working in harmony with each other and their natural world. (Allman and Wallis 1990b:242)

Allman's and Wallis' critique of New Times thinking thus culminates in a ringing endorsement of their vision of communism. In their 1995 polemic against New Times they focus more closely on the role of the political party.

Allman's and Wallis's direction to adult educators to read Gramsci and Marx is welcome in a field which is acknowledged to be undertheorized. However, they represent the New Times project as rather more monolithic than it is in reality, the result, perhaps, of basing their critique (1995b:136–9) on the *Manifesto for New Times* (Communist Party of Great Britain 1990) and Stuart Hall's article (1989), "The Meaning of New Times," rather than on the wide range of publications and other activity since—much of it, I would argue, developing, rather than misreading Gramscian themes.[2] I also find their claim to speak "on behalf of Gramsci" troubling. Gramsci's legacy is disputed and will no doubt remain so. Commentators have every right to argue for their interpretation of Gramsci's writing, but surely no one can claim to speak on his behalf.

The year 1995 also saw the publication of *Adult Learning, Critical Intelligence and Social Change* (M. Mayo and J. Thompson eds. 1995), conceived, as Jane Thompson makes clear in her Preface, as a review of radical adult education in the United Kingdom since the publication of *Adult Education for a Change* (J. Thompson ed. 1980). It may therefore serve as a useful benchmark of the influence of Freire and Gramsci in the field of adult education in the mid-1990s, as viewed from the United Kingdom.

Some contributors to the Mayo and Thompson collection make reference to Gramsci; for example, John McIlroy on trade union education and John Grayson on tenant training. David Alexander and Ian Martin, in their excellent chapter on "Competence, Curriculum and Democracy" draw on Gramsci, on the contemporary Scottish philosopher George Davie, and on the strong tradition of independent working class education in Scotland, in order to construct a democratic resistance to the currently ascendant competency movement in education and training. This they regard as dangerous "because its technicising, reductive and individuating nature lends itself to [the] process of hegemonic reconstruction" by the New Right (Alexander and Martin 1995:82). They call instead for "the critical unity of democracy and intellect" (Alexander and Martin 1995:86) and quote Gramsci in support of their argument that adult and community educators need "to construct an intellectual-moral bloc which can make politically possible the intellectual progress of the masses and not only small intellectual groups" (Gramsci quoted in Alexander and Martin 1995:93).

Some contributors refer to Freire; for example, Wilma Fraser on making experience count and Keith Jackson on community education. In addition, Allman and Wallis use Marx, Gramsci, Freire and others in their challenge to the postmodernist condition, which is discussed below. There are some noticeable changes; for example, in the tenor of McIlroy's chapter about trade union education, indi-

cated in his title, "The Dying of the Light," when compared with
the confident tone of Doyle's and Yarnit's chapters on the same subject in the earlier book, and Barratt Brown's review, outlined above.
This needs to be seen in context: trade union education in Britain
has inevitably been affected by the loss of one third of union members since 1979.

Elsewhere, Ursula Apitzsch (1993) uses Gramsci in her interesting article on "Gramsci and the Current Debate on Multicultural
Education," arguing that multicultural education is a vehicle for the
marginalization of subaltern groups. Instead, she argues that it should
be seen in terms of a Gramscian understanding of subaltern social
strata and his critique of the concept of "national culture." However
tantalizing, as Peter Mayo points out, Apitzsch does not draw out
the implications of her argument for radical adult education practice "in areas where the issue of multiculturalism has to be confronted,
notably language classes for immigrants or community development
projects among specific ethnic groups" (Mayo 1995:7).

Gelsa Knijnik uses Gramsci in her challenging discussion of the
role of the intellectual in relation to social movements, focusing on
her research and teaching in mathematics with the landless people's
movement in Brazil (Knijnik 1993, 1996). This is discussed in the
next chapter in the context of a discussion about the role of the
adult educator as intellectual. Gramsci's concept of common sense
is central to my discussion of the meanings of mathematics in adults'
lives, in particular the relationship between mathematics and common sense implicit in many adults' "mathematics life histories"
(Coben 1997; Coben and Thumpston 1996). I have argued (Coben
1992, 1994, 1995) that it is time to revisit Gramsci in rethinking
the politics of the education of adults—an argument continued here.

Gramsci and Freire: The Case for Synthesis

As we have seen, a large number of educationists cite Freire and
Gramsci, either separately or in association. Such references are com-
monplace—almost the hallmark of the discourse of radical adult
education over the last twenty years. In a field noted for its diversity,
different writers have focused on different aspects of their work and,
of course, a number of other thinkers are also referred to, including
Marx, Althusser, Habermas and Foucault.

Some commentators, including Peter Mayo, Paula Allman and John Wallis and Peter Leonard, propose a more systematic linking of Freire's and Gramsci's ideas; their arguments are examined next.

Peter Mayo: Synthesizing Gramsci and Freire

Peter Mayo (1994) proposes a synthesis of the ideas of Gramsci and Freire in order to lay a foundation for a radical theory of adult education. He poses a series of questions which he considers should form the basis of an assessment of the potential of an educationist's work for incorporation in a theory of radical adult education for social transformation. First, does the work contain a "language of critique"? By this he means "a process of analysis which ties educational systems to systemic and structural forms of domination in the wider society," while allowing educational systems a "relative autonomy" (Mayo 1994:126). Second, does it contain a "language of possibility," meaning, does it allow room for agency, and if so, whose? On the basis of these questions, Mayo puts forward a framework for analysis in terms of sites of practice, content and social relations to determine how the kind of pedagogy proposed differs from the norm and to explore its educational and political implications.

In the course of this analysis, Mayo emphasizes that Freire denies the possibility of a neutral pedagogy and demands commitment of educators to the cause of the oppressed and to the possibility of social transformation. Mayo sees adult education, in particular, popular education, as an important forum for social transformation, with Freirean adult educators facilitating rather than directing the education process. He points out that, for Freire, the educator's role entails direction, even authority, but not authoritarianism (Freire in Horton and Freire 1990:181). He also points out that Freire has become more flexible with regard to teaching style, conceding that it may include elements of both traditional and democratic teaching under appropriate circumstances, for example, during initial meetings with students who are used to prescriptive methods (Freire in Horton and Freire 1990:160). Mayo concludes that, although in Freire's early work agency for change lay with the peasantry rather than the urban proletariat, in his more recent work "Freire's oppressed vary from context to context" (Mayo 1994:137). Mayo identifies social movements as constituting, for Freire in his later work and in his work as Secretary for Education in São Paulo, the larger context within which transformative educational initiatives can be effectively carried out (Mayo 1994:138). He concludes that Freire's writings are imbued with a language of critique and a language of possibility, indeed, of hope, which Mayo attributes to the influence of Liberation Theology (Mayo 1994:134–5).

Mayo considers that both Gramsci and Freire engage in a "war of position" and therefore their chosen sites of educational practice vary (Mayo 1994:138). As regards content, Mayo does not see Freire as primarily a literacist, rather as someone concerned with the attainment of political literacy. Freire's codification/decodification method, he considers, "can constitute an effective method to reconsider critically 'taken for granted' aspects of one's 'reality', therefore converting one's Gramscian 'common sense' to 'good sense'" (Mayo 1994:139). Mayo notes that Freire focuses exclusively on popular culture whereas Gramsci explores both high and low culture. However, he notes that they both resist the "over-romanticising" of popular culture and acknowledge "the presence, within it, of such potentially disempowering elements as superstition, magic and traditional religious beliefs" (Mayo 1994:139). He discerns the "common cause" in Gramsci's and Freire's writings as "the struggle against oppression caused by the exploitation of 'subaltern' groups by dominant, hegemonic ones" (Mayo 1994:139).

For Gramsci, transformative education can take place in a variety of sites of social practice (Mayo 1994:131) and the social relations of adult education must be "participative and radically democratic" (Mayo 1994:132). Mayo cites Gramsci's advocacy of an "active and reciprocal" relationship between teacher and student (SPN:350). This he interprets to mean that the intellectuals act in a directive capacity with the masses while allowing them some directive capacity; in this context, "a certain degree of information needs to be imparted to render any dialogical education taking place an informed one" (Mayo 1994:132).

Mayo concludes that Gramsci's writings, also, are imbued with a language of critique (Mayo 1994:127) and a language of possibility, with the organic intellectuals of the revolutionary proletariat as agents of social transformation (Mayo 1994:130). He draws the following inference for a theory of radical adult education:

The pedagogy is directive (it is intended towards a political goal) and the organic intellectual/adult educator is equipped with a body of knowledge and theoretical insight which, nevertheless, needs to be constantly tested and renewed through contact with the learner/masses. (Mayo 1994:133)

Mayo concludes that Gramsci and Freire offer combined insights for a theory of radical adult education in three main ways.

First, "radical adult education initiatives should be rooted in a commitment to confronting oppression in its different forms" (Mayo 1994:140). Second, radical adult education initiatives can play an important role in the struggle for hegemony by problematizing taken-for-granted notions concerning what is defined as reality, exposing their hidden ideologies and promulgating democratic and dialogical social relations in opposition to the legitimized power relations in society (Mayo 1994:140). Third, radical adult education initiatives derive a greater sense of agency if they are carried out in "the context of a social movement or, better still, an alliance of movements" both in nonformal education and within the state system (Mayo 1994:140).

Mayo's formulation raises many important questions. For example, how should oppression be identified? This is not always a straightforward matter, as the discussion of Freire's bipolar oppressor/oppressed model in Chapter 3 illustrates. Mayo agrees but considers this a problem for both Gramsci and Freire: he submits that

failure to take account of the complexity of the nature of oppression, and of the interchangeability of roles between oppressor and oppressed, is one of the lacunae in both Gramsci's and Freire's writings. (Mayo 1994:144)

But if this is so, how does Gramsci's and Freire's work help us to understand how oppression should be confronted through radical adult education?

Also, how are "democratic and dialogical social relations" defined? I have argued that Freire's work does not give an adequate basis for such a definition. Arguably Gramsci does not do so either, since for him many aspects of social relations, including those of the adult education group, would be regulated by the revolutionary political party.

Furthermore, on what basis are "hidden ideologies" identified and exposed? Borrowing a term from the London, Edinburgh Weekend Return Group (1979, 1980), Mayo contends that committed adult educators can

become mediating influences in the process of cultural transmission, reinterpreting mandates in the light of their own hidden, radical agendas—being "in and against the state," especially where there is a concentration of people from a particularly oppressed social category, such as the unemployed. (Mayo 1994:141)

While this may be an accurate picture of the aspirations of many radical adult educators, it points up the problem: agency does not lie with the oppressed in Freire's formulation, but with the educators. This is because, however much they engage in dialogue, they are deemed to hold the knowledge that counts, they are the ones with the agendas, hidden or otherwise. What are these radical agendas? In Gramsci's case the agenda is clear (but nonetheless problematic for that), but in Freire's less so. Also, from whom is the educator's agenda hidden? The answer is presumably the educator's employer or sponsor (the state or an agency of the state). It is perhaps not surprising that, as Torres (1993:127) points out (noted above), the main proponents of Freire's pedagogy, including Freire himself, work in relatively autonomous institutions. But the problem is that the agenda must therefore also be hidden from the learner, at least at the outset, so it is difficult to see how "democratic and dialogical social relations" can be established by subterfuge.

Mayo's emphasis on social movements rather than political parties is perhaps more Freirean than Gramscian, although Freire is a relatively recent convert to the idea of social movements and they do not sit entirely happily with his notion of people as trapped in their "culture of silence" until "conscientized" by the Freirean educator. But do the new social movements constitute potential elements of a Gramscian revolutionary hegemonic settlement? Where is the organizing principle, the (post)modern equivalent of Gramsci's "Modern Prince"? How should the adult educator relate to the social movements (an important question addressed in different ways in very different contexts by Ball 1992 and Knijnik 1993, 1996)? On what grounds should the adult educator distinguish between competing social movements? Faced with a possibility of working with a tenants' association, an antiabortion group, or a group opposed to the building of a new highway, with whom should the radical adult educator engage, given that he or she should, according to Mayo, identify totally with the group's cause (Mayo 1994:142)? What if the tenants' association were seeking to exclude nonwhite residents, or residents with a history of antisocial behavior from the housing estate? Real life is messy in ways that are not catered to in this formulation.

Mayo argues that "Gramsci's concept of a 'historic bloc' [sic][3] must transcend its 'national-popular' character to begin to signify an alliance of social movements across national boundaries" (Mayo 1994:144–5). There is an important point here: in a way (blurring for a moment the distinction between social movements and political parties and leaving aside problems about Mayo's conception of a "historic bloc") Gramsci was part of just such a movement—the Comintern. However, his focus was, undeniably, on the nation-state: on the prospects for—and then the failure of—revolution in Italy. In this age of globalization it is tempting to dismiss the nation-state as no longer relevant but this would be premature. Those who, like the Kurds and the Palestinians, are without a nation-state can testify to its continuing political and economic importance. It is the specificity of Gramsci's focus, his recognition of the contingent quality of events and human agency, that marks his departure from the determinist Marxism of the Second International. It is also part of what makes him useful in envisaging a radical theory of adult education: any such theory must have regard for the particularities of place, person and circumstance, while seeing these in the global context. Mayo's central point is valid: a radical adult education theory worthy of the name must transcend national boundaries. But Freire's vision of a Third World redeemed through revolution is not transcendent of place so much as utopian—without place, as the subsequent histories of Nicaragua, Guinea-Bissau and Grenada indicate.

On the question of language and culture, Mayo points to Gramsci's argument that subordinated people should learn the dominant language in order to survive in the power struggle, but he over-looks Gramsci's important notes on the development of a new common language (SCW:183; Gramsci 1984). Mayo offers a "combined" view in which radical adult educators "critically appropriate elements from the dominant culture in their attempts to empower learners to engage successfully in a 'war of position' with socially transformative ends in mind" (Mayo 1994:143).

The problem is that, however sincere their commitment to socially transformative ends, in this formulation the educators hold all the cards. Mayo's contention that the adult educator must be totally committed to the learner's cause (Mayo 1994:142) is contradictory here, as it denies agency to the educator by subordinating his or her agency to that of the learner. For Mayo the problem does not arise, perhaps because he reads the "organic" in Gramsci's "organic intellectual" to mean primarily someone who is organically part of the group with which he or she is working as an educator. In this reading the analogy is biological—specifically, botanical—rather than political, implying that the organic intellectual is rooted in the group in the same way that a plant is rooted in the soil. There is evidence for this in Mayo's discussion of the relationship of educators, as change agents, with the class or group with which they are working (Mayo 1994:137), where he cites Freire's use of words like "growing" (1971:61) and "in communion" (Freire in Freire and Faundez 1989:56). But this is at best a partial reading of Gramsci. I have argued in Chapter 2 that Gramsci's primary meaning of "organic" is functional rather than positional; he emphasizes the organic intellectual's role in organizing and mediating the revolution, not his or her rootedness.

Mayo contends that Gramsci's organic intellectual and Freire's facilitator can be combined to produce an adult educator "equipped with a theoretical understanding of the adult learners' predicament" who "engages in a directive form of adult education" (Mayo 1994:141). He goes on to say:

The culture of the learner makes its presence felt through a dialogical teaching process. The educator's task is to facilitate the means whereby this culture is examined critically by the learners themselves, so that the "common sense," which is a hallmark of this culture, is converted to "good sense." (Mayo 1994:141)

But Gramsci does not—quite—say that common sense is the hallmark of the learner's culture: it is *"common* sense" at least partly because it is common to us all. Mayo contends that one means of overcoming common sense is through Freire's codification/ decodification process, but he does not question the fact that it is the educators who hold the key to the code. Mayo leaves unaddressed the vital question of what constitutes good sense, the question that Gramsci devoted his life to trying to answer—and that has been thrown into sharp relief by the collapse of Soviet communism in 1989–90.

This is a problem built into Mayo's analytical framework: he does not explicitly address the question of the purpose of the educational activity. His point about a "language of critique" implies a recognition of issues of purpose but does not address them directly. Thus an educational activity might fulfill all of Mayo's criteria to be considered radical (it might be intrinsically radical in educational terms) and represent a "language of critique" with respect to existing social forms, but contribute toward a nonradical cause (it might not be extrinsically radical). Without a consideration of purpose we cannot judge a specific example of educational practice in terms of the legitimacy of its explicit aims, how far it has achieved them and whether these are intrinsic or extrinsic. Neither can we appreciate the tensions between the purposes of the organization, which may be different at different locations within the organization and those of the educators and their students. And if we cannot identify these we cannot identify—and use—what Gramsci would call "terrains of struggle."

Without adequate criteria for considering the purpose of the educational activity, the scope for misunderstanding between learners, trapped in their Freirean culture of silence and their Gramscian common sense, and radical adult educators armed with their hidden agendas seems limitless. Freire's vision of the oppressed as humanized (civilized? redeemed?) through a process of conscientization initiated and controlled by a born-again leader/educator, motivated by love, may be inspirational for those who identify with the educator/

leader/lover, but what of the other, the oppressed, who has not sought—and may not want—the educator's love or leadership?

Paula Allman and John Wallis: Conceptualizing Freire and Gramsci Together

Also proposing what Mayo would call a synthesis of Gramsci's and Freire's ideas, are Paula Allman and John Wallis, who acknowledge their debt to Gramsci, Freire and Marx as inspiration for their work over the last decade and more (Allman and Wallis 1995a:21). In a series of articles and conference papers, Allman and Wallis develop this theme (see, for example, Allman 1987, 1988, 1994; Allman and Wallis 1988, 1990a, 1990b, 1995a, 1995b).

Allman makes the case for Freire and Gramsci to be conceptualized together in a project of "education for socialism" in a chapter published in 1988 (Allman 1988:92). Her argument is briefly outlined here, since it underpins her later writing on this topic, both as a single author and in her collaborations with Wallis. In Allman's formulation, Gramsci's ideas set the philosophical framework wherein Freire's approach may bear fruit specifically in educational practice. Gramsci "enables us to understand the need for an educative relationship in every aspect of political practice" and "Freire offers us a specific approach by which we can seek to establish an appropriate set of socialist educative relationships" (Allman 1988:105). Freire's approach is underpinned by two interrelated assumptions: first, that to be fully human means to have the potential to overcome one's conditioning through critically conscious agency; second, that education can serve "either to maintain that conditioning or to enable people to become critically aware of it and critically engaged in transforming the relations which sustain it" (Allman 1988:96). On this basis, Freire's educational approach entails

a critical investigation of the way in which ideology is embedded in common sense, magical consciousness (what Gramsci terms folklore) and sometimes even revolutionary consciousness and practice. (Allman 1988:94)

For Allman, Freire's approach "strikes at the heart of the relations which sustain ideology" and Gramsci "offers us a strategy by which we can begin the conscious struggle to create the ethical political leadership that will lead to a will and a collective understanding of the need for socialist revolution" (Allman 1988:109). Gramsci's strategy entails two tasks: the replacement of ideology with a more advanced or developed method of thinking; and, during the struggle to establish hegemony within civil society, the expression of socialist ideology, a conception of the world and human beings through transformed social relationships. This, she contends, is entirely compatible with Freire's emphasis on transforming relations, although Freire takes us much further in understanding which relations need to be transformed and in understanding what these transformations would entail.

Allman states that while "Gramsci takes us a long way forward in understanding the dominant ideology of our own society and how this ideology works" (1988:103), neither Freire nor Gramsci takes us far enough in our understanding of ideology, and for further clarification she turns to Marx, Althusser, Hall and Poulantzas. Contrasting "ideology" with "science," she cites Marx's use of "science" to mean both "a conceptual method" and "knowledge, truth or a fixed body of content;" it is with science as method that Allman is most concerned (Allman 1988:105). Allman describes ideology as characterized by processes of displacement and concealment which mask or conceal reality (Allman 1988:108). On this basis, Allman proposes "dialectic thinking," as opposed to "ideological thinking," as a means of unmasking reality. It follows that "dialectic thinking" is "scientific," although as "a new form of cognition" it is not yet fully understood. Allman urges socialists to work together to explicate the dialectic method more fully (Allman 1988:109).

In their 1990 article Allman and Wallis spell out the implications for "really" radical education of their reading of Gramsci, Freire and Marx. They base their "praxis" on "Marx's 'theory of consciousness'" (Allman and Wallis 1990a:16) encapsulated in the statement in *The German Ideology:* "Life is not determined by consciousness, but consciousness by life" (Marx and Engels in McLellan ed. 1977:164). Really radical education, they contend, must be based on an understanding of the relationship between surface appearances and "current developments in the dialectic contradictions of capitalism." Tactics ("short-term or immediate struggles") must be linked with "strategy (the longer-term plan for social transformation)." Radical education is "one of our tactical struggles and must be a site of critical, revolutionary praxis." Against this background, radical adult and community educators must struggle "to transform two interconnected relations": their relationship to knowledge and the relationship between teacher and learner (Allman and Wallis 1990a:21). Finally, Allman and Wallis argue that really radical education entails three elements: the political commitment of intellectuals as educators; the generation of prefigurative education on a wide scale to create a sense of the human potential for genuine change; the fusion of knowledge and action so that the "'logics' of racism and other oppressions are neither tenable nor socially necessary" (Allman and Wallis 1990a:27).

Allman and Wallis (1990a:24) warn against interpreting Freire's work as dichotomizing method and content, a point reiterated in Allman's 1994 article in which she stresses the need for a Marxist reading of Freire in order to avoid the "damaging tendency" to associate Freire with pedagogy or process and Gramsci with knowledge, content and organization and thus to regard Freire's work as incompatible with Gramsci's (Allman 1994:145).

In their "challenge to the impasse in radicalism created by the post-modern condition" (Allman and Wallis 1995a:31), Allman and Wallis expand on this theme and propose the following line of action for radicals. First, they call for a reclamation of "the original theoretical sources that can inform a radical praxis of education and politics" (primarily Marx, Gramsci and Freire, as well as primary-source historical studies of radical education). This would help radicals to "fully develop a dialectical theory of consciousness and a critical concept of ideology as well as the ability to analyze the world dialectically." Second, they want to preserve the recognition of human difference and diversity "whilst also strongly promoting the common needs and goals of humanity and the natural world." Third, they argue that the relativization of truth characteristic of postmodernism must be challenged. Radicals must distinguish between "dialectical/radical concepts of truth and other, ultimately conservative, enlightenment concepts of truth" which "focus solely on universal, trans-historical, static or finite truths." The kinds of truth for which radicals must search fall into four types "which are valuable only in relation to one another": metatranshistorical truths (truths which it is difficult to think could be otherwise than as they are); truths which conceivably might be otherwise; truths which pertain to the foundation of a particular social formation; conjuncturally specific truths. Taken together, Allman and Wallis (1995a:31–2) contend that these four types of truth constitute a dialectical concept of truth, necessary if radicals are to challenge the "abandonment of the quest for truth so characteristic of postmodern relativism."

Armed with this concept of truth, radicals can challenge "the postmodernist condition and the oppressive experiences within capitalism by initiating educational/political projects in which participants can experience, even if only briefly, the meaning of a socialist/radical vision." This must include challenging "every form of oppression and the ideological praxes that legitimate them, e.g. patriarchy, racism, ageism" (Allman and Wallis 1995a:32).

Allman's and Wallis's sustained attempt to elucidate the principles of a radical project of adult education is to be welcomed for its seriousness and its emphasis on original theoretical sources. It represents a significant contribution to the development of theory in what is acknowledged to be an undertheorized field. There is much in their arguments which I find valuable, but also several key aspects with which I take issue.

For example, I certainly agree that Freire's work should not be depoliticized—or, at least, that this is contrary to his intention; after all, he constantly stresses that his is a political pedagogy. Where I disagree is on the nature of Freire's politics. Allman and Wallis see Freire as primarily a Marxist; I see him, as I have argued in Chapter 3, as *Marxisante*, rather than Marxist, a Brazilian Catholic radical, in many ways typical of his class, gender and generation. I see the depoliticization of Freire's ideas (for example, the pseudo-Freireanism described by Archer and Costello 1990) as symptomatic of the lack of clarity of political focus in much of his writing. It therefore does not surprise me that depoliticization has been a feature of the interpretation of Freire's ideas, together with politicizations in ways of which he might disapprove.

I also agree that Freire should not be seen as dichotomizing method and content and, like them, I reject the tendency to associate Freire with pedagogy or process and Gramsci with knowledge, content and organization. Freire's method is always secondary to his pedagogical purpose of conscientization, which entails, as Allman and Wallis contend, a critical engagement with content. However, for Freire, content varies according to the context; he is rather more specific on method, so again it is perhaps not surprising if his method has been seized upon by educators and policy makers anxious for something that might work where other methods have failed. The association of Gramsci with content rather than process is justified partially by reference to his writings on education, but is less viable if his writings on the factory councils or the editorial board of a political journal are taken into account, as I have argued they should be (see Chapter 2). Arguably, Gramsci is vague on process or method actually in the adult classroom, but then his concept of the educative revolution is not primarily a matter for the classroom. Unlike Allman and Wallis, I do not see Freire's and Gramsci's approaches to content or method as compatible simply because their ideas have been wrongly dichotomized in this fashion. Instead, I suspect Gramsci would find Freire's pedagogical method rather too reminiscent of the "romantic phase" of the French *nouvelle education* which Taylor persuasively argues was an important inspiration for it. I also think he would find the Freirean approach to content too arbitrary, too much at the mercy of the educators' agendas in setting the parameters of research into the learners' reality.

On oppression, I agree with Allman and Wallis that radical adult education must challenge oppression in all its forms or else be party to them. However, I find Allman's and Wallis's concept of oppression reductionist; that is, they appear to believe all forms of oppression (by race, gender, and so on) may be reduced to one cause: capitalism, hence their insistence that particular oppressions should always be seen in the wider context of the oppression of the capitalist system. Rather, I would argue that oppressions of race, gender and so forth are manifest in particular forms under capitalism and may be manifest in other forms under different forms of social organization. For example, patriarchy is a feature of feudal as well as capitalist societies; similarly, capitalists did not invent racial oppression, for all that they frequently support and profit from it, and under certain circumstances they may even decide it is bad for business.

Oppression by race, gender and so on would not automatically be eliminated by the eradication of capitalism—that would depend on the nature of the socialism inaugurated by the epochal transformation they propose.

To me the nature of socialism is a wide open question. I find Allman's and Wallis's certainty on the subject rather alarming. I find no real grounds for certainty about the nature of the desired society in Gramsci, whose writing and other political activity were all directed at trying to answer that very question: nowhere does he announce that he has found the answer. Nor, indeed, are there grounds for certainty in Marx, whose own critique of capitalism was unfinished when he died, leaving only scattered references to the nature of the communist society that would displace it. It seems to me to stem more from Freire, who is a prophetic thinker, constantly looking ahead to the state of grace in which humankind will have achieved its ontological vocation, as he sees it, to be more fully human.

Allman's and Wallis's point that radical adult education must entail the transformation of our relationship with knowledge, together with the transformation of the relationship between teacher and learner, lies at the heart of their argument and is profoundly important in the delineation of a theory of radical adult education. On the latter point, I find Gramsci's organic intellectual a better model for adult educators than the self-sacrificing Freirean educator, as I have made clear in the discussion above. Seeing both the educator *and learner* as, at least potentially, Gramscian organic intellectuals, is, I consider, an important safeguard for the learner against incorporation into any hidden agenda the educator may have. This is an ethical point in that it seems to me particularly important in situations in which educators and learners are putting themselves at mortal risk, as is likely to be the case in a revolution (a "war of manoeuvre" in Gramsci's terms). But it is important in both the "war of position" and the "war of manoeuvre," since hegemony cannot be built on ignorance: the learner must have some idea of the nature of the educational enterprise. For the educator, the organic intellectual role must force him or her to consider the political purpose of the educational encounter and his or her own organizing role within it, as well as focusing attention on the potential interchangeability of teacher and learner.

The transformation of the relationship of the learner and educator (in Allman's and Wallis's—and Freire's—formulation, the learners/educators) with knowledge is the key to the radical education process—and warrants a book in itself. Allman and Wallis agree with Gramsci and Freire that that relationship must be critical and I agree, although I find more support for this idea in Gramsci's writing, and his example, than in Freire's, despite the latter's insistence that his is a critical pedagogy. Freire's commitment to criticality seems to me to rest too heavily on notions of authenticity and reality which cannot be verified outside his frame of reference. As such, it strikes me as a sincere but nonetheless ultimately rhetorical quality in his work.

But the relationship to knowledge postulated by Gramsci is also problematic in that it rests on his unfinished philosophical project. We can read Gramsci as far as he got with the prison notebooks, although even this is difficult for nonreaders of Italian, and, for English speakers, will remain so until Buttigieg's mammoth task of producing an English edition of the notebooks is completed. Even then, the scope for interpreting Gramsci in different ways will hardly diminish, since his is an irremediably open text, and inevitably new readers will bring new understandings to bear on his writings. In that Gramsci's project is a development of Marxism, we can return to the source, Marx himself, with the advantage over Gramsci that we have access to *The German Ideology* and other of Marx's and Marx and Engels's writings which were not available to him. We also have the historical advantage that, with the collapse of the Soviet bloc regimes with their particular fetishizations of Marx and Engels, we have the opportunity to look afresh at Marxism.

Looking afresh at—and beyond—Marxism is what New Times thinking is about and it is what Laclau and Mouffe and others are doing in their project of post-Marxism, which I would characterize as a left strand of postmodernism. But these attempts are decried by Allman and Wallis, who seek instead to reclaim Gramsci from the postmodernists, post-Marxists and New Timers. I find their description of the postmodern condition suffers from the same tendency to oversimplification that characterized their critique of New Times thinking, outlined above. They tend to conflate postmodernism, as an intellectual project, with the postmodern condition, as a descriptive category, and characterize both as irredeemably relativistic, rather than as complex phenomena encompassing a range of political, philosophical and other tendencies, including relativism.

Allman's and Wallis's (1995a:31) elaboration of four kinds of "dialectical/radical concepts of truth" as alternatives to both the postmodern abandonment of truth and the enlightenment concept of truth as "universal, transhistorical, static or finite" I find unconvincing because it is based on a false dichotomy. Not all post-modernists have abandoned the search for truth; rather, many would say that they interrogate received notions of truth. Also, the enlightenment was as much about the testing of truths through scientific experiment as it was about the assertion of truths as "universal, transhistorical, static or finite." Furthermore, in Allman's and Wallis's formulation, how does an understanding of truths as meta-transhistorical (truths which it is difficult to think could be otherwise than as they are) do more than indicate the limits of the thinker's imagination? Do they mean that it is important to be aware that our conceptions of truth are limited by our imaginations? But how is that different from a relativist view of truth which insists that it varies depending on whose truth it is? Allman's and Wallis's other categories of truth are also problematic: without the benefit of hindsight, how are we to distinguish truths which hold across history to date but which conceivably might change in the future, from meta-transhistorical truths which do not? Truths which pertain to the foundation of a particular social formation would include racist and sexist "truths" and "conjuncturally specific truths" likewise (Allman and Wallis 1995a:31–2). Taken together, these four types of truth constitute an unsound basis for a dialectical concept of truth, which in turn calls into question Allman's and Wallis's chosen tools of dialectical analysis and ideology critique. If their conceptualization of truth (or rather, truths) is flawed, what does this say about their concept of ideology, as the inverse of truth? Allman and Wallis seem to me trapped in a true/false dichotomy which owes far more to Freire than Gramsci.

Too many questions are begged here. So, also, when they state (Allman and Wallis 1995a:31): "We need to develop a new and concrete idea of equality that celebrates our individuality, our diversity, and considers these as qualitative riches which could benefit both individuals and the 'common good'"; I ask how is the common good defined and by whom?

Peter Leonard: Freire and Gramsci Considered Together

Finally, to Peter Leonard, who reflects on his work with a group who might be considered to have the common good as a professional goal: social workers (Leonard 1993).

Unlike Mayo, or Allman and Wallis, Leonard is not here arguing *for* the synthesis of Gramsci and Freire; rather he is reflecting on the ways in which Freire and Gramsci, "*especially when considered together*" (Leonard 1993:160) figured in his and his colleagues' attempts to develop a critical pedagogy of social work education from 1974 to 1986 at the University of Warwick, England. His account may thus serve as a coda to the discussion above.

Leonard traces his intellectual encounters with Gramsci and Freire in the mid-1970s, in "a political climate which was increasingly encouraging broad left alliances" within which "the conjunction of ideas originating from both Marxism and the social gospel of the church seemed especially interesting" (Leonard 1993:160). Gramsci and Freire fitted very well with this orientation. In addition, Leonard points out that both Gramsci and Freire believe that collectively organized cultural action can make a difference and that both are voluntarists, opposed to left determinism (Leonard 1993:160–1). The "connection between individual consciousness and subordination" emphasized by both Gramsci and Freire, also served to encourage "the struggle against fatalism," a professional hazard of social workers (Leonard 1993:161).

Against this background, Leonard (1993:164) describes the attempt to make operational Freire's conception of dialogical education. He recalls frequent references to organic intellectuals of the working class, but the idea that was grasped "most fiercely was that of ideological struggle, the ongoing 'war of position'" (Leonard 1993:166).

Although Gramsci's and Freire's ideas were influential, Leonard reflects that "no complete alternative single *model* of social work practice was established," and in this respect practice at the Warwick School of social work education differs from that of Allman and Wallis, who describe their "sustained effort to engage in radical education" in the university context in terms of their model, outlined above (Allman and Wallis 1995a:22–5). Instead, Leonard describes how the school "became an arena in which various critical perspectives—feminist, socialist, antiracist—could be tried out and argued." Leonard welcomes this critical pluralism, stating, in Freirean terms, that the educational process was thereby "able to maintain its dialogical character, for no single orthodoxy ruled and no single banking system could be established" (Leonard 1993:164).

However, maintaining dialogical relationships between students and teachers in this context was "always problematic, always needing renewed commitment" (Leonard 1993:164). In particular, there was a continuing challenge from radical and socialist feminism, which "confronted what was seen as the 'male Marxism' of many teachers and students." This "male Marxism" was accused of "objectification, economism, workerism and commitment to monolithic party organizations as the vehicles for revolutionary change" (Leonard 1993:164–5). Leonard describes how "the emphasis in the feminist critique on consciousness-raising and its attack on 'fatalism' resonated with Freire's work, as did its humanism and its emphasis on the role of ideology in social change." But feminism is not a unified entity either, and "the separatist radical tendency within feminism [. . .] served to provide a continuous critique of the socialist enterprise of the School" (Leonard 1993:165). Meanwhile, the "anti-racist critique" was "critical of both Marxism and feminism." Furthermore, "the connection of Freire with the Third World struggle, with liberation theology, and with Marxism" all featured in the dialogue of the Warwick School. Leonard reports that

It enabled, eventually, the recognition of the similarity and "equality" of the various oppressions resulting from the social divisions of race, gender, and class, and so formed the basis of discourse concerning the interconnection between the various social divisions and their implications for social work practice. (Leonard 1993:165)

Nevertheless, Leonard warns that "the attempt to use ideas generated in different cultural contexts or different historical periods is always fraught with dangers: dangers of oversimplification, vulgarization, distortion" (Leonard 1993:165). Furthermore, he reminds us that "the continued vitality of a triumphal, nature-destroying capitalism shows us that the critical perspectives of Freire and Gramsci are having little impact on mass politics" (Leonard 1993:165).

Leonard concludes that the three issues which deserve most attention in the development of a critical socialist practice are: "The role of the intellectual, the development of critical pluralism, and the place of subjectivity" (Leonard 1993:166).

The first of these, the role of the intellectual, he sees as personally and professionally problematic: rather than Gramscian organic intellectuals, he considers himself and his colleagues to have been Gramscian intellectual defectors "left-wing traditional academics who have an initial role to play in the interregnum between the old order and the establishment of new developed class forces which can push revolutionary activity forward." As intellectual defectors, he and his colleagues "faced, but never fully escaped from, the dangers inherent in traditional bourgeois intellectual activity—élitism, the cult of the expert, the belief in the superiority of mental over manual labor" (Leonard 1993:166). On the second point, the pluralist discourse of the Warwick School may have enabled Leonard and his colleagues to avoid dogma, but "in spite of their humanism, Freire and Gramsci present us always with the dangers of charisma, the certainty, the dominance of ideas over practice, the compelling belief system" (Leonard 1993:166). Finally, Leonard concludes that Freire and Gramsci "show us the necessity for a theory of social construction of individuality without actually articulating one themselves" (Leonard 1993:167).

I suspect that many radical adult educators would recognize the dilemmas that Leonard outlines. Many would also identify, if a little ruefully, with his point about being an "intellectual defector." But I do not find his pluralist solution entirely convincing. In what ways is there "'equality' of the various oppressions resulting from the social divisions of race, gender, and class"? Does he mean that these are all reducible to one cause, as it seems to me Allman and Wallis are saying? Is it rather that oppressions based on race, gender, and class are equal in their effects on the individual or on society? This is manifestly not so, and who should know this better than social workers, who are dealing precisely with the unequal effects of differential oppressions? A "discourse concerning the interconnection between the various social divisions and their implications for social work practice" sounds to me exactly what is needed in education for social work, but why does it have to be based on a notion of equality of the effects of oppression? Such a notion is not Gramscian—Gramsci's emphasis on specificity and contingency in his concept of hegemony runs counter to any homogenization of the effects of oppression. Is it Freirean? Not exactly. Neo-Freirean, perhaps, insofar as Freire's bipolar concept of oppression lends itself to a dichotomized view of the effects of oppression.

Leonard's final point, that Freire and Gramsci "show us the necessity for a theory of social construction of individuality without actually articulating one themselves" is well made. A related need is for a theory of the constitution of knowledge taking full account of adults' informal learning and the constitution of knowledge by adults with little or no formal education.[4] Without these it is difficult to see how a truly radical politics of adult education can be created, one that can explore the particular features of adult learning and articulate the relationship of knowledge and understanding to social and political change.

Conclusion

Leonard gives us a glimpse, in microcosm, of similar debates in other arenas in which feminist, socialist and antiracist ideas are being tried out and argued, and into which Gramsci's and Freire's names are inexorably drawn. To the extent that those debates are reflected in the literature reviewed here they reveal a popularity poll headed by Freire—as the radical adult educator's adult educator. Both Gramsci and Freire emerge as radical heroes, but by this reckoning, Gramsci is in second place with a more specialist following (in participatory research and trade union education, for example) and frequently appears in the literature as an adjunct of Freire, either in casual association or more systematically linked, as by Mayo and Allman and Wallis.

The literature on Freire is noticeably polarized, for and against, with the majority for. Some of those against have been vitriolic in their condemnation (*viz.* Berger 1976). Against this background it is noticeable that commentators on Freire are often at pains to place any negative comments in the context of overall approval—continuing a tradition of the "loving critic" set by Boston (1972). The result is that criticism is muted on key issues such as the nature of racist and sexist oppression and the role of adult educators in response to it. That cannot be good for the health of the debates into which Freire's name is drawn and ultimately it must impede the development of a radical political theory of adult education.

The Gramsci literature is noticeably less polarized than that on Freire. While Gramsci is not immune from negative criticism it seems likely that those who might disagree with him are just not citing him, rather than citing him in order to argue against him. In this sense Gramsci is in the wings while Freire is center stage—adult educators who want to signal their support for a radical politics of adult education have to take account of Freire; there is not the same imperative to engage with Gramsci.

Unlike Freire, Gramsci is not specifically addressing adult educators per se, so there is a work of translation between fields to be done and much of the adult education literature on Gramsci is of this type. Translation inevitably involves putting some kind of gloss on the work in question and commentators can and do disagree on matters of interpretation. Where Gramsci's work has been used inappropriately (most notably by Entwistle in his polemic against the "new sociology of education") his supporters have sprung to his defence. Allman's and Wallis's polemic against postmodernist relativism is of a different order. Although both are using Gramsci to shore up positions they perceive as under threat, Entwistle seems to have been deliberately provoking the Left in education in his choice of Gramsci to support his argument against a position espoused by Gramsci's natural constituency. By contrast, Allman and Wallis are attempting to reclaim the left ground from postmodernists and Marxist revisionists by reference to Gramsci's, and increasingly in their more recent work, Marx's writings, which take on a scriptural quality in their work.

If Freire is the radical adult educator's adult educator, Gramsci is the radical adult educator's political theorist. This is the nub of Allman's, and Allman's and Wallis's argument—that Gramsci supplies the political theory needed to underpin Freire's radical political pedagogy. Mayo's proposal to "synthesize" Gramsci and Freire is an integral, rather than a compensatory project; that is, he is not using

Gramsci or Freire to complement each other and compensate for holes in each other's theoretical fabric. Although, as I have argued, his critical framework is flawed, Mayo's project is considerably redeemed by the openness of his approach and his willingness to interrogate both Freire's and Gramsci's texts; Mayo's is not a scriptural reading. Nevertheless, I have argued that Gramsci's and Freire's ideas are not sufficiently compatible to be usefully conjoined in the construction of a political theory of radical adult education.

The persistence of the linkage of Gramsci's and Freire's ideas can be explained in part by the particular historical factors outlined in Leonard's account. For a time Gramsci and Freire "considered together" as Leonard puts it, seemed to fill a need for radical left theory of the education of adults (in this case, in social work in Britain) in a period when broad left alliances seemed to offer a way forward. But Gramsci's and Freire's place in the pantheon of radical heroes has always been contested—in Leonard's account, more vigorously in the field than in the literature.

Leonard's warning about the "dangers of charisma" is timely here. Do we—should we—need radical heroes—or heroines—in order to think through issues of the education of adults in relation to social change? This question is considered in the next, and final chapter.

Notes

1. The concept of "anomie" as a social condition characterized by the breakdown of norms governing social interaction was developed by Emile Durkheim (1952) in his work on suicide and enlarged by R.K. Merton (1967) into a general theory of deviant behavior.

2. See, for example, Laclau and Mouffe (1990), Showstack Sassoon (1994), Holub (1992) and others. An example of the "other activity" referred to is Signs of the Times, an independent discussion group committed to "remaking the political" through an exploration of the "New Times" analysis. The London-based group runs seminar series and conferences and publishes discussion papers and books (Perryman ed. 1994, 1996). Details of Signs of the Times seminars, conferences and discussion papers are available from Signs of the Times, PO Box 10684, London N15 6XA, UK.

3. This should be "historical bloc" (see Chapter 2, p. 15). Boothman, in the General Introduction to FSPN points out that the English translation of Gramsci's term *blocco storico* is everywhere rendered "historical bloc," as in the text of SPN. However, the index to SPN gives the misleading translation "historic bloc," "as if the emphasis were on the momentous nature of such a bloc [. . .] compounded by the mistaken impression among some people that by this term Gramsci meant a bloc of social alliances" (FSPN:xi). This seems to be precisely the mistake that Mayo is making here.

4.   Important work on adults' informal learning processes has been done by Jean Lave (1988) and on the constitution of knowledge by adults with little or no formal education by Juan Carlos Llorente (1996). The classic study of adults' informal learning projects is by Allen Tough (1979).

Chapter 6
Gramsci and Freire: Radical Heroes?

Despite the best efforts of commentators reviewed in the previous chapter, I suspect that the majority of adult educators, while they may be aware of Freire and Gramsci (especially Freire) as important figures in the field, may not know their work in any detail. Freire's prizes and honorary doctorates reflect and add to his international prestige and raise the public profile of adult education. But his popularity among adult educators may derive less from a careful reading of his texts (although most have probably read *Pedagogy of the Oppressed*) than from a more casual second-hand acquaintance, mediated through ideas of "good practice." Freire's eclecticism means that he is known to different constituencies: his politics, his educational techniques, his theology, his philosophy, are all stressed by different commentators and read (literally and metaphorically) by practitioners from a variety of perspectives. In the First World also, Freire's popularity among adult educators may reflect romantic yearnings for faraway places where good and evil, progressive and reactionary, Left and Right, and right and wrong seem to stand in sharper relief; where the stakes are higher and adult education might make a real contribution to social justice and social change.

Gramsci, likewise, is emblematic of monumental struggles. He is a tragic figure, enormously important in the development of Marxist thought and increasingly influential in a wide range of fields. He seems to offer a noble vision of adult education as a key element in the creation of revolutionary hegemony. He was a real revolutionary, but the cause he lived and died for seems to have all but collapsed and it is futile to wonder whether history would have taken a different course if he had been at liberty during the 1930s and survived into the period after World War II. Nevertheless, his ideas are very important for anyone seeking to understand the education of adults in terms of its political purpose. But reading Gramsci requires some effort on the part of the anglophone reader—hence the importance of selections of his writings such as Hoare and Nowell Smith's selection from the prison notebooks (SPN) and Forgacs's *Gramsci Reader* (GR), and hence, also, the disproportionate influence of Entwistle's (1979) book. Unlike Freire, Gramsci is not an eclectic or syncretic thinker, but the openness of his most important text, the prison notebooks, means that his work, like Freire's, has been subject to various and sometimes starkly divergent interpretations.

Since their work is in the public domain, both Freire and Gramsci must submit to the enthusiastic promulgation or refutation of their ideas by people with strong convictions, some of whom may have very different agendas from their own. Their names figure in debates on issues they may not have addressed in their published work and if their ideas are misinterpreted, they cannot speak for themselves to set the record straight. It is as if their ideas have taken on a life of their own, so that merely to mention "dialogue" or "praxis" in the company of adult educators triggers an expectation of a certain set of "Freirean" attitudes and beliefs that might not have been approved by Freire himself. Indeed, Freire's ideas seem to be particularly vulnerable to misappropriation and a considerable amount of energy has gone into efforts by some of his supporters to distinguish the real from the pseudo-Freirean practice; Freire himself seemed constantly to be trying to explain what he meant. Similarly, "organic intellectuals," "hegemony," "terrains of struggle" are all hallmarks of a Gramscian discourse of adult education that may be used to legitimize practice that Gramsci himself might disown. The "dangers of charisma, the certainty, the dominance of ideas over practice, the compelling belief system" that Leonard (1993:166) warns us of, seem to me to apply more to Gramsci's and Freire's ideas in this reified sense than to what either has actually written or said. But these are real dangers nonetheless.

Freire's ideas—and Freire himself—seem particularly vulnerable to mythification. To his many admirers, Freire seems to offer a noble vision of adult education as politically liberating and spiritually redemptive, shot through with poetic insights, imbued with hope and crowned with love. Not surprisingly, he is regarded as inspirational (Field et al. 1991:13), charismatic, a prophetic figure, of huge symbolic importance to a marginalized and underresourced field.

Something of Freire's impact may be gauged from his reception at his personal appearances around the world, where he frequently received standing ovations. One example, from my own experience, may suffice to give an impression of such occasions. I was part of a packed audience which had come to hear Freire speak at the Institute of Education in London in 1993.[1] The atmosphere was electric, strangely reminiscent of a religious revival meeting. I found the experience troubling, not so much because of anything Freire said, but because of the enraptured response his presence elicited from the audience. Freire spoke of the qualities needed by a progressive teacher, of the love he felt as a teacher for his students and of his "pedagogy of hope" (Freire in de Figueiredo-Cowen and Gastaldo 1995:17–24). Afterward, a succession of members of the audience stood up to acclaim him or question him with what I can only describe as reverence. One man said, "Professor Freire, last year I met Nelson Mandela, today I am in a room with Professor Paulo Freire. This is the greatest day of my life." Others confessed their pedagogical sins, like the woman who began her question with: "I am not a sufficiently dialogical teacher. . . ."

I was reminded of Max Weber's definition of charisma, a word often used of Freire:

an extraordinary *quality of a person, regardless of whether this quality is actual, alleged or presumed. [. . .] The legitimacy of charismatic rule thus rests upon the belief in magical powers, revelations and hero worship. (Weber quoted in Hughes 1979:289)*

While charisma is imputed to the individual, it resides rather in the charged relationship between the charismatic individual and the mass. That certainly seemed to be the case at the Institute of Education. Nor does the effect only occur in the charismatic individual's presence. The "belief in magical powers" mentioned by Weber may sound extreme, but it is exactly what Freire's pedagogical method was accorded in the pseudo-Freirean aberrations described by Archer and Costello (1990) and others. It seems to me that under certain circumstances, for example, when educators feel demoralized and marginalized, as many do in Britain in the 1990s, the charisma factor can turn hero worship into something pathological, into fetishism. That is what I felt happening all around me in the audience at the Institute of Education. The desperate need for something—someone—to believe in was palpable. Freire did not seem disturbed by it; he seemed to accept the adulation as normal, which rendered the experience all the more disturbing.

Reflecting on the occasion now, it seems to me to epitomize the problematic, sacrificial relationship in Freire's pedagogy between leader and led, teacher and student. It also highlights a more general problem with the radical hero phenomenon. Once ideas and individuals are fetishized in this way they cease to be open and productive of new insights. Challenge becomes inadmissable and debate dies. The cult of personality is a beguiling and insidious phenomenon, as stultifying for the object of desire as it is for the worshiper. As a martyred hero of the Left, Gramsci has his own cult following; I like to think he would be horrified if he knew.

The point is that ideas matter. Theory should be something that we use to think through difficult issues, such as the relationship of adult education to social and political change. I should like to end this book with an example of theory used in this positive way in Gelsa Knijnik's account of her work with the landless people's movement in Brazil (1993, 1996). I have chosen it also because it seems to me to illuminate important issues pertinent to Gramsci and Freire and the possibility of a radical politics of adult education in the context of a social movement.

Adult Education with the *Movimento dos Sem-Terra* in Brazil

Gelsa Knijnik's work with the *Movimento dos Sem-Terra* (MST), part of the landless people's movement, is discussed in two papers she presented at the second and third International Conferences of Political Dimensions of Mathematics Education (PDME) (Knijnik 1993, 1996). Land reform is a very sensitive issue in Brazil, where 1 percent of landowners control 50 percent of the economically productive farmland and there is international concern over the loss of the rainforest. MST, with its motto "Occupying, Resisting, Producing," is one of the most important rural movements in Brazil, aiming to prevent the exodus from rural areas to the cities and improve the standard of living of rural people through redistribution of the country's wealth. In April 1993 approximately 124,000 people were living in MST camps and settlements spread among nineteen of the twenty-six states of Brazil (Knijnik 1993:149). By March 1997 there were approximately fifty coordinators running MST education projects of adult and youth literacy and numeracy in nineteen states, with 600 monitors and more than 11,000 adults and young people.[2]

MST recognizes that education is a strategic issue for the movement and Knijnik's work, teaching and researching in the field of ethnomathematics,[3] was part of a project to train MST members, called "monitors," to run an educational project involving 2,000 illiterate adults and young people. Mathematical competence is one of the three areas covered in the training and focuses on the mathematics involved in the living and production problems of the MST settlements. The other areas are "political qualification," where the monitors study land reform and MST's struggle, and Freire's approach to literacy work (Knijnik 1993:149–50).

The MST leadership considers mathematics a priority—with good reason. In the words of one of the monitors,

Well my friends, in the research we have done in the settlements and campings where we were, we could observe the deficiencies among our companions. Then we realized that what our settlement companions really need is mathematics. They also need reading and writing but, mainly mathematics. They search for mathematics the same way they search for a medicine for a wound. Because they know where the bullet hole is, from which side they are exploited. (Knijnik 1993:150)

Against this background, Knijnik starts by rejecting the idea that academic neutrality is a guarantee of scientific rigor. She emphasizes her commitment to the aims of the MST in its struggle for land and works with the movement on this basis.

The initiative for the involvement of educators came from MST itself, a fact that must have influenced the relationship between the educators and the movement. Knijnik quotes an MST leader, confirming this: "We ourselves have to take the initiative of going to get people who know, to give a contribution. [. . .] The fact that you are with us is our achievement as workers" (Knijnik 1996:99).

Having "got" the educator, all is not necessarily plain sailing. Knijnik quotes an extract from her interview with one of her MST students, Ivori, which "gives us a glimpse, from the perspective of a member of the movement, of the complexity of the process of an intellectual's insertion in a social movement" (Knijnik 1996:100). It is in her discussion of the nature of that complexity that Knijnik's insights are most relevant in this context.

At the beginning, the students, members of the social movement, cannot know whether the educator is trustworthy and this must affect the relationship. In the words of Ivori,

We want these people [. . .], but, at the same time, when this relationship begins [. . .] we are not going to tell all we are experiencing, all we are feeling because one does not know the person, one does not know whether the person can help, one does not know whether they really want to get involved in our problems, or whether they simply want to perform a study in their specific field. (Knijnik 1996:100)

He might have added "or whether the person is an informer for the police or military." MST's is a militant struggle: according to news reports, nineteen MST members died in a police massacre in April 1996 (Buchanan 1996).

It is easy to see how the reluctance to "tell all we are experiencing" could be taken as symptomatic of the "culture of silence" by an outsider. But trust is clearly essential if a relationship is to develop, so is Freire right to insist on it? Yes, but trust cannot be asserted, it must be created between the parties to the educational endeavor. The possibility of trust depends on the student's assessment of the educator's motives. The educator must be aware of this and must act accordingly, with integrity, but the ball is in the student's court.

Indeed, withholding or withdrawing trust is one of the few means of self-defense the student has available, especially when the initiative for the involvement of educators has not come from the students themselves, as might well be the case in the Freirean context.

Ivori's statement shows that even in the optimum situation, when the initiative has come from the social movement, there is still initial wariness. There is also the possibility that the leadership of the social movement might have taken the initiative of inviting educators in without ensuring that the members were happy with that decision. In that situation (which might be very difficult for the educator to gauge) the students might also withhold trust.

So what *should* the educator's motives be? In terms of the stark either/or presented by Ivori, should they "really want to get involved" in the problems of the social movement or should they "simply want to perform a study in their specific field"? In response, Knijnik problematizes these alternatives. She quotes Popkewitz (1991:241) in support of her point that the commitments of intellectuals are "'historically situated, provisional and connected to regional practices, through which social life is structured'." In other words, she recognizes that she brings the historical and cultural baggage of her own intellectual formation into the relationship. She acknowledges that she cannot avoid the implications of the privileged position from which she speaks: that of "a white woman, from the city, a researcher and teacher of mathematics at the university," but she can problematize her "voice" and try to make it permeable to other "voices" (Knijnik 1996:108).

Knijnik (1996:91) follows Gramsci in considering intellectual activity in functional terms, rather than as an intrinsic quality of some individuals. She considers educators as intellectuals and their teaching activities as intellectual work (Knijnik 1996:92). But the intellectual, in her formulation, is not the universal intellectual of the left, guided by "ideals and utopias" who was "everyone's conscience," a being dismissed by Foucault as passé (Knijnik 1996:107). Neither is the intellectual simply a cipher of the group with whom he or she works. Knijnik cites Bourdieu's injunction that in order to make explicit the way in which society is constituted, social scientists (and hence, by extension, intellectuals generally), must have an attitude of disengagement and "distance themselves from the practical experience of the world," while acknowledging that Bourdieu privileges the role of intellectual as she does not. So Knijnik recognizes the need for the intellectual to exercise a degree of autonomy, consistent with the fact that, even if intellectuals and social movements "function homologously," the fields in which they fight for power do not coincide (Knijnik 1996:109).

One way in which this noncoincidence of fields manifests itself is in the tension between what is of interest to the educator in research terms and the student's more immediate, practical interest in the knowledge mediated between them. As Ivori puts it, if something goes badly wrong for the group (if, for example, the crops fail), the way the group handles the resulting crisis may be interesting to the researcher, but

it does not change his wage, it does not change his living conditions, whereas for us [. . .] it is not a matter of knowledge. It is our life. This knowledge is our life (Knijnik 1996:110).

Knijnik agrees, but points out that the research could still benefit the members of the group through increasing their understanding of the symbolic power relationships brought into play by the crisis. At stake also is the wider issue, in the case of research into ethnomathematics, of "what mathematics is considered legitimate and, therefore, can be taught in school" (Knijnik 1996:110). In other words, the educator is a channel through which the implications of the immediate crisis may be drawn out and become available to the group itself and to other groups elsewhere.

Both educator and student also have an interest in the relationship that extends beyond the pedagogical encounter. Ivori describes how the rural worker may pretend to accept the advice of the agricultural extension agent, for example, because to do so opens doors. As he says:

When one goes to the city one can use the technician's phone, one can go to the bank with the technician, one can get a loan. [. . .] So, actually, everyone would like to have these people on one's side. (Knijnik 1996:100)

Knijnik points out that Ivori's hypothetical account shows that while the students may fear being used as an object of study, they also use the intellectual to their own advantage: "In this sense they appropriate to themselves the technician's power to obtain power." For the intellectuals, also, the relationship opens doors in that it allows them "the possibility of obtaining greater symbolic benefits" in their scientific field (Knijnik 1996:100).

Thus the question of trust and the motivations of both parties to the educational endeavor are problematized. The educator does not only give and the student does not only take, and they both give and take benefits and costs other than the ostensible educational ones in the course of the relationship. In Freire's terms (although this is a possibility Freire does not discuss in the sources I have reviewed), the worker subverts the technician's "banking" aim of disseminating the introduction of modern farming techniques by operating another agenda—that of exploiting the relationship with the technician in order to gain benefits other than those which the technician intends to bestow. Of course, the technician might be well aware of what is happening and allow the exploitation to proceed for reasons of his or her own—it might be regarded as a necessary on-cost, payable in return for the cooperation of the local population, which, even if not real in this instance, might have longer-term benefits. It might even be the only way the technician can justify his or her salary—to be seen to be doing something and to be on good terms with the rural workers. In that case, the elaborate game being played out leaves Freire's distinction between banking and problem-posing education, with its assumed transparency of motivation, far behind.

So, if the educator/intellectual is committed to the cause of the social movement, aware that the fields in which he or she fights for power do not coincide and aware of the complexities of motivation and agenda involved, is he or she, at least potentially, "organic" to the social movement in Gramscian terms? Knijnik sees the MST's Education Sector, and the participation of academics and researchers in its activities, as contributing to the preparation of militants "who, to a certain extent, are similar to those "new type" intellectuals referred to by Gramsci, intellectuals-workers, who, with their work would try to overcome the contradictions between manual work and intellectual work" (Knijnik 1996:105). But what of the academics and researchers themselves? How do they fit within the Gramscian schema?

Knijnik's answer is that they do not fit. She illustrates her point with reference to her own position, describing her relationship with

MST as that of a Foucauldian "specific intellectual" (Knijnik 1996:108). As such, she is "involved in the specific educational problems of the Movement" (Knijnik 1996:98). So why does she identify with Foucault's specific intellectual—why not with Gramsci's organic intellectual?

Part of the reason is that Knijnik's role is specific in relation to MST. Her role is limited to MST and specific to her area of expertise; she does not seek to unify or organize the class, the movement, or the group, nor does she undertake manual work in the MST context. Also, MST itself is a movement with a specific set of aims related to its struggle for land reform, rather than broader class struggles. In this specificity of focus it is typical of the so-called new social movements. As Knijnik points out,

The particular aims around which some of the movements are organized—ethnic, racial or gender questions—indicate divisions of the social space which cut transversally across its division into classes, which is more structural in nature. (Knijnik 1996:106)

In this context, "the space for 'universal' intellectuals, who, with their powerful narratives will act as 'awareness makers' and leaders of the 'masses' diminishes" (Knijnik 1996:107). Gramsci's revolutionary organic intellectual is thus ruled out of play, but is he or she irredeemably universal in Foucault's terms? In that Gramsci's organic intellectual's role is the totalizing one of organizing disparate elements into a coherent whole and discerning a route in the light of Marxist principles, there is undeniably a universalist project at work here. However, "conscience" and "ideals and utopias" are not Gramscian concepts. Gramsci may have been used as the conscience of the left, but he did not set himself up as such, neither did he envisage such a role for the organic intellectuals. His concept of the intellectual-moral bloc is more dynamic, more diffuse, less personal. Revolutionary organic intellectuals are the organizers of a new hegemony with its own intellectual and moral character rather than prophets of a new morality per se. Also, that the space for universal intellectuals is diminishing may be true, but it does not mean there is no space in which disparate specificities can be addressed together, rather than separately. Indeed, a valuable aspect of the intellectual's role could be to problematize the multiplicitousness of social movements and find ways of drawing out connections between them which are of practical as well as theoretical significance. But this brings us up against the question of who would sponsor such an endeavor and how would it be organized so as to have a practical impact? In Gramsci's formulation the answer is the "Modern Prince," the revolutionary political party. In the absence or inadequacy of such a "monarch" the role may fall to academics, but with consequent problems of an unbridgeable gap between academic interests and practical politics.

Knijnik considers Gramsci's concept to be less appropriate to her situation than Foucault's also because she argues that Gramsci privileges the role of the organic intellectual of the subaltern classes "as the one who will perform the process which would lead these classes to 'higher levels of culture', one of the conditions to build up a counter-hegemony" (Knijnik 1996:105). She points out that this raises two questions: first, she regards Gramsci's concept of common sense (as fragmented, yet capable of becoming unified and homogenous), as "a concept which has been appropriately problematized by postmodern thought." Second, the leadership position occupied by the Gramscian intellectual is problematic: the MST want the researchers to be "participants in their struggles," not to be their leaders (Knijnik 1996:105). In support of the latter point, she cites Bourdieu's (1989:103) argument that "the 'myth' of the organic intellectual reduces the role of the intellectuals to that of fellow travellers of the proletariat 'preventing them from taking on the defense of their own interests'" (Knijnik 1996:110).

These are serious indictments. With respect to Knijnik's first point, it is true that Gramsci differentiates between different types of culture; indeed he was one of the first to analyze popular culture with the seriousness previously reserved for high culture. In doing so, he helped to open up the field of cultural studies as an academic discipline, and to make us all more aware of the cultural complexities of our lives and how these articulate to produce hegemonic relations. He also anticipates the development of a sociology of knowledge. His distinction between good sense and common sense is both epistemological and sociological; both a distinction between different forms of knowledge and a distinction between the knowledges characteristic of different social groups. But the distinctions are not mutually exclusive in either case. In epistemological terms, common sense includes elements of good sense. In sociological terms, good sense is not the preserve of an elite, and common sense is common to us all.

The full ramifications of Gramsci's distinction between good sense and common sense are not fully worked out in the prison notebooks. The distinction may be taken as one between real knowledge and dross, or between order and chaos—between unified knowledge and fragmented knowledge. It is certainly possible to interpret it as a distinction between higher and lower forms of knowledge, and, by implication, between higher and lower forms of consciousness. This interpretation resonates with my objection to Freire's staged theory of consciousness and I consider it would be a misinterpretation of Gramsci.

In postmodern thought, to which Knijnik alludes in her rejection of Gramsci's formulation, all sense is inevitably and irredeemably fragmented; unified and homogenous good sense is an illusion. To this I answer: perhaps so, but does this mean that there are no degrees of coherence? In writing this book I am trying to order my thoughts, to make coherent and intelligible to others ideas which would otherwise remain scattered, incoherent and unexpressed. I know I cannot achieve an ultimate order but that does not prevent me from trying to be as coherent as possible. I see Gramsci's distinction between good sense and common sense as conceptual rather than empirical since the categories are not mutually exclusive, as Hoare (1980:321) rightly argues is also the case in Gramsci's distinction between organic and traditional intellectuals.

Knijnik's second point, that the MST do not want the intellectuals as leaders but as "participants in their struggles" is telling. It resonates, again, with my misgivings about Freire's pedagogic process, in which the educator/leaders could be seen as foisting their leadership on the people. Bourdieu's objection to the organic intellectual as fellow traveler, preventing the proletariat from looking after their own interests, strikes me as a criticism to be leveled at Freire rather than at Gramsci. But does Knijnik's point resonate also with my reading of Gramsci? Perhaps. I could say that if the intellectuals were really organic to the movement they would emerge as leaders anyway, but that would be too contrived. My reading of Gramsci's primary meaning of "organic" as functional to the process of building hegemony means that the intellectual's function in organizing the revolution is actively consented to and participated in by the group. The intellectuals' organizing function is thus sanctioned by the group, not passively, but through their actions, in Gramsci's formulation. Knijnik states that MST does not reject the possibility of intellectuals becoming militants, but says that that is not her focus in this paper (Knijnik 1996:105 n10). If so, then presumably Knijnik is implicitly choosing a more limited role as a participant; she could seek to extend it to a leadership role if she chose, but that would clearly entail a different kind of commitment. From MST's point of view, it seems that for an intellectual in Knijnik's position to become a militant would be the exception rather than the rule. Giroux (1992:82) offers another formulation. He states that the educator should be a combination of Gramsci's organic intellectual and Foucault's specific intellectual, and it is conceivable that this could happen in the case of educators in Knijnik's position.

But perhaps we need to shift our focus to find the Gramscian revolutionary organic intellectuals involved in MST. In a footnote, Knijnik states that Ivori had been a student in the various stages of the Monitor Training Course for the MST Literacy Movement for Youths and Adults and later participated in a Vacation Teachers course. He is now "a leader in the Sector of Education of the state of Rio Grande do Sul" (Knijnik 1996:90–1 n). Knijnik acknowledges that the MST Education Sector produces Gramscian "intellectuals-workers," who "try to overcome the contradictions between manual work and intellectual work" (Knijnik 1996:105). People like Ivori must also perform a technical and political organizing role on behalf of the movement, which would make him an organic intellectual, albeit of the social movement, rather than of his class as a whole. It may be stretching the point, but it seems to me in keeping with Gramsci's highly differentiated and contingent concept that organic intellectuals should be differently located in a movement; that the movement might be fragmented and have its own internal conflicts and contradictions; and that its relationship with wider groupings, for example, on the basis of class, gender or race might be highly problematic.

But if Knijnik's role as an intellectual is specific, it is not necessarily uncomplicated. She states that she experiences "permanent tension" between her social function as an intellectual, which entails "dimensions of autonomy," and her commitment to the demands of the MST (Knijnik 1996:109). Knijnik is torn between two apparently contradictory forces: responsibility to her academic field and commitment to the cause of the social movement. I suggest the tension for a Gramscian revolutionary organic intellectual would be threefold: between responsibility to the academic field; engagement with, rather than commitment to, the cause of the social movement; and commitment to the revolutionary political party and through that to the class and society as a whole. In some readings of Gramsci the social movement would be subsumed within the party—I prefer to give him the benefit of the doubt and opt for a more libertarian reading.

Knijnik's responsibility to her field, ethnomathematics, raises other issues pertinent to a discussion of Gramsci's and Freire's ideas. Knijnik describes her ethnomathematical approach to the question of estimating the area of a piece of land and estimating the volume of a tree trunk, both clearly key issues for MST (Knijnik 1996:104). Knijnik discusses the role of the educator in this situation, stating that from a Gramscian point of view this could be considered as raising the "'simple ones' to a higher elaboration of their own reality" (Gramsci quoted in Knijnik 1996:104). Knijnik rejects this proposition as privileging the intellectual and the intellectual's knowledge.

Knijnik recounts how, when she first encountered the informal, popular mathematical methods used by the group to tackle these problems she was inclined to reject them as inaccurate, the more so in that their inaccuracy disadvantaged the group financially. The problem appeared to Knijnik at this stage to be the search for more-satisfactory mathematical methods from the economic standpoint, "as though this lack of precision were simply the product of lack of mathematical knowledge." The fact that the group was part of an organized movement, with well-defined production targets, made this seem even more imperative and "caused my traditional mathematical training to appear," as Knijnik wryly notes. Eventually,

It was the development of field research and the deliberate attitude of listening to what the group had to say about the interrelations between different land measurement methods that allowed me to gather elements which redirected my initial assessment. (Knijnik 1996:108)

While she did not use this approach in order to ease the "intellectual-social movement relationship" she reports that it did have that effect (Knijnik 1996:101). She discovered later that her early pedagogical interventions, based on her initial assessment of the situation, had been "pulverized by the group." Ivori's description of Knijnik's revised, ethnomathematical approach is illuminating:

The way you worked, especially with these questions in Maths, challenging: "But what is your problem? How do you get to think this? How have you solved this or that question?" [. . .] So we began to talk about what we were feeling, the problems we really had. (Knijnik 1996:99)

Knijnik tells this story, against herself, to indicate the inappropriateness of an approach based in a hierarchical conception of knowledge, as she takes Gramsci's to be. But is this the only interpretation of what happened? Her early interventions could certainly be interpreted as illustrating the pitfalls of the banking mode of education, as described by Freire, in which the gap between what the students know and what they need to know is first identified and then filled by knowledge transmitted by the educator. Knijnik's alternative, questioning approach could be seen as Socratic, an approach also favored by Gramsci (*viz.* his 1916 article on "Socialism and Culture," Gramsci 1994b:8–12; SPWI:10–3). It could also be interpreted, in Gramsci's terms, as an illustration of the need to engage with the students' common sense, in Gramsci's terms, insofar as that was what Knijnik was doing when she learned the students' informal, popular methods.

The difference is that having engaged with their common sense, Knijnik does not seek to unify or organize the students' mathematical knowledge at the expense of their popular knowledge, which might be the logical next step in a Gramscian approach, although Gramsci does not specifically say so. Instead, the students learned academic mathematics as well as popular methods, although Knijnik is careful to point out that "popular knowledge was taken into account, it was not exalted" (Knijnik 1993:151).

The students who knew the popular methods taught them to the group during the mathematics classes. As she remarks "the 'informants' were 'teachers' as well as 'students'" (Knijnik 1993:151). This was literally true, in that they taught their methods to their fellow students, rather than metaphorically so, as in Freire's approach. Knijnik quotes one of the students as saying, "Before our mathematics class I knew the counts, now I know mathematics." She concludes, using the Freirean concept of decoding, that he was aware that in the mathematics class he became capable of understanding and decoding the mathematical ideas involved in his social practices (Knijnik 1993:151). The decoding in this case, though, was done by the student, the educator did not hold the key to the code.

Knijnik's papers—and my review of them here—do not attempt an evaluation of the effectiveness of her educational approach, or of the ethnomathematics approach more generally—although I am sympathetic to both. From the enthusiasm of Ivori's description, and from the student's quote above, it seems possible that students might emerge from her courses with a much stronger idea of the costs and benefits of different methods on the basis of the ethnomathematics approach rather than the more traditional approach. Potentially, at least, they would have an enlarged repertoire of mathematical techniques and a much deeper understanding of processes of measurement—and a degree of enhanced self-respect consequent upon the fact that their knowledge was taken seriously and had made a real contribution to the educational endeavor. They would probably be better equipped to contribute to production, organization and education in MST and would be less easily duped by unscrupulous people seeking to limit their incursions or cheat them in the sale of their produce. But would they be conscientized in Freire's terms? Would they be contributing to the creation of revolutionary hegemony in Gramsci's terms? Possibly. From what I have said so far it will come as no surprise that I think the possibility of the latter is greater than that of the former, but in either case we should have to agree upon criteria by which outcomes could be measured in terms of their conscientizatory or revolutionary potential. I find that easier to conceive of in relation to revolution than conscientization, although some readings of Freire, as we have seen, would deny that there is any difference—the conscientized individual is in a position to contribute to the revolution by virtue of his or her conscientization.

But there is a difference. For example, if land reform were to be achieved without a fundamental disruption of existing power relations, that is, *within* the existing hegemonic settlement, that would not constitute revolution. If land reform triggered a fundamental change in those power relations, then that would be revolutionary, although whether the revolution would be considered Marxist or not would depend on a range of other factors elucidated by Marx and Gramsci, among others. It would be possible, for example, to conceive of a religious group espousing the issue of land reform, winning the struggle and instituting a religious autocracy.

An Analysis—and Some Open Questions in Lieu of a Conclusion

In terms of Peter Mayo's framework for analysis of radical adult education, outlined in Chapter 5, Knijnik's work contains a "language of critique" in several ways: in the fact that it is taking place at all among people with little or no formal education; in its location and consequent political orientation as part of MST's education project; in its problematization of the subject (mathematics). It also seems, in Mayo's terms (1994:126), to "tie educational systems to systemic and structural forms of domination in the wider society," while allowing educational systems a "relative autonomy." In this case, the "systemic and structural forms of domination" with which MST is concerned relate specifically to landlessness rather than to the complex of other oppressions, but Knijnik's description of her educational approach seems to justify the "relative autonomy" tag. Knijnik's account illustrates my point that questions of political purpose must be defined by adults themselves and not by adult educators on behalf of their students. The educators may decide whether or not to engage with the social movement, but, in the first place, the social movement decides whether to approach the educators.

It also contains a "language of possibility" in that it allows room for agency in several "locations." The educator exercises agency in her teaching and research. The students exercise agency in their contributions to the teaching of popular methods and in their active engagement with the education process (*viz.* Ivori's statement "we began to talk about what we were feeling, the problems we really had"). The students also have the opportunity to exercise agency in (potentially) becoming MST militants. The MST leaders exercise agency in that they initiate contact with the intellectuals and invite them to work with the movement on the MST's terms.

Mayo's framework also allows for analysis of Knijnik's work with MST in terms of sites of practice, content and social relations. The site of practice, the social movement of landless people, seems ideal for radical practice, yet, as Knijnik's account of her first attempt to work with the MST group shows, this need not be the case—it is quite possible to undertake nonradical adult education in an apparently radical context. Mayo (1994:138) asks, "Do social movements constitute the larger context within which transformative educational initiatives can be effectively carried out?" and on the basis of this brief enquiry, the answer must be yes. Social movements would seem to provide excellent opportunities for the practice of radical adult education, not least because they are organizations of adults, setting their own agendas, rather than of adult educators setting them for others. But Knijnik's account indicates that the educator's commitment to the cause of the movement must always be problematic, even if, as in this case, the educator is in agreement with the movement's aims.

Are social movements then the only site of practice where radical adult education can take place? Are universities and colleges hopelessly compromised by their status as hegemonic institutions and their reliance on state or other official funding? What about factories or offices or trade unions or voluntary organizations or churches, mosques or synagogues? This brings us up against the need for an element of Mayo's analytical framework which I have argued in the previous chapter is conspicuous by its absence: the question of the purpose of the educational activity. Here we must remember that although "radical" is generally used as a short-hand term for leftwing it can also be used of and by the Right (Williams 1990).

In the case of MST, the radical heroes of the movement are Mao, Guevara and the Brazilian radical, Zumbi (Buchanan 1996). There is not space here for a full examination of MST's political complexion but these names tell us something of how the MST militants conceive of their struggle: as a guerrilla movement of peasants and the landless poor with the immediate aim of land reform, but the distinct possibility of something even more radical and revolutionary in the wings. The first two names certainly feature on Freire's list of radical heroes (the third may also, but I have not found it in Freire's writings in English translation). I suspect that, of the three, Mao's name will be the most difficult for radical adult educators in the First World to swallow, and it is interesting that Freire's rapprochement with Mao is so little commented on in the English language literature. There has been much discussion of whether Freire is a Marxist but very little indeed about whether he is a Maoist (and I am not suggesting he is—although perhaps *Maoisante* might capture it, if there is such a word).

So could radical adult education be undertaken in accord with conservative, right-wing or reactionary aims? I have argued in Chapter 3 that Freire's method is readily adaptable to reactionary purposes, although that is clearly not what Freire intended. Whether Gramsci's approach could be so traduced is harder to say. There is plenty of evidence of revolutions devouring their children, but none so far has been Gramscian in nature. Gramsci's concept of revolutionary leadership ought, in theory, to make the abuse of power more difficult, but that is not to say no way could be found of perverting Gramsci's intentions. Manipulative leaders often find the gap between rhetoric and reality a convenient space in which to operate. Conversely, Gramsci does enable us to pose the question of what "spaces" exist within even the most conservative organizations for radicals of the Left to explore and exploit.

In terms of content, ethnomathematics invalidates—or at least problematizes—dichotomies between different knowledges, formal and informal, academic and popular, high and low and the consequent allocation of power to preferred forms of knowledge. In so doing it provides a useful litmus test for questions concerning the compatibility of a hierarchical concept of the organization of knowledge with a commitment to radical democratic principles. Gramsci's distinction between common sense and good sense, when reviewed in that light, emerges as problematic but endlessly suggestive.

The final category in Mayo's analytical framework, social rela-

tions, is highlighted in Knijnik's account in terms of the key relationship between intellectuals and members of the social movement.
The more limited role of the Foucauldian specific intellectual that
she espouses may be a more realistic aspiration for many radical adult
educators than the whole-hearted revolutionary commitment required by Gramsci, although, as Giroux (1992:82) argues, the two
are not incompatible. Knijnik (1996:107) also stresses the permanent need for intellectuals to practice their capacity for self-reflection and her papers seem to me to exemplify this capacity in action.
This seems to me a more sound basis for honest and effective educational activity than the hidden agendas that Mayo proposes for educators working "in and against the state" on the basis of his synthesis
of Gramsci and Freire, or the love and trust that Freire insists educators should have for their students, and students for their teachers. It
seems more compatible with Gramsci's vision of the educator and
student working toward the possibility of exchanging their roles in
the process of pursuing their common aims. But what are the common aims worth fighting for? Is a common aim still conceivable?
How should adult educators relate both to the diverse aims of the
so-called new social movements and to wider issues of social and
political change and social justice?

Neither Gramsci nor Freire can provide us with the answers,
but I believe Gramsci can help us to explore the questions. It is by
exploring such questions in both theory and practice that we shall
begin to move beyond hero worship, however admirable our radical
heroes might be, toward a politics of adult education which engages
with difficult issues of purpose, process and content in the education of adults in relation to social and political change.

Postscript

In a letter to his younger brother Carlo, written from prison and
dated September 12, 1927, Gramsci wrote:

*My moral position is very good; some people think of me as a devil,
others think of me as almost a saint. I don't want to be either a martyr or
a hero. I believe I am simply an average man who has his own deep
convictions and will not trade them away for anything in the world.
(Gramsci 1994a vol.1:140)*

Notes

1.   The main speeches (by Freire and others) at the seminar are recorded in de Figueiredo-Cowen and Gastaldo (1995).

2.   These figures, which are approximate, were given me in a private communication from Professor Knijnik, 6 March 1997.

3.   Knijnik (1996:101) describes her ethnomathematics approach as follows:

> the investigation of the traditions, practices and mathematical concepts of a subordinate social group [. . .] and the pedagogical work which is developed so that the group will interpret and decode its knowledge; acquire the knowledge produced by academic mathematicians and establish comparisons between its knowledge and academic knowledge, thus being able to analyze the power relations involved in the use of both these kinds of knowledge.

The term "ethnomathematics" was coined by Ubiratan D'Ambrosio in the mid-1970s. See D'Ambrosio (1985). See also Frankenstein and Powell (1994) for an interesting discussion on ethnomathematics in relation to Freire's epistemology.

Bibliography

List of Abbreviations of Works by Freire and Gramsci

CAF   *Cultural Action for Freedom*, by Paulo Freire. Harmondsworth: Penguin (1972).

EPF   *Education: The Practice of Freedom*, by Paulo Freire, translated by Myra Bergman Ramos. London: Writers and Readers (1976).

FSPN   *Further Selections from the Prison Notebooks/Antonio Gramsci*, edited and translated by D. Boothman. Minneapolis: University of Minnesota Press (1995).

GR   *A Gramsci Reader: Selected Writings 1916–1935 by Antonio Gramsci*, edited by D. Forgacs. London: Lawrence and Wishart (1988).

LGB   *Pedagogy in Process: The Letters to Guinea-Bissau*, by Paulo Freire, translated by C. St. John Hunter. London: Writers and Readers (1978).

LP   *Letters from Prison by Antonio Gramsci*, selected, translated and introduced by L. Lawner. London: Jonathan Cape (1975).

PE   *The Politics of Education*, by Paulo Freire, translated by Donaldo Macedo. London: Macmillan (1985).

PH   *Pedagogy of Hope: Reliving Pedagogy of the Oppressed*, by Paulo Freire, translated by Robert R. Barr. New York: Continuum (1995).

PNI   *Antonio Gramsci: Prison Notebooks* (Volume 1), edited with Introduction by Joseph A. Buttigieg, translated by J. A. Buttigieg and A. Callari. New York: Columbia University Press (1992).

PNII   *Antonio Gramsci: Prison Notebooks* (Volume 2), edited and translated by J. A. Buttigieg. New York: Columbia University Press (1996).

PO   *Pedagogy of the Oppressed,* by Paulo Freire, translated by Myra Bergman Ramos. Harmondsworth: Penguin (1972).

SCW   *Selections from Cultural Writings,* by Antonio Gramsci, edited by D. Forgacs and G. Nowell Smith, translated by W. Boelhower. London: Lawrence and Wishart (1985).

SPN   *Selections from the Prison Notebooks of Antonio Gramsci,* edited and translated by Quintin Hoare and Geoffrey Nowell Smith. London: Lawrence and Wishart (1971).

SPWI   *Selections from Political Writings (1910–20),* by Antonio Gramsci, edited by Quintin Hoare, translated by John Matthews. London: Lawrence and Wishart (1977).

SPWII   *Selections from Political Writings (1921–26),* by Antonio Gramsci, translated and edited by Quintin Hoare. London: Lawrence and Wishart (1978).

Bibliography of Other Sources

Alden, H. (1981) "Antonio Gramsci: Conservative Schooling for Radical Politics" (review article), *Convergence,* **XIV**, 3: 91–4.

Alexander, D. and Martin, I. (1995) "Competence, Curriculum and Democracy," Chapter 7 in M. Mayo and J. Thompson (eds.) *Adult Learning, Critical Intelligence and Social Change.* Leicester: National Institute of Adult Continuing Education. 82–96.

Allman, P. (1994) "Paulo Freire's Contributions to Radical Adult Education," *Studies in the Education of Adults,* **26**, 2: 144–61.

Allman, P. (1988) "Gramsci, Freire and Illich: Their Contributions to Education for Socialism" in T. Lovett (ed.) *Radical Approaches to Adult Education: A Reader,* Radical Forum on Adult Education. London: Routledge and Kegan Paul. 85–113.

Allman, P. (1987) "Paulo Freire's Education Approach: A Struggle for Meaning" in G. Allen et al. (eds.) *Community Education: An Agenda for Educational Reform.* Milton Keynes: Open University Press.

Allman, P. and Wallis, J. (1995a) "Challenging the Postmodern Condition: Radical Adult Education for Critical Intelligence,"

Chapter 2 in M. Mayo and J. Thompson (eds.) *Adult Learning, Critical Intelligence and Social Change.* Leicester: National Institute of Adult Continuing Education. 18–33.

Allman, P. and Wallis, J. (1995b) "Gramsci's Challenge to the Politics of the Left in 'Our Times'" *International Journal of Lifelong Education,* **14**, 2 (March–April): 120–43.

Allman, P. and Wallis, J. (1990a) "Praxis: Implications for 'Really' Radical Education," *Studies in the Education of Adults,* **22**, 1 (April): 14–30

Allman, P. and Wallis, J. (1990b) "1992 and New Times: A Critical Reading," *Towards 1992: Education of Adults in the New Europe,* Proceedings of the Twentieth Annual Conference SCUTREA. Sheffield: University of Sheffield. 234–45.

Allman, P. and Wallis, J. (1988) "Karl Marx's Theoretical Contributions to Radical Education" in M. Zukas (ed.) *Transatlantic Dialogues.* Leeds: School of Continuing Education, University of Leeds.

Anderson, P. (1976–77) "The Antinomies of Antonio Gramsci," *New Left Review,* **100** (November 1976–January 1977): 5–78.

Anderson, P. (1964) "Origins of the Present Crisis," *New Left Review,* **23** (January–February): 26–53.

Apitzsch, U. (1993) "Gramsci and the Current Debate on Multicultural Education," *Studies in the Education of Adults,* **25**, 2: 136–45.

Apple, M.W. (1982) *Education and Power.* London: Routledge and Kegan Paul.

Apple, M.W. (1980) "Review of Antonio Gramsci, Conservative Schooling for Radical Politics, by Harold Entwistle," *Comparative Education Review* (October): 436–8.

Archer, D. and Costello, P. (1990) *Literacy and Power: The Latin American Battleground.* London: Earthscan.

Archer, D. and Cottingham, S. (1996a) *Action Research Report on REFLECT, Regenerated Freirean Literacy through Empowering Community Techniques: The experience of three REFLECT pilot projects in Uganda, Bangladesh, El Salvador.* Serial no. 17. London: Overseas Development Agency.

Archer, D. and Cottingham, S. (1996b) *REFLECT Mother Manual: Regenerated Freirean Literacy through Empowering Community Techniques.* London: ACTIONAID.

Armstrong, P. (1988) *"L'Ordine Nuovo:* The Legacy of Antonio Gramsci and the Education of Adults," *International Journal of Lifelong Education,* 7, 4: 249–60.

Arnove, R.F. (1987) "The 1980 Nicaraguan National Literacy Crusade," Chapter 12 of R.F. Arnove and H.J. Graff (eds.) *National Literacy Campaigns: Historical and Comparative Perspectives.* New York and London: Plenum Press.

Arnove, R.F. (1986) *Education and Revolution in Nicaragua.* New York: Praeger.

Ball, W. (1992) "Critical Social Research, Adult Education and Anti-Racist Feminist Praxis," *Studies in the Education of Adults,* 24, 1: 1–25.

Barratt Brown, M. (1980) "Adult Education and Social Change," *Convergence,* XIII, 4: 89–92.

Bee, B. (1993) "Critical Literacy and the Politics of Gender" in C. Lankshear and P. McLaren (eds.) *Critical Literacy: Politics, Praxis and the Postmodern.* Albany: State University of New York Press.

Bee, B. (1980) "The Politics of Literacy" in R. Mackie (ed.) *Literacy and Revolution: The Pedagogy of Paulo Freire.* London: Pluto Press. 39–56.

Benseman, J. (1978) "Paulo Freire: A Revolutionary Alternative," *Delta,* 23 (November): 27–40.

Berger, P. (1976) *Pyramids of Sacrifice.* London: Allen Lane.

Berggren, L. and Berggren C. (1975) *The Literacy Process: A Practice in Domestication of Liberation?* London: Writers and Readers.

Bobbio, N. (1996) *Left and Right: The Significance of a Political Distinction,* translated with an Introduction by A. Cameron. Cambridge: Polity Press.

Bocock, R. (1986) *Hegemony.* Chichester: Ellis Horwood, and London: Tavistock.

Boff, L. (1985) *Church, Charism, and Power: Liberation Theology and the Institutional Church.* New York: Crossroad.

Boston, B. (1972) "Paulo Freire: Notes of a Loving Critic" in S.M. Grabowski *Paulo Freire: A Revolutionary Dilemma for the Adult Educator.* Syracuse: Eric Clearing House on Adult Education.

Bourdieu, P. (1989) "The Corporatism of the Universal: The Role of Intellectuals in the Modern World," *Telos,* 81: 99–110.

Brady, J. (1994) "Critical Literacy, Feminism and a Politics of Representation," Chapter 8 of P. McLaren and P. Lankshear (eds.)

Politics of Liberation: Paths from Freire. London and New York: Routledge and Kegan Paul.

Brookfield, S.D. (1987) *Developing Critical Thinkers: Challenging Adults to Explore Alternative Ways of Thinking and Acting*. Milton Keynes: Open University Press.

Brown, C. (1975) *Literacy in 30 Hours: Paulo Freire's Process in North-East Brazil*. London: Writers and Readers. First published as Brown, C. "Literacy in Thirty Days: Paulo Freire's Process" in *Urban Review*, 7, 3 (July 1974): 245–56.

Brown, D. (1994) *Strategies of Social Development: NGOs and the Limitations of the Freirean Approach*. The New Bulmershe Papers. Reading: Faculty of Education and Community Studies, University of Reading.

Bruneau, T. (1980) "The Catholic Church and Development in Latin America: The Role of Basic Church Communities," *World Development*, **8**: 535–44.

Bruss, N. and Macedo, D. (1985) "Toward a Pedagogy of the Question: Conversations with Paulo Freire," *Journal of Education, Boston University*, **167**, 2: 7–21.

Buchanan, E. (1996) *Dying for Land* (television documentary), BBC 2, screened 24 November 1996.

Buci-Glucksmann, C. (1980) *Gramsci and the State*, translated by D. Fernbach. London: Lawrence and Wishart.

Cammett, J.M. (1991) *Bibliografia Gramsciana 1922–1988*. Rome: Editori Riuniti.

Cammett, J.M. (1967) *Antonio Gramsci and the Origins of Italian Communism*. Stanford, CA: Stanford University Press.

Cammett, J.M. and Righi, M.L. (1995) *Bibliografia Gramsciana: Supplement Updated to 1993*. Rome: Fondazione Istituto Gramsci.

Cannistraro, P.V. (ed.) (1982) *Historical Dictionary of Fascist Italy*. Westport, CT: Greenwood Press.

Cardenal, F., SJ and Miller, V. (1981) "Nicaragua 1980: The Battle of the ABCs," *Harvard Educational Review*, **51**, 1 (February): 1–26.

Carnoy, M. (1982) "Education, Economy and the State" in M.W. Apple (ed.) *Culture and Economic Reproduction in Education: Essays on Class, Ideology and the State*. London: Routledge and Kegan Paul. 79–126.

Cavalcanti, P. and Piccone, P. (eds.) (1975) *History, Philosophy and Culture in the Young Gramsci.* St. Louis: Telos Press.

Chain, B.C. (1974) "An Examination of Three Paulo Freire–Inspired Programs of Literacy Education in Latin America," *Literacy Discussion,* 5, 3: 393–408.

Chambers, R. (1993) *Challenging the Professions: Frontiers for Rural Development.* London: IT Publications.

Chambers, R. (1983) *Rural Development: Putting the Last First.* Harlow: Longman.

Charters, A.N. (1989) *Landmarks in International Adult Education.* London: Routledge and Kegan Paul.

Clark, M. (1977) *Antonio Gramsci and the Revolution That Failed.* New Haven and London: Yale University Press.

Coben, D. (1997) "Mathematics Life Histories and Common Sense," *Adults Learning Mathematics—a Research Forum—3 (ALM-3), Proceedings of the Third International Conference of Adults Learning Mathematics—a Research Forum,* University of Brighton, UK, 5–7 July 1996. London: Goldsmiths College, University of London, in association with Adults Learning Mathematics—a Research Forum (ALM).

Coben, D. (1995) "Revisiting Gramsci," *Studies in the Education of Adults,* 27, 1 (April): 36–51.

Coben, D. (1994) "Antonio Gramsci and the Education of Adults" *Adult Education and Social Change,* a collection of papers presented at the European Research Seminar of the European Society for Research into the Education of Adults (ESREA), 7–11 August, Lahti, Finland.

Coben, D. (1992) "Radical Heroes: Gramsci, Freire and the Liberal Tradition in Adult Education," unpublished Ph.D. thesis, University of Kent at Canterbury, Faculty of Social Science.

Coben, D. and Thumpston, G. (1996) "Common Sense, Good Sense and Invisible Mathematics" in T. Kjærgård, A. Kvamme, N. Lindén (eds.) *Numeracy, Race, Gender and Class: Proceedings of the Third International Conference of Political Dimensions of Mathematics Education (PDME) III, Bergen, Norway.* Landås, Norway: Caspar Publishing Company. 284–98.

Cohen, N. (forthcoming) "Dilemmas in the Theory and Practice of Popular Education in Latin America: Participation and Empowerment under the Microscope," *Goldsmiths Journal of Education.* London: Goldsmiths College, University of London.

Collins, D. (1977) *Paulo Freire: His Life, Works and Thought.* New York: Paulist Press.

Communist Party of Great Britain (1990) *Manifesto for New Times: A Strategy for the 1990s.* London: The Communist Party in association with Lawrence and Wishart.

Cooper, G. (1995) "Freire and Theology," *Studies in the Education of Adults,* **27,** 1 (April): 66–7.

Cowburn, W. (1986) *Class Ideology and Community Education,* Radical Forum on Adult Education. Beckenham: Croom Helm.

Cozens, P. (1977) *Twenty Years of Antonio Gramsci: A Bibliography of Gramsci and Gramsci Studies Published in English 1957–1977.* London: Lawrence and Wishart. 3–12.

D'Ambrosio, U. (1985) "Ethnomathematics and Its Place in the History and Pedagogy of Mathematics," *For the Learning of Mathematics,* **5,** 1: 44–8.

da Silva, T. T. and McLaren, P. (1993) "Knowledge under Seige: The Brazilian Debate," Chapter 3 of P. McLaren and P. Leonard (eds.) *Paulo Freire: A Critical Encounter.* London and New York: Routledge and Kegan Paul.

Davidson, A. (1977) *Antonio Gramsci: Towards an Intellectual Biography.* London: Merlin Press.

De Castro, J. (1969) *Death in the North-East.* New York: Vintage.

De Figueiredo-Cowen, M. and Gastaldo, D. (1995) *Paulo Freire at the Institute.* London: Institute of Education, University of London.

De Kadt, E. (1970) *Catholic Radicals in Brazil.* London: Oxford University Press.

De Kadt, E. (1967) "Religion, the Church and Social Change" in C. Veliz (ed.) *The Politics of Conformity in Latin America,* Royal Institute of International Affairs. London: Oxford University Press.

Durkheim, E. (1952) *Suicide: A Study in Sociology,* translated by J.A. Spaulding and G. Simpson, edited and with an Introduction by G. Simpson. London: Routledge and Kegan Paul.

Eley, G. (1984) "Reading Gramsci in English: Observations on the Reception of Antonio Gramsci in the English-Speaking World 1957–82," *European History Quarterly,* **14:** 441–78.

Elias, J.L. (1994) *Paulo Freire: Pedagogue of Revolution.* Malibar, FL: Krieger.

Elias, J.L. (1976) *Conscientization and Deschooling: Freire's and Illich's Proposals for Reshaping Society.* Philadelphia: Westminster.

Entwistle, H. (1979) *Antonio Gramsci: Conservative Schooling for Radical Politics.* London: Routledge and Kegan Paul.

Fanon, F. (1967) *The Wretched of the Earth,* translated by C. Farrington. Harmondsworth: Penguin.

Fernandes, L.B. (1985) "Basic Ecclesiastic Communities in Brazil," *Harvard Educational Review,* 55, 1: 76–85.

Field, J., Lovell, T. and Weller, P. (1991) *Research Quality in Continuing Education: A Study of Citations Patterns.* Coventry: University of Warwick Research Paper in Continuing Education, No. 3.

Finger, M. (1989) "New Social Movements and Their Implications for Adult Education," *Adult Education Quarterly,* 40, 1: 15–22.

Fiori, G. (1970) *Antonio Gramsci: Life of a Revolutionary,* translated by T. Nairn. London: NLB.

Forgacs, D. (1989) "Gramsci and Marxism in Britain," *New Left Review,* 176 (July–August): 70–88.

Frank, A.G. (1969) *Capitalism and Underdevelopment in Latin America: Historical Studies of Chile and Brazil.* New York and London: Monthly Review Press.

Frankenstein, M. (1989) *Relearning Mathematics: A Different Third R—Radical Maths.* London: Free Association Books.

Frankenstein, M. (1987) "Critical Mathematics Education: An Application of Paulo Freire's Epistemology" in I. Shor (ed.) *Freire for the Classroom: A Sourcebook for Liberatory Teaching.* New York and London: Heinemann.

Frankenstein, M. and Powell, A. (1994) "Toward Liberatory Mathematics: Paulo Freire's Epistemology and Ethnomathematics," Chapter 4 in P.L. McLaren and C. Lankshear (eds.) *Politics of Liberation: Paths from Freire.* London: Routledge and Kegan Paul. 74–99.

Freire, P. (1995) *Pedagogy of the Oppressed,* translated by M. Bergman Ramos (New Revised 20th Anniversary Edition). New York: Continuum.

Freire, P. (1993) *Pedagogy of the City.* New York: Continuum.

Freire, P. (1981) "The People Speak Their Word: Learning to Read and Write in São Tomé and Príncipe," *Harvard Educational Review,* 51, 1 (February): 27–30.

Freire, P. (1979) "To Know and to Be," *Indian Journal of Youth Affairs* (June): 1–13.

Freire, P. (1976a) "A Few Notions about the Word Conscientization," translated by Manuel Vaquerizo, in R. Dale, G. Esland, M. MacDonald, (eds.) *Schooling and Capitalism*. London: Routledge and Kegan Paul and Open University. 224–27.

Freire, P. (1976b) "Literacy and the Possible Dream," *Prospects,* **VI**, 1: 68–71.

Freire, P. (1975) "Pilgrims of the Obvious," *Risk,* **11**, 1.

Freire, P. (1974) "Authority versus Authoritarianism," *Thinking with Paulo Freire* (audio tape series). Australian Council of Churches.

Freire, P. (1972a) "The Educational Role of the Churches in Latin America," LADOC, **3**: 14.

Freire, P. (1972b) "A Letter to a Theology Student," *Catholic Mind,* **LXX**, 1265: 6–8.

Freire, P. (1971) "To the Coordinator of a Cultural Circle," *Convergence,* **IV**, 1: 61–2.

Freire, P., Escobar, M., Fernandez, A. and Guevara-Niebla, G. (1994) *Paulo Freire on Higher Education*. Albany: State University of New York Press.

Freire, P. and Faundez, A. (1989) *Learning to Question: A Pedagogy of Liberation*. Geneva: World Council of Churches.

Freire, P. and Macedo, D. (1993) "A Dialogue with Paulo Freire" in P. McLaren and P. Leonard (eds.) *Paulo Freire: A Critical Encounter*. London: Routledge and Kegan Paul. 169–76.

Freire, P. and Macedo, D. (1987) *Literacy: Reading the Word and the World*. London: Routledge and Kegan Paul.

Furter, P. (1985) "Profile of Educators: Paulo Freire," *Prospects,* **15**, 2: 301–10.

Furter, P. (1974) "On the Greatness of Being Utopian," *Literacy Discussion* (Spring): 117–24.

Gadotti, M. (1994) *Reading Paulo Freire: His Life and Work*, translated by J. Milton. Albany: SUNY Press.

Geras, N. (1987) "Post-Marxism?" *New Left Review,* **163** (May-June 1987): 40–82.

Gerhardt, H.-P. (1993) "Paulo Freire (1921–)," *Prospects,* **XXIII**, 3/4 (87/88): 439–58.

Germino, D. (1990) *Antonio Gramsci: Architect of a New Politics*. Baton Rouge and London: Louisiana State University.

Gheebrant, A. (1974) *The Rebel Church in Latin America.* Harmondsworth: Penguin.

Giddens, A. (1994) *Beyond Left and Right: The Future of Radical Politics.* Cambridge: Polity Press in association with Blackwell Publishers.

Giroux, H.A. (1993) "Paulo Freire and the Politics of Postcolonialism," Chapter 10 of P. McLaren and P. Leonard (eds.) *Paulo Freire: A Critical Encounter.* London and New York: Routledge and Kegan Paul. 177–88.

Giroux, H.A. (1992) *Border Crossings: Cultural Workers and the Politics of Education.* New York and London: Routledge and Kegan Paul.

Giroux, H.A. (1985) "Introduction" in P. Freire *The Politics of Education,* translated by D. Macedo. London: Macmillan. xi–xxv.

Giroux, H.A. (1980) "Review of Antonio Gramsci, Conservative Schooling for Radical Politics by Harold Entwistle," *British Journal of Sociology of Education,* **1**, 3: 307–15.

Golding, S. (1992) *Gramsci's Democratic Theory: Contributions to a Post-Liberal Democracy.* Toronto: University of Toronto Press.

Gorman, R.A. (ed.) (1986) *Biographical Dictionary of Marxism.* London: Mansell.

Grabowski, S.M. (1972) *Paulo Freire: A Revolutionary Dilemma for the Adult Educator.* Syracuse: Eric Clearing House on Adult Education.

Gramsci, A. (1995) *The Southern Question,* translation, introduction and notes by P. Verdicchio. Lafayette, IN: Bordighera Inc.

Gramsci, A. (1994a) *Letters from Prison,* edited by F. Rosengarten and translated by R. Rosenthal (two volumes). New York: Columbia University Press.

Gramsci, A. (1994b) *Pre-prison Writings,* edited by R. Bellamy, translated by V. Cox. Cambridge: Cambridge University Press.

Gramsci, A. (1988) *Gramsci's Prison Letters.* Lettere dal Carcere. Selected, translated and introduced by H. Henderson. London: Zwan in association with the Edinburgh Review.

Gramsci, A. (1984) "Notes on Language," Special Section, selected and edited by S.R. Mansfield, translated by S.R. Mansfield and L. Alchini with an introduction by S.R. Mansfield, *Telos,* **59** (Spring): 119–50.

Gramsci, A. (1957a) *The Modern Prince and Other Writings,* translated and with an introduction by L. Marks. New York: International Publishers.

Gramsci, A. (1957b) *The Open Marxism of Antonio Gramsci*, translated and annotated by C. Marzani. New York: Cameron Associates.

Green, A. (1990) *Education and State Formation.* London: Macmillan.

Griffith, W.S. (1974) "Paulo Freire: Utopian Perspective in Literacy Education," *Literacy Discussion* (Spring): 93–115.

Gutiérrez, G. (1973) *A Theology of Liberation.* New York: Orbis Books.

Hadjor, K.B. (1993) *Dictionary of Third World Terms.* London: Penguin.

Hall, S. (1989) "The Meaning of New Times" in S. Hall and M. Jacques (eds.) *New Times: The Changing Face of Politics in the 1990s.* London: Lawrence and Wishart in association with *Marxism Today.* 116–34.

Hall, S. and Jacques, M. (eds.) (1989) *New Times: The Changing Face of Politics in the 1990s.* London: Lawrence and Wishart in association with *Marxism Today.*

Harasim, L.M. (1983) "Literacy and National Reconstruction in Guinea-Bissau: A Critique of the Freirean Literacy Campaign," Ph.D. dissertation, Ontario Institute for Studies in Education (OISE), University of Toronto.

Harris, D. (1992) *From Class Struggle to the Politics of Pleasure: The Effects of Gramscianism on Cultural Studies.* London and New York: Routledge and Kegan Paul.

Harvey, D. (1993) "Class Relations, Social Justice and the Politics of Difference" in J. Squires (ed.) *Principled Positions: Postmodernism and the Rediscovery of Value.* London: Lawrence and Wishart. 85–120.

Hawthorn, R. (1980) "Pedagogy, Oppression and Us," *Basic Education* (May): 30–1.

Hebdige, D. (1989) "After the Masses" in S. Hall and M. Jacques (eds.) *New Times: The Changing Face of Politics in the 1990s.* London: Lawrence and Wishart in association with *Marxism Today.* 76–93.

Hirshon, S. (1983) *And Also Teach Them to Read.* Westport: Lawrence Hill and Co.

Hoare, Q. (1980) "Review of Antonio Gramsci, Conservative Schooling for Radical Politics by Harold Entwistle," *British Journal of Sociology of Education*, 1, 3: 319–25.

Hobsbawm, E. (1987) "Speaking at Gramsci '87 Conference," organized by *Marxism Today* (April).

Holly, D. (1980) "Review of Antonio Gramsci, Conservative Schooling for Radical Politics by Harold Entwistle," *British Journal of Sociology of Education*, 1, 3: 315–9.

Holub, R. (1992) *Antonio Gramsci: Beyond Marxism and Postmodernism.* London: Routledge and Kegan Paul.

hooks, b. (1993) "bell hooks Speaking about Paulo Freire—the Man, His Work," Chapter 7 of P. McLaren and P. Leonard (eds.) *Paulo Freire: A Critical Encounter.* London and New York: Routledge and Kegan Paul.

Horton, M. and Freire, P. (1990) *We Make the Road by Walking: Conversations on Education and Social Change.* Philadelphia: Temple University Press.

Hughes, H.S. (1979) *Consciousness and Society.* Brighton: Harvester.

International Gramsci Society (1995) *Newsletter* 5 (November). Notre Dame, IN: University of Notre Dame, English Department.

Ireland, T.D. (1987) *Antonio Gramsci and Adult Education: Reflections on the Brazilian Experience*, Manchester Monographs. Manchester: The Centre for Adult and Higher Education, University of Manchester.

Jackson, K. (1980) "Foreword" in J.L. Thompson (ed.) *Adult Education for a Change.* London: Hutchinson.

Jackson, T. (1981) "The Influence of Gramsci on Adult Education," *Convergence*, **XIV**, 3: 81–6.

James, M.D. (1990) "Demystifying Literacy: Reading, Writing, and the Struggle for Liberation," *Convergence*, **XXIII**, 1: 14–26.

Jarvis, P. (1995) *Adult and Continuing Education: Theory and Practice* (2nd edition). London: Routledge and Kegan Paul.

Jarvis, P. (1993) *Adult Education and the State: Towards a Politics of Adult Education.* London: Routledge and Kegan Paul.

Jarvis, P. (1990) "Adult Education As a Field of University Study" in C. Duke and R. Moseley (eds.) *Quality and Control: Widening High Quality University Continuing Education through the Nineties.* Coventry: Universities Council for Adult and Continuing Education.

Jarvis, P. (1989) *The Sociology of Adult and Continuing Education.* London: Routledge and Kegan Paul.

Jarvis, P. (1987) *Adult Learning in the Social Context.* Beckenham: Croom Helm.

Jarvis, P. and Walters, N. (eds.) (1993) *Adult Education and Theological Interpretations.* Malabar, FL: Krieger.

Joliffe, J. (1983) "The Exile's Appeal," *Guardian* (newspaper interview with Luis Cabral), 16 September.

Kidd, R. and Byram, M. (1982) "Demystifying Pseudo-Freirean Development: The Case of Laedza Batanani," *Community Development,* **17**, 2: 91–105.

Kidd, R. and Kumar, K. (1981) "Coopting Freire: A Critical Analysis of Pseudo-Freirean Adult Education," *Economic and Political Weekly,* **XVI**, 1 and 2: 27–36.

Kirkwood, C. and Kirkwood G. (1989) *Living Adult Education: Freire in Scotland.* Milton Keynes: Open University Press in association with the Scottish Institute of Adult Education.

Knijnik, G. (1996) "Intellectuals and Social Movements: Examining Power Relations" in T. Kjærgård, A. Kvamme, N. Lindén, (eds.), *PDME III Proceedings: Numeracy Gender Class Race.* Landås, Norway: Caspar Publishing Company. 90–113.

Knijnik, G. (1993) "Culture, Mathematics, Education and the Landless of Southern Brazil" in C. Julie, D. Angelis, Z. Davis (eds.) *Political Dimensions of Mathematics Education PDME 2: Curriculum Reconstruction for Society in Transition.* Cape Town: Maskew Miller Longman and National Education Coordinating Committee (NECC) Mathematics Commission (South Africa). 149–53.

Kohl, H. (1973) *Reading, How To.* New York: Dutton.

Kosík, K. (1976) *Dialectic of the Concrete.* Dordrecht: Reidel.

Kozol, J. (1978) "A New Look at the Literacy Campaign in Cuba," *Harvard Educational Review,* **48**, 3 (August): 341–77.

La Belle, T.J. (1987) "From Consciousness Raising to Popular Education in Latin America and the Caribbean," *Comparative Education Review,* **31**: 201–17.

La Belle, T.J. (1986) *Non-Formal Education in Latin America and the Caribbean—Stability, Reform or Revolution?* New York: Praeger.

Laclau, E. (1990) *New Reflections on the Revolution of Our Time.* London: Verso.

Laclau, E. with Mouffe, C. (1990) "Post-Marxism without Apologies" in E. Laclau *New Reflections on the Revolution of Our Time.* London: Verso. 97–132.

Laclau, E. and Mouffe, C. (1987) "Post-Marxism without Apologies," *New Left Review,* **166** (November–December): 79–106.

Laclau, E. and Mouffe, C. (1985) *Hegemony and Socialist Strategy: Towards a Radical Democratic Politics.* London: Verso.

Landy, M. (1994) *Film, Politics and Gramsci.* Minneapolis: University of Minnesota Press.

Lankshear, C. (1993) "Adult Literacy in Nicaragua 1979–90," Chapter 7 of P. Freebody and A.R. Welch (eds.) *Knowledge Culture and Power: Interational Perspectives on Literacy As Policy and Practice.* London and Washington, DC: Falmer Press.

Lankshear, C. (1987) *Literacy, Schooling and Revolution.* Lewes and Philadelphia: Falmer Press.

Lankshear, C. and McLaren, P. (eds.) (1993) *Critical Literacy: Politics, Praxis and the Postmodern.* Albany: State University of New York Press.

Laponce, J.A. (1981) *Left and Right: The Topography of Political Perceptions.* Toronto: University of Toronto Press.

Lather, P. (1986) "Research As Praxis," *Harvard Educational Review,* **56**: 257–77

Lave, J. (1988) *Cognition in Practice: Mind, Mathematics and Culture in Everyday Life.* Cambridge: Cambridge University Press.

Leach, T. (1982) "Paulo Freire: Dialogue, Politics and Relevance," *International Journal of Lifelong Education,* **1**, 3: 185–201.

Leiner, M. (1987) "The 1961 National Cuban Literacy Campaign," Chapter 8 of R.F. Arnove and H.J. Graff (eds.) *National Literacy Campaigns: Historical and Comparative Perspectives.* New York and London: Plenum Press.

Lenin, V.I. (1947) *What Is to Be Done?* Moscow: Progress Publishers.

Leonard, P. (1993) "Critical Pedagogy and State Welfare: Intellectual Encounters with Freire and Gramsci, 1974–86," Chapter 8 of P. McLaren and P. Leonard (eds.) *Paulo Freire: A Critical Encounter.* London and New York: Routledge and Kegan Paul.

Llorente, J.C. (1996) *Problem Solving and Constitution of Knowledge at Work*, Research Bulletin 92. Helsinki, Finland: Department of Education, University of Helsinki.

Lloyd, A.S. (1972) "Freire, Conscientization and Adult Education," *Adult Education*, **XXIII**, 1: 3–20.

London, Edinburgh Weekend Return Group (1979, 1980) *In and against the State*. Bristol: Pluto Press.

Lovett, T. (1982) *Adult Education, Community Development and the Working Class* (2nd edition). Nottingham: Department of Adult Education, University of Nottingham.

Lovett, T. (1978) "The Challenge of Community Education in Social and Political Change," *Convergence*, **XI**, 1: 42–51.

Lovett, T., Clarke, C. and Kilmurray, A. (1983) *Adult Education and Community Action: Adult Education and Popular Social Movements*, Radical Forum on Adult Education. London: Croom Helm.

MacEoin, G. (1973) "Latin America's Radical Church" in C. Harding and C. Roper (eds.) *Latin America Review of Books*. London: Latin American Newsletters Ltd. and Books of Leeds, 1 (Spring): 67–74.

MacEoin, G. (1972) "Conscientization for the Masses," *The National Catholic Reporter*, 17 March.

Machiavelli, N. (1965) *The Prince*, translated by C.E. Detmold. New York: Airmont.

Mackie, R. (1980a) "Introduction" in R. Mackie (ed.) *Literacy and Revolution: The Pedagogy of Paulo Freire*. London: Pluto Press. 1–11.

Mackie, R. (1980b) "Contributions to the Thought of Paulo Freire" in R. Mackie (ed.) *Literacy and Revolution: The Pedagogy of Paulo Freire*. London: Pluto Press. 93–119.

Manzoni, A. (1956) *The Betrothed*, translated by A. Colquhoun. London: Dent.

Marx, K. and Engels, F. (1974) *The German Ideology*, edited and introduced by C.J. Arthur (2nd edition). London: Lawrence and Wishart.

Mashayekh, F. (1974) "Freire, the Man, His Ideas and Their Implications," *Literacy Discussion*, 5, 1: 1–62.

Mayo, M. and Thompson, J. (eds.) (1995) *Adult Learning, Critical Intelligence and Social Change*. Leicester: NIACE.

Mayo, P. (1995) "The 'Turn to Gramsci' in Adult Education: A Review of the English-Language Literature," *International Gramsci Society Newsletter*, 4 (April): 2–9. Notre Dame, IN: University of Notre Dame, English Department.

Mayo, P. (1994) "Synthesizing Gramsci and Freire: Possibilities for a Theory of Radical Adult Education," *International Journal of Lifelong Education*, 13, 2 (March–April): 125–48.

Mayo, P. (1993) "When Does It Work? Freire's Pedagogy in Context," *Studies in the Education of Adults* 25, 1 (April): 11–30.

Mayo, P. (1991) "Review of Learning to Question—a Pedagogy of Liberation by Paulo Freire and Antonio Faundez," *Convergence*, **XXIV**: 80–82.

McGinn, N.F. (1973) "The Psycho-social Method of Paulo Freire: Some Lessons from Experience," *World Education*: 9–13.

McLaren, P. (1994) "Postmodernism and the Death of Politics: A Brazilian Reprieve," Chapter 11 of P. McLaren and C. Lankshear (eds.) *Politics of Liberation: Paths from Freire*. London and New York: Routledge and Kegan Paul.

McLaren, P. and Lankshear, C. (eds.) (1994) *Politics of Liberation: Paths from Freire*. London: Routledge and Kegan Paul.

McLaren, P. and Leonard, P. (eds.) (1993) *Paulo Freire: A Critical Encounter*. London and New York: Routledge and Kegan Paul.

McLellan, D. (1987) *Marxism and Religion*. London: Macmillan.

McLellan, D. (1986) *Ideology*. Milton Keynes: Open University Press.

McLellan, D. (1979) *Marxism after Marx*. London: Macmillan.

McLellan, D. (ed.) (1977) *Karl Marx: Selected Writings*. Oxford: Oxford University Press.

McRobbie, A. (1994) "Feminism, Postmodernism and the Real Me" in M. Perryman (ed.) *Altered States: Postmodernism, Politics, Culture*. London: Lawrence and Wishart.

Merriam, S. (1977) "Philosophical Perspectives on Adult Education: A Critical Review of the Literature," *Adult Education*, **XXVII**, 4: 195–203.

Merton, R.K. (1967) *On Theoretical Sociology*. New York: The Free Press.

Mezirow, J. (1977) "Perspective Transformation," *Studies in Adult Education*, 9, 2: 153–64.

Miliband, R. (1973) *The State in Capitalist Society*. London: Quartet.

Miller, V. (1985) *Between Struggle and Hope: The Nicaraguan Literacy Campaign.* Boulder: Westview Press.

Morales, A.P. (1981) "The Literacy Campaign in Cuba," *Harvard Educational Review,* **51**, 1 (February): 31–9.

Morgan, W.J. (1996) "Antonio Gramsci and Raymond Williams: Workers, Intellectuals and Adult Education," *Convergence,* **XXIX**, 1: 61–73.

Morgan, W.J. (1987) "The Pedagogical Politics of Antonio Gramsci—Pessimism of the Intellect, Optimism of the Will," *International Journal of Lifelong Education,* **6**, 4 (October–December): 295–308.

Mouzelis, N. (1988) "Marxism or Post-Marxism?" *New Left Review,* **167** (January–February): 107–23.

Nairn, T. (1964a) "The British Political Elite," *New Left Review,* **23**, (January–February): 19–25.

Nairn, T. (1964b) "The English Working Class," *New Left Review,* 24 (March–April): 43–57.

Nairn, T. (1964c) "The Nature of the Labour Party," *New Left Review,* **27** (September–October): 38–65; **28** (November–December): 33–62.

Nemeth, T. (1980) *Gramsci's Philosophy: A Critical Study.* Brighton: Harvester Press.

Nisi, C. and Mascia, V. (1985) "Gramsci, Antonio (1891–1937)" in J.E. Thomas, and B. Elsey (eds.) *International Biography of Adult Education.* Nottingham: Department of Adult Education, University of Nottingham. 210–2.

O'Gorman, F. (1978) "Conscientization—Whose Initiative Should It Be?" *Convergence,* **XI**, 1: 52–58.

Organization for Economic Cooperation and Development (1992) *Education at a Glance: OECD Indicators.* Paris: Organization for Economic Cooperation and Development (OECD).

Pantham, T. (1986) "Proletarian Pedagogy, Satyagraha and Charisma: Gramsci and Gandhi," Chapter 8 of R. Roy (ed.) *Contemporary Crisis and Gandhi.* New Delhi: Discovery Publishing House.

Perryman, M. (ed.) (1996) *The Blair Agenda.* London: Lawrence and Wishart in association with Signs of the Times.

Perryman, M. (1994) "Introduction: The Remaking of the Political" in M. Perryman (ed.) *Altered States: Postmodernism, Politics,*

Culture. London: Lawrence and Wishart in association with Signs of the Times. 1–19.

Perryman, M. (ed.) (1994) *Altered States: Postmodernism, Politics, Culture*. London: Lawrence and Wishart in association with Signs of the Times.

Piccone, P. (1983) *Italian Marxism*. Berkeley and Los Angeles: University of California Press.

Popkewitz, T.S. (1991) "A Political Sociology of Educational Reform: Power/Knowledge" in *Teaching, Teacher Education and Reform*. New York: Teachers College.

Robertson, D. (1986) *The Penguin Dictionary of Politics*. Harmondsworth: Penguin.

Sanders, T.G. (1973) "The Paulo Freire Method: Literacy Training and Conscientization," *Dialogue*, 7, 1.

San Juan Jr., E. (1995) *Hegemony and Strategies of Transgression: Essays in Cultural Studies and Comparative Literature*. Albany: State University of New York Press.

Senese, G.B. (1991) "Warnings on Resistance and the Language of Possibility: Gramsci and a Pedagogy from the Surreal," *Education Theory*, 41, 1: 13–22.

Shor, I. (1988) *Working Hands and Critical Minds: A Paulo Freire Model for Job Training*. Chicago: Alternative Schools Network; also published in *Language Issues*, journal of NATESLA, Spring and Summer 1988.

Shor, I. (1987) *A Pedagogy for Liberation: Dialogues on Transforming Education*. New York: Bergin and Garvey.

Shor, I. (ed.) (1987) *Freire for the Classroom: A Sourcebook for Liberatory Teaching*. Portsmouth: Boynton/Cook.

Shore, C. (1990) *Italian Communism: The Escape from Leninism*. London: Pluto Press.

Showstack Sassoon, A. (1994) "Rethinking Socialism—New Processes, New Thinking" in M. Perryman (ed.) *Altered States: Postmodernism, Politics, Culture*. London: Lawrence and Wishart in association with Signs of the Times.

Skidmore, T. E. (1973) "Brazil: From Revolution to Miracle" in C. Harding and C. Roper (eds.) *Latin America Review of Books*, 1 (Spring): 103–9.

Skidmore, T.E. (1967) *Politics in Brazil 1930–1964: An Experiment in Democracy*. London: Oxford University Press.

Spriano, P. (1975) *The Occupation of the Factories: Italy 1920,* translated and introduced by G.A. Williams. London: Pluto Press.

Squires, J. (ed.) (1993) *Principled Positions: Postmodernism and the Rediscovery of Value.* London: Lawrence and Wishart.

Stanley, M. (1973) "Literacy: The Crisis of a Conventional Wisdom," *Convergence,* **VI,** 1: 62–77.

Street, B. (1991) "Misreading the Signs," *Times Higher Education Supplement,* 25 January.

Street, B. (1984) *Literacy Theory and Practice,* Cambridge Studies in Oral and Literate Culture. Cambridge: Cambridge University Press.

Taylor, P.V. (1993) *The Texts of Paulo Freire.* Buckingham: Open University Press.

Thomas, J.E. (1982) *Radical Adult Education: Theory and Practice.* Nottingham: Department of Adult Education, University of Nottingham.

Thompson, E.P. (1978) *The Poverty of Theory.* London: Merlin Press.

Thompson, E.P. (1963) *The Making of the English Working Class.* London: Victor Gollancz.

Thompson, J.L. (1983) *Learning Liberation: Women's Response to Men's Education.* London: Croom Helm.

Thompson, J.L. (ed.) (1980) *Adult Education for a Change.* London: Hutchinson.

Tight, M. (1996) *Key Concepts in Adult Education and Training.* London and New York: Routledge and Kegan Paul.

Titmus, C.J. (ed.) (1989) *Lifelong Education for Adults: An International Handbook.* Oxford: Pergamon Press.

Togliatti, P. (1979) *On Gramsci and Other Writings.* London: Lawrence and Wishart.

Torres, C.A. (1993) "From the Pedagogy of the Oppressed to *A Luta Continua:* The Political Pedagogy of Paulo Freire," Chapter 6 of P. McLaren and P. Leonard (eds.) *Paulo Freire: A Critical Encounter.* London and New York: Routledge and Kegan Paul. 119–45.

Torres, C.A. (1991) "The State, Nonformal Education, and Socialism in Cuba, Nicaragua, and Grenada," *Comparative Education Review,* **35,** 1: 110–30.

Torres, C.A. (1990a) "Adult Education and Popular Education in Latin America: Implications for a Radical Approach to Comparative Education," *International Journal of Lifelong Education*, **9**, 4: 271–87.

Torres, C.A. (1990b) *The Politics of Non-formal Education in Latin America*. New York: Praeger.

Torres, C.A. and Freire, P. (1994) "Twenty Years after Pedagogy of the Oppressed: Paulo Freire in Conversation with Carlos Alberto Torres," Chapter 5 of P.L. McLaren and C. Lankshear (eds.) *Politics of Liberation: Paths from Freire*. London and New York: Routledge and Kegan Paul.

Tough, A. (1979) *The Adult's Learning Projects* (2nd edition). Toronto, Canada: Ontario Institute for Studies in Education.

Tuckett, A. (1995) "Scrambled Eggs: Social Policy and Adult Learning" in P. Raggatt, R. Edwards and N. Small (eds.) *The Learning Society: Challenges and Trends*. London: Routledge and Kegan Paul in association with the Open University. 45–58.

Walker, J. (1980) "The End of Dialogue: Paulo Freire on Politics and Education" in R. Mackie (ed.) *Literacy and Revolution: the Pedagogy of Paulo Freire*. London: Pluto Press. 120–50.

Weiler, K. (1996) "Myths of Paulo Freire," *Educational Theory*, **46**, 3: 353–71 (Summer).

Weiler, K. (1994) "Freire and a Feminist Pedagogy of Difference," Chapter 1 of P. McLaren and P. Lankshear (eds.) *Politics of Liberation: Paths from Freire*. London and New York: Routledge and Kegan Paul. 12–40.

Welton, M. (1993) "Seeing the Light—Christian Conversion and Conscientisation" in P. Jarvis and N. Walters (eds.) *Adult Education and Theological Interpretations*. Malabar, FL: Krieger.

Westwood, S. (1990) "Adult Education and 'New Times'" in *Towards 1992: Education of Adults in the New Europe*, Proceedings of the Twentieth Annual Conference SCUTREA, University of Sheffield, 14–19.

Westwood, S. (1980) "Adult Education and the Sociology of Education" in J.L. Thompson (ed.) *Adult Education for a Change*. London: Hutchinson. 31–44.

Williams, G.A. (1960) "Gramsci's Concept of Egemonia," *Journal of the History of Ideas*, **XXI**, 4 (October–December): 586–99.

Williams, R. (1990) *Keywords: A Vocabulary of Culture and Society*. London: Fontana/Croom Helm.

Williams, R. (1961) *The Long Revolution.* London: Chatto and Windus.

Williams, R. (1958) *Culture and Society.* London: Chatto and Windus.

Wilson, W. (1978) *Towards Industrial Democracy in Britain,* Manchester Monographs 10. Manchester: Department of Adult and Higher Education, University of Manchester.

Wynia, G.W. (1990) *The Politics of Latin American Development* (3rd edition). Cambridge: Cambridge University Press.

Yarnit, M. (1980) "Second Chance to Learn," in J.L. Thompson (ed.) *Adult Education for a Change.* London: Hutchinson. 174–91.

Youngman, F. (1986) *Adult Education and Socialist Pedagogy.* Radical Forum on Adult Education. Beckenham: Croom Helm.

Index

.